CATALOGING NONPRINT AND INTERNET RESOURCES

A How-To-Do-It Manual for Librarians

Mary Beth Weber

HOW-TO-DO-IT MANUALS FOR LIBRARIANS

NUMBER 113

NEAL-SCHUMAN PUBLISHERS, INC.
New York, London

Published by Neal-Schuman Publishers, Inc.
100 Varick Street
New York, NY 10013

Printed and bound in the United States of America.

ISBN 1–55570–435–2

CONTENTS

LIST OF FIGURES

PREFACE

The world of cataloging continues to develop in interesting new ways. The cataloging of nonprint resources is sometimes overlooked entirely or mentioned only very briefly in cataloging courses (which themselves are no longer required in many library science Master's programs). Library schools offer service-oriented information courses on the use of nonprint resources, yet may not deal with the starting point of access for these resources, which is cataloging. Although many nonprint resources may be as common as their print counterparts in the collections of libraries, the standards for cataloging nonprint resources continues to evolve. *Cataloging Nonprint and Internet Resources: A How-to-Do It Manual for Librarians* is designed to help hard-working professionals master this constant challenge.

PURPOSE

Cataloging is essential for access to nonprint resources, particularly in cases when they are housed in noncirculating, closed collections, or they do not exist in a physical manifestation, such as Internet resources. Without a bibliographic record, access is severely limited or nonexistent. Since nonprint resources may not be browsed in the manner of books and other print resources, reliance on the bibliographic record for access to their contents is of particular importance. To emphasize the importance of cataloging to nonprint resources, it is noteworthy to include a portion of the rationale provided by the Online Audiovisual Catalogers (OLAC):

> "Full and standardized bibliographic description of nonprint resources facilitates: a heightened awareness of the full range of information resources a library offers its user population; a consistent means for both the local and remote user of the catalog to search the entire collection through a single interface; identification of material that represents a significant expenditure of library funds; international efforts in cooperative cataloging by sharing bibliographic records in the utility databases...." (Online Audiovisual Catalogers, Cataloging Access and Policy Committee, 1998).

Cataloging Nonprint and Internet Resources also reflects other changes in the field including the nature of new materials being cataloged and categories of new users searching for materials. The proliferation of nonprint resources (most notably, Internet resources) over the past decade has increased the necessity for effective access to them. Libraries now typically serve user communities outside of the physical structure in addition to onsite users. Increased reliance on the World Wide Web (hereafter referred to as "the Web") has led in some cases to a situation in which users may choose to use a library's resources only via remote access. For this reason, the manner in which a library publicizes and makes available these resources through its online catalog and/or Web page is of particular importance. Many libraries have attempted to reach all categories of users by cataloging nonprint resources as well as providing hyperlinked lists of resources arranged by title, subject, etc. on their Web pages.

Cataloging Nonprint and Internet Resources completely updates *Cataloging Nonbook Resources* published in 1993. (To clear up any cataloging confusion in the author field between the first edition of this guide and this revised edition, my last name has changed legally and officially, since my marriage, from Fecko to Weber.) At that time standards were being developed for electronic resources (formerly referred to as "computer files"), and musical CDs were first becoming available. Since then, new formats have emerged, and the Internet has grown tremendously. Cataloging of most types of electronic resources, sound recordings, and video recording formats have reached some level of standardization. Standards continue to evolve for the newer formats, such as Internet resources, serials provided through aggregator services, and digital video discs (DVDs). In addition, libraries have often canceled print subscriptions or have developed creative solutions permitting both versions of resources to coexist in the library and to be fully available to patrons as resources have become increasingly available electronically—on disk or via the Web. This type of access (permitting both versions of a resource to coexist in the OPAC), while very beneficial to users, presents many challenges to catalogers, including the decision to provide one record to accommodate all versions of a resource, or separate records for each version. Other issues include record maintenance, recataloging when providers/aggregators change, and usage restrictions.

RATIONALE FOR WRITING THE GUIDE

When I began cataloging nonprint resources, I found that, while standard cataloging sources provided excellent guidance in general cataloging principles, they often lacked information and examples covering the unique challenges nonprint cataloging presents. Texts dealing with nonprint cataloging also existed, yet posed their own problems. These guides were specific to one format, which is not always helpful to individuals who handle several formats; they were not completely up-to-date regarding current standards; or, successive editions to excellent texts were never published.

Cataloging Nonprint and Internet Resources was written in response to the need for the most clear, up-to-date guidance and examples in the area of nonprint cataloging. While other texts are available on this topic, many were published in the late 1990s. Standards and material types have significantly evolved even since that time. This revised edition provides timely information and examples, including new resources available on the Web and the *Amendments 2001* to the *Anglo-American Cataloging Rules Second Edition, 1998 Revision* (hereafter referred to as *AACR2R (1998)*).[1] The *Amendments 2001* were agreed to by the Joint Steering Committee for the Revision of AACR (hereafter referred to as "the JSC") at their meeting in San Diego in March, 2000 and their meeting in London in September, 2000. The *Amendments 2001* have been incorporated into *AACR-E* (the electronic version of *AACR2R [1998]*), and paper copies became available in October, 2001. The changes outlined in the *Amendments 2001* became effective December, 2001. All changes outlined in the *Amendments 2001* are included in this text.

HOW IT WAS DEVELOPED

Cataloging Nonprint and Internet Resources was developed during the course of my involvement with pivotal groups and experiences in the world of nonprint cataloging. It summarizes the answers I discovered by my position as a cataloger and the corresponding lack of available information to guide my work. It is an outgrowth of my involvement with the American Library Association's Association for Library Collections and Technical Services' (ALCTS) Computer Files Discussion Group, the Media

Resources Committee (formerly Audiovisual Cataloging Committee), and the Committee on Cataloging: Description and Access (CC:DA) when standards were being developed to meet the changing needs of catalogers, and my experience with OCLC's landmark Internet Cataloging Experiment. My experiences led me to recognize the need for a text to provide timely guidance in the area of cataloging nonprint resources.

SCOPE

The guide covers a wide-ranging area. To reflect the shifts in cataloging, it does not cover some information (such as printed music, globes, and electronic cartographic materials) and instead focuses on Internet resources and the many other cutting-edge challenges in cataloging today. Classification, for example, is not covered since it varies by type of library, type of collection, and local practice. Series treatment is covered briefly in this manual since series are not as prevalent in nonprint resources as they are for monographs. Likewise, subject analysis is only briefly covered since this practice is also unique to type of library and local practices.

Another feature included in this new manual is an examination of the appropriateness of MARC format versus metadata schemes for certain categories of nonprint resources. All examples included in this text are provided in MARC format since this currently is the predominant scheme used by libraries. In some cases, it is the only bibliographic scheme supported by some online catalogs. It is also the scheme currently used by Rutgers University Libraries, my place of employment, and all of my bibliographic records are created using MARC format. Please note that the examples provided in this text are not in RLIN or OCLC MARC format. Rather, they are in the MARC format provided by the online catalog currently used by Rutgers University Libraries, which is similar in appearance to RLIN MARC.

SKILLS FOR TODAY'S CATALOGERS

This manual concentrates on deciphering the challenges of descriptive cataloging. It will guide catalogers of all skill levels in how to:

- choose main entry (which is particularly important for resources such as sound recordings);
- provide descriptive cataloging treatment necessary for creating a basic MARC record;
- enter basic series information;
- formulate a wide variety of notes (which are of special importance for nonprint resources), with an emphasis on notes specific to particular formats;
- provide subject added entries (personal, corporate, and topical); and
- provide name (personal and/or corporate) and title added entries.

Cataloging Nonprint and Internet Resources: A How-To-Do-It Manual for Librarians focuses on the specific information needed to catalog a broad range of nonprint resources that are likely to be handled by the average cataloger in everyday situations. It presents easy-to-use instructions for cataloging a wide array of nonprint resources. This guide to descriptive cataloging is designed to be used in conjunction with standard cataloging sources such as *AACR2R (1998)* and the *Amendments 2001*, the *Library of Congress Rule Interpretations*, and the *Library of Congress Subject Cataloging Manuals. Cataloging Nonprint and Internet Resources* emphasizes the practical over the theoretical by providing realistic examples and actual bibliographic records created by catalogers working in a real world library setting. While this guide illustrates some portion of the MARC bibliographic record (classification fields and subject headings, for example) with Library of Congress examples, it may also be used by individuals who do not adhere to these practices.

ORGANIZATION OF THE MANUAL

Chapters 1 through 8 form the core of the book. Chapter 1 provides a general discussion of nonprint cataloging, including the various levels of cataloging description. Subject analysis and subject heading schemes are covered briefly in Chapter 1, "Essential Background," since the emphasis of this text is on descriptive cataloging procedures. Chapters 2 through 8 discuss format specific cataloging, and formats are covered in the order which they are presented in *AACR2R (1998)*. Chapter 9 provides a comparison of MARC format and metadata, and includes a discussion of standards and applications. "A Final Word" concludes the guide. The appendix, "Suggested Readings," offers a useful list of resources to be consulted for further information.

The chapters devoted to format specific cataloging cover: cartographic materials, sound recordings, visual materials, electronic resources, microforms, and Internet resources. Each chapter begins with an overview that discusses cataloging issues specific to that format. The overview is followed by an outline of the elements that may be included in bibliographic records for the format, including chief and prescribed sources of information, elements of descriptive cataloging, series, notes, subject access, added entries, and classification. Bibliographic records that serve as examples to illustrate the points outlined in the chapter are included at the end of each format specific chapter. The examples included in this text are original, are taken from my own work or work done by my staff, and were not taken from bibliographic records submitted by other libraries to the RLIN and OCLC online union databases. Any examples taken from work other than my own have been used with prior permission from all involved parties; sources of information are noted in the acknowledgments. In the event an example is similar to a record available in RLIN or OCLC, it was submitted to the union databases after my record was created.

I trust that you will find *Cataloging Nonprint and Internet Resources: A How-to-Do It Manual for Librarians* a useful and engaging tool as you explore the changes and innovative evolution of this very challenging area of librarianship.

ACKNOWLEDGMENTS

I would like to acknowledge those individuals who provided support and guidance as this text was written: my friend and colleague Valerie Weinberg, who is a member of the cataloging team in the Library of Congress's Sound Recordings Division; my friends and colleagues in Technical and Automated Services, Rutgers University Libraries: Ruth Dyer and Charlotte Toke, who provided encouragement and support as well as cataloging examples; Margaret Papai, who provided encouragement and support; and Rhonda Marker, who lent me her copy of the *Amendments 2001 to AACR2R (1998)*.

REFERENCES

Online Audiovisual Catalogers, Cataloging Policy Committee. "Rationale for Cataloging Nonprint Collections" (November 2000) Available at: *http://ublib.buffalo.edu/libraries/units/cts/olac/rationale2.html*.

ENDNOTE

1. Email correspondence in October, 2001, with Dr. Barbara Tillett, Director, Cataloging Policy and Support Office, Library of Congress, and Member, Joint Steering Committee to Revise *AACR2*.

1 ESSENTIAL BACKGROUND

OVERVIEW

This chapter outlines the basic elements of bibliographic records for all nonprint resources. It also includes a brief discussion of the various levels of cataloging as described in *AACR2R (1998)* and the *Amendments 2001*. Notes, MARC fields, choice of main entry, descriptive cataloging, and order of information as presented in bibliographic records are covered. Each successive chapter covers information specific to type of format, including chief and prescribed sources of information. The chapters include format specific sources of information that were consulted when writing this book. Additionally, a separate bibliography is included after the main body of work.

LEVELS OF CATALOGING DESCRIPTION

This text focuses on descriptive cataloging and places less emphasis on subject access and classification. It is intended to provide catalogers with guidance and examples in creating a physical description and notes for nonprint resources.

AACR2R (1998) outlines three possible levels of cataloging that may be used to describe resources. The level of cataloging depends on a particular library's needs, available staff, and the emphasis given to a specific collection and/or material type.

The first level of description, as per Rule 1.0D1, *AACR2R (1998)*, is comparable to minimal level cataloging that may be used when libraries are unable to do full-scale retrospective conversion but wish to have some access, however limited, to older resources in their collections. This level of cataloging may also be used for items of a temporary nature that libraries may wish to make available in their online catalogs, including reserve resources, recent acquisitions that have not yet been cataloged, gifts/donations, or interlibrary loan resources. Or, it may be used by libraries with limited staff and monetary resources that have a minimum of time to provide cataloging treatment for nonprint resources. As prescribed by *AACR2R (1998)*, the following elements should be included in a first level description:

title proper; first statement of responsibility if different from main entry heading in form or number or if main entry heading is lacking; edition statement, material or type of publication specific details; first publisher, etc., date of publication, etc.; extent of item; notes; standard number

An example of a first level description follows:

Figure 1–1, Example of First Level of Description Cataloging

0792156188
The Truman show / ‡c[presented by] Paramount Pictures.
Widescreen ed.
Hollywood, CA : ‡bParamount, ‡c[1999]
1 videorecording (113 min.) : ‡bsd., col. ; ‡c1/2 in.
Close captioned.
Originally released as a motion picture in 1998.

The second level of description, as per Rule 1.0D2, *AACR2R (1998)*, is fuller, and might be compared to full-level cataloging. It is perhaps the closest of the three in the degree of detail provided by most libraries in their bibliographic records. It is also comparable to those records created by the Project for Cooperative Cataloging, or PCC.

The core record standard was defined in 1994 by a Task Group appointed by the Cooperative Cataloging Council, which later became the PCC. The Task Group was charged to develop cost-effective bibliographic standards that would be acceptable to a wide range of libraries. Core records are created by BIBCO, the bibliographic record component of the PCC. BIBCO is composed of institutions that are independent NACO libraries, which means that they submit authority records (personal, corporate, and geographic names, and series) for inclusion in the Library of Congress's Name Authority File. The BIBCO FAQ defines core records as a level of cataloging between minimal- and full-level. The core record standard specifies a minimum set of data elements. Records lacking this minimum are not considered to be core level.

Since core records are created by NACO institutions, access points on all core records are supported by an authority record in the Name Authority File. This guarantees that core records can be accepted as is, and require no additional authority work. Core records are identified by an encoding level of 4 (Leader/17, the fixed field EL: in RLIN, and ELvl: in OCLC, and 042 field), **Authentication Code,** with the letters "pcc." Information on the PCC and BIBCO are included in "Suggested Readings" in the Appendix.

As prescribed by *AACR2R (1998),* the following elements should be included in a second level description:

> *title proper and general material designation(if applicable); parallel title (if applicable); other title information (such as subtitle); first statement of responsibility; subsequent statements of responsibility; edition statement and first statement of responsibility relating to the edition (if applicable); material or type of publication specific details; first place of publication, etc., first publisher, etc., date of publication, etc.; extent of item, other physical details, and dimensions; title proper of series, statement of responsibility for series, ISSN of series, numbering for series (if applicable), title of subseries, ISSN of subseries, numbering within subseries (if applicable); notes; standard number*

An example of a second level description follows:

Figure 1-2, Example of Second Level of Description Cataloging

---

L'Homme sur les quais ‡h[videorecording] = ‡bThe man by the shore / ‡ca co production of Frouma Films International, Blue Films, Les Productions Du Regard, Velvet Film GmbH Berlin ; director, Raoul Peck ; producer, Pascal Verroust ; screenplay, Andre Graill and Raoul Peck.
New York : ‡bKJM3 Entertainment Group [distributor], ‡c1993.
1 videocassette (105 min.) : ‡bsd., col. ; ‡c1/2 in.
VHS.
A foreign film (France)
In French with English subtitles.
Cast: Jennifer Zubar, Toto Bissainthe, Jean Michel Martial, Patrick Rameau.
Credits: Cinematography, Armand Marco ; edited by Jacques Comets ; music by Amos Coulanges and Dominque Dejean.
Set in Haiti in the 1960's, 8-year-old Sarah and her two sisters are victims of Francois "Papa Doc" Duvalier's reign of terror.

The third level of description, as per Rule 1.0D3, *AACR2R (1998)*, is the fullest and most complete, and might be compared to enhanced cataloging. Libraries may lack the staff resources and time to routinely provide this level of cataloging. This type of cataloging may also be purchased through a vendor service, such as Blackwell's MARC Plus, which includes full-level cataloging plus an enhanced contents note, or by special agreement through a service like OCLC's TechPro. An item given third level descriptive treatment would include all elements outlined in the rules that are applicable to the item being cataloged. Since this varies greatly depending on library and the resource being cataloged, the various elements that might possibly be included in a third level description are not outlined in the manner provided for levels one and two. For this reason, a record using the third level of description will not be provided.

ELEMENTS OF BIBLIOGRAPHIC RECORDS

The following information may be used to create bibliographic records for nonprint resources:

- **Chief Source of Information** (described in detail in following chapters)
- **Prescribed Sources of Information** (described in detail in following chapters)
- **Choice of Main Entry**
- **International Standard Book Number (ISBN)**
- **Cataloging Source**
- **Language Code**
- **Geographic Information**
- **Library of Congress Call Number**
- **Title**
- **Title Variations**
- **General Material Designation (GMD)**
- **Statement of Responsibility**
- **Edition**
- **Place of Publication and/or Distribution, or Manufacture, etc.**
- **Name of Publisher(s) and/or Distributor(s)**
- **Date of Publication, Distribution, Copyright, Manufacture, etc.**
- **Physical Description**

- Series
- Notes
- Subject Access
- Added Entries (Personal and/or Corporate Names, Title Added Entries)
- Classification

The information listed above and detailed in the following paragraphs is repeated in each format specific chapter to enable the chapters to function as self-contained units. The format specific chapters also provide information pertaining specifically to the format under discussion.

All examples and sample records are in MARC format.

Chief and Prescribed Sources of Information are described in format specific chapters.

CHOICE OF MAIN ENTRY

Main entry may be under personal authorship or corporate authorship, or title main entry may be chosen. Some library professionals feel that the issue of main entry is not as pressing in an online environment where a variety of types of searches may be performed to locate an item. However, Rule 21.1A1, *AACR2R (1998)* defines a personal author as the individual chiefly responsible for a resource's intellectual or artistic content. Rule 21.1B1, *AACR2R (1998)* defines a corporate author as an organization or group of persons with a particular name that functions as an entity. Lastly, Rule 21.1C1, *AACR2R (1998)* states that a resource should be entered under title proper (or uniform title if appropriate) when: personal authorship is unknown or shared by a large number of individuals and authorship can not be attributed to one particular individual or when a resource is not issued by a corporate body; or when a resource is a collection of works by different individuals or corporate bodies.

For some resources, title main entry is the most logical choice since the nonprint resource is the result of the work of many individuals and/or corporate bodies, and it is not possible to attribute authorship to a particular individual or corporate body. Lack of a statement of responsibility is another reason why title main entry is chosen for some nonprint resources.

Choice of main entry is covered in more detail in the format specific chapters.

Physical Description

Physical description is provided both in fixed fields and the 300 field, **Physical Description**. The 007 field, **Physical Description**

Fixed Field—General Information provides information on physical description in alphabetic coded form. Some bibliographic utilities and cataloging modules display the 007 field at the top of the bibliographic record with other fixed fields; other utilities and modules provide this information in the bibliographic record with the variable fields. In this text, the 007 field is displayed with the variable fields in examples of bibliographic records. There are no subfields or indicators defined for the 007 field.

The 007 field for each material type begins with a different letter.
c = electronic resource (floppy disks, CD-ROMs, and Internet resources)
e = cartographic materials
h = microforms (microfiche, microfilm, etc.)
m = motion picture (reel to reel films)
o = kit
s = sound recording (sound cassettes, vinyl discs, CDs)
v = videorecordings (videocassettes, laser discs, DVDs)

The number of characters included in the 007 field varies for each format, and ranges from 6 to 14. The characters provide information on SMD, color characteristics, sound characteristics, dimensions, reduction ratio, etc. The 007 field is covered in greater detail in the format specific chapters.
example

electronic resource
007   cr cn
c = electronic resource
r = remote (in this case, an Internet resource)
blank
c = multicolored
n = no sound (silent)

microform
007   hc bfu bucu
h = microform
c = microfilm cassette
blank
b = negative
f = 35 mm.
u = reduction ratio unknown
Three blanks = reduction ratio; since unknown, spaces are left blank
b = black and white
u = emulsion on film unknown
c = service copy
u = base of film unknown

A full list of values for the 007 field is available on the USMARC Web page at http://lcweb.loc.gov/marc/bibliographic/ecbd007s.html.

International Standard Book Number (ISBN)

Monographic resources are often assigned ISBNs. Provide this information in the 020 field, **International Standard Book Number,** which is repeatable. This information can be helpful in identifying specific versions of a resource.

The following subfields are used in the 020: ‡a ISBN; ‡c terms of availability (price).

There are no indicators defined for the 020 field.
example

020	0780619900 (set) :‡c$300.00
020	0333776151 (Macmillan ISBN)

Cataloging Source

Information on the origin of a bibliographic record, plus any institutions that have modified a record, is provided in the 040 field, **Cataloging Source,** which is not repeatable.

The following subfields are available for use in the 040 field: ‡a original cataloging agency; ‡c transcribing agency (which is typically the institution in ‡a); and ‡d modifying agency. There are other subfields that may be used in the 040; this discussion is limited to those which are most predominantly used.

There are no indicators defined for the 040 field.
example

Original cataloging record created and transcribed by Rutgers University Libraries
040   NjR‡cNjR

Original cataloging record created and transcribed by Rutgers University Libraries, modified by Library X.
040   NjR‡NjR‡dXyZ

Original cataloging record created and transcribed by Rutgers University Libraries, modified at a later date by Rutgers University Libraries.
040   NjR‡NjR‡dNjR

Language Code

Provide information on language(s) present in a resource in the 041 field, **Language Code,** which is not repeatable. Information in the 041 is provided in alphabetic coded form. The 041 works in conjunction with the 546 field, **Language Note**.

Codes are provided according to their predominance in the resource (Network Development and MARC Standards Office, Library of Congress, 1999). The 041 field can provide codes for a maximum of six languages. If more than six languages are present in the resource, the language for the title is coded as "mul"(multiple) to represent all the languages.

The following subfields are used in the 041: ‡a language code for text, sound track, or separate title; ‡b language code for summary or subtitle; ‡d language code for sung or spoken text; ‡e language code for librettos; ‡g language code for accompanying materials other than librettos; ‡h language code for original and/or intermediate translations of text.

The initial indicator value indicates whether a resource is or includes a translation. An initial indicator of 0 indicates that the resource is not a translation and does not include a translation; a value of 1 indicates that the item is a translation or includes a translation.

example

041	0	‡beng
546		Silent with captions in English.
041	1	freita‡gengfreita
546		In French and Italian; program notes in English, French, and Italian.
041	0	
		‡dgerita‡egeritaengfre‡hgerita‡genggerfreitaspa‡henggerfre
546		Program notes by Alan Newcombe, Richard Osborne, Klaus Bennert, and Francis Drêsel, in English, German and French, with Italian and Spanish translations, and texts of the vocal works, in German and Italian, with English and French translations (16 p. : ill.) included.

Geographic Information

Provide information on the geographic area presented, described, covered, etc. by the resource in the 043 field, **Geographic Area Code**, which is not repeatable. The 043 can accommodate 1-3 codes, which are represented in alphabetic coded form. Multiple geographic codes are separated by a ‡a.

Indicator values are not defined for the 043 field.

example

Resource contains information pertaining to New Jersey, in the United States

043		n-us-nj

Resource contains information pertaining to the Great Plains region in the United States

043   np- - - - -

Resource contains information pertaining to Japan

043   a-ja- - -

Resource contains information pertaining to Spain and Mexico

043   e-sp- - -‡an-mx- - -

A full list of geographic area codes is available on the USMARC Web page at http://lcweb.loc.gov/marc/geoareas/.

Library of Congress Call Number

Provide a Library of Congress Call Number (if applicable according to the cataloging agency's policies and procedures for nonprint resources) in the 050 field, **Library of Congress Call Number**, which is repeatable. Some institutions have policies governing whether an LC Call Number is included in the bibliographic portion of a record when their records are submitted to a national online bibliographic utility such as RLIN or OCLC.

The following subfields are available for use in the 050 field: ‡a classification number; ‡b item number.

The initial indicator value indicates whether the item is in Library of Congress's collection. An initial value of blank indicates that no information is provided, and is used when libraries other than the Library of Congress provide classification numbers. The second indicator value indicates source of call number. Classification numbers provided by Library of Congress have a second indicator value of zero; classification numbers provided by other libraries have a second indicator value of 4.

example

| 050 | 0 | HB1335‡b.M84 |
| 050 | 4 | GB1399.4.N5‡bF566 1971 |

TITLE INFORMATION

Includes title, general material designation, remainder of title, and statement of responsibility.

Title

Consult the chief source of information first. If it is lacking or provides limited or no information, consult the prescribed sources of information. In the absence of chief or prescribed sources of information, a title may be supplied by the cataloger. The supplied title must be bracketed, and the source of title must be documented in a general note.

Title information is provided in the 245 field, **Title Statement**. The following subfields are available for use in the 245 field: ‡a title; ‡b remainder of title; ‡c statement of responsibility; ‡h GMD; ‡n number of part/section; ‡p name of part/section. One method of presenting subfields is to discuss them in the order in which they are used in bibliographic records, rather than alphabetically. However, the alphabetic approach is used in this text, and has been modeled after authoritative sources of information, such as *Concise MARC Format* and the RLIN and OCLC cataloging manuals. Placement of the subfields is illustrated in examples and illustrations. There are additional subfields that may be used in the 245; this text focuses discussion and examples on those that are most predominantly used.

Rule 1.1B1, *AACR2R (1998)*, instructs catalogers to transcribe the title proper exactly as to wording, order, and spelling, but not necessarily to capitalization and punctuation. Titles are provided in the 245 field, ‡a, which is not repeatable.

Indicator values in the 245 field indicates if a title added entry will be generated. Many nonprint resources are cataloged using title main entry since responsibility for creation of the resource is diffuse and can not be attributed to one individual or corporate body. (A discussion of choice of main entry for nonprint resources is provided in the following paragraph.) For this reason, many nonprint resources will have a first indicator value of 0. A first indicator value of 1 is used when a title added entry will be generated. The second indicator specifies number of nonfiling characters, with a range of 0-9 available.
example

Title from chief source of information
245   00   Kyushu-Okinawa Summit 2000 official guide

Title supplied by cataloger
245   00   [Documentary on Douglass College, Rutgers University]
500   Title supplied by cataloger.

Remainder of Title

The 245 field also provides the remainder of a title or other information, such as parallel titles. Provide this information in the ‡b, which is not repeatable.
example

| 245 | 00 | Powwow songs :‡bmusic of the Plains Indians |
| 245 | 03 | L'Homme sur les quais‡h[videorecording] =‡bThe man by the shore |

Title Variations

Provide title variations in the 246 field, **Varying Form of Title**, which is repeatable. The 246 provides other titles by which a resource may be known; this includes abbreviations or acronyms, parallel titles in another language, or when one title appears on external packaging and another title is given in the chief source of information. Providing access to title variations permits users to search for a resource in multiple ways.

The following subfields are available for use in the 246 field: ‡a title; ‡b remainder of title or parallel title; ‡h medium; ‡i display text; ‡n number of part/section of a work; ‡p name of a part/section of a work. There are additional subfields that may be used with the 246; this text focuses discussion and examples on those that are most predominantly used.

The initial indicator value indicates note or added entry. The second indicator value is used to provide information on type of title. A complete list of indicator values is available on the USMARC Web page at http://lcweb.loc.gov/marc/bibliographic/ecbdtils.html#mrcb246.
example

Portions of the main title

245	10	Kyushu-Okinawa Summit 2000 official guide CD-ROM‡h[electronic resource].
246	30	Kyushu-Okinawa Summit 2000 official guide‡h[electronic resource]
246	30	Kyushu-Okinawa Summit 2000‡h[electronic resource]

Remainder of title

| 245 | 00 | To steal or not to steal‡h[videorecording] :‡bthat is the copyright question. |
| 246 | 30 | That is the copyright question‡h[videorecording] |

Title on chief source and container differ

| 245 | 04 | The Beatles live at the Star Club in Hamburg, Germany, 1962‡h[sound recording]. |
| 246 | 1 | ‡iTitle on container:‡aLingasong Records presents the Beatles live at the Star Club in Hamburg, Germany, 1962 |

Portion of the main title

| 245 | 00 | Excavating the Bible.‡nVolume two,‡pMarine archaeology ‡h[videorecording]. |
| 246 | 30 | Marine archaeology‡h[videorecording] |

General Material Designation (GMD)

Use of a GMD is deemed optional by Rule 1.1C, *AACR2R (1998)*. There are several reasons why a library may choose to use GMDs. It indicates to users the format of a resource when a search is done in an online catalog since all resources with a specific GMD will cluster together. Additionally, the resource described in an online catalog may not readily be apparent to users even when the bibliographic record includes a physical description that includes type of resource and characteristics. Use of a GMD helps users to distinguish between different formats in which a title is available. For example, *Midnight Express* is the title of a book, as well as a motion picture, a motion picture sound track, and is also available on videorecording. However, there is a growing sentiment that GMDs are no longer useful, particularly in a Web-based environment in which some libraries use one bibliographic record to represent multiple manifestations of a title (a paper and an electronic version of a serial title, for example), or that the existing list of GMDs needs to expand to accommodate changing formats and needs of users. A survey was conducted by Jean Weihs concerning usage of GMDs in the twenty first century. The survey and results are available on the Web at http://ublib.buffalo.edu/libraries/units/cts/olac/capc/gmd.html.

The GMD is included in the 245 field, ‡h and is enclosed in brackets. It immediately follows the information provided in ‡a and precedes the ‡b. It is not repeatable.

Two lists of GMDs are provided in *AACR2R (1998)*. The first list is for British cataloging agencies; Australian, Canadian, and American cataloging agencies use terms from the second list. The following terms from the second list are used in this text: *electronic resource, kit, microform, motion picture, sound recording,* and *videorecording.*

example

| 245 | 00 | Kyushu-Okinawa Summit 2000 official guide‡h[electronic resource] |
| 245 | 00 | Cities for Utopia‡h[videorecording] |

Statement of Responsibility

The statement of responsibility provides names of corporate bodies and/or individuals responsible for production, creation, manufacture, etc. of a nonprint resource. This information is taken from the chief or prescribed sources of information.

The statement of responsibility is included in the 245 field, ‡c, is preceded by a forward slash, and is not repeatable. Each corporate body or individual presented in the statement of responsibility is separated by semicolons. Per Rule 1.1F1, *AACR2R (1998)*, statements of responsibility are to be transcribed as they appear. Information taken from sources other than the chief source of information will be bracketed.

example

| 245 | 00 | Kyushu-Okinawa Summit 2000 official guide‡h[electronic resource] /‡cpresented by the Government of Japan ; produced by Nippon Koho Center and NHK Enterprises 21. |
| 245 | 00 | Organized crime‡h[videorecording] /‡cproduced by Rutgers University, Newark, Graduate Department of Public Administration and Suburban Cablevision TV3 ; [producers, Steve Adubato, Karla Kasper ; director, Michael I. Butler]. |

EDITION

Provide edition information in the 250 field, **Edition Statement**, which is not repeatable. Edition information for nonprint resources is not limited to the term "edition," and includes "version," "release," "revision," or other terms deemed appropriate by the cataloging agency. Rule 1.2B1, *AACR2R (1998)*, instructs catalogers to transcribe edition statements in the form found on the item.

The following subfields are available for use in the 250 field: ‡a edition statement; ‡b remainder of edition statement. There are additional subfields that may be used with the 250; this text focuses discussion and examples on those that are most predominantly used.

There are no indicators defined for the 250 field.

example

250	Japanese/English version.
250	Version 1.00.
250	Windows version.
250	Director's cut.

PUBLICATION AND/OR DISTRIBUTION, OR MANUFACTURE INFORMATION

Consult the chief and/or prescribed sources of information to obtain information on where and when a resource was published, distributed, manufactured, etc. Publication, distribution, manufacture, etc. information is provided in the 260 field, **Publication, Distribution, etc. (Imprint)**, which is not repeatable.

Place of Publication, Distributions, Manufacture, Etc.

The place of publication, distribution, manufacture, etc. is provided in the 260 field, ‡a. It is repeatable if there is more than one place of publication, or if a resource is published in one location and distributed in another, for example.

Generally, the city and country or state of publication are given. If only a city name is given, and it is necessary to record the country, state, etc., for purposes of identification and clarification, record the supplied information in brackets, as per Rule 1.4C3, *AACR2R (1998)*.
example

260	Detroit, Mich.
260	Schmalkalden [Germany]

If a place of publication, distribution, manufacture, etc. is not provided, but may be ascertained, record in brackets with a question mark. Consult Rule 1.4C6, *AACR2R (1998)*, for further discussion of this topic.
example

260	[Denver?]

If no place of publication, distribution, manufacture, etc. is provided, and may not be ascertained, the abbreviation for the term "Sine loco," [S.l.], is used per Rule 1.4C6, *AACR2R (1998)*. The abbreviation is always bracketed.
example

260	[S.l.] :‡bMedia Mix Productions

Name of Publisher, Distributor, Manufacturer, Etc.

Consult the chief and/or prescribed sources of information first. Record the publisher's name following the place of publication as per Rule 1.4D1, *AACR2R (1998)*. If the distributor (or another body with a function related to the material being described) is included, transcribe the distributor, etc. name as it appears in the chief or prescribed sources of information. If the distributor's location differs from that of the publisher, record both locations.

Provide this information in the 260 field, ‡b, which is repeatable when there is more than one publisher, distributor, etc.

example

260	[S.l.] :‡bMedia Mix Productions ;‡aChicago :‡bDistributed by Light Pharmacy Films

The term "distributor" is added in brackets following distributor information only when this function (or other related functions) is not clear in the chief or prescribed sources of information, as per Rule 1.4E1, *AACR2R (1998)*. If distributor information is taken from a label affixed to the resource, external packaging, etc., this must be noted.

example

260	New Brunswick, N.J. :‡bT. Meyer Publishers ;‡aRobinson Media Group [distributor]
260	San Francisco, CA :‡bNan Hai Co., Inc. [distributor], ‡cc1988.
500	Distributor information from label affixed to external container.
500	Distributor information from cassette label.

If there is no information provided for publisher, distributor, etc., and it may not be ascertained, use the abbreviation for the term "sine nomine," [s.n.], as per Rule 1.4D7, *AACR2R (1998)*. The abbreviation is always bracketed.

example

260	Chicago :‡b[s.n.]

Date of Publication, Distribution, Manufacture, Etc.

Provide this information in the 260 field, ‡c, which is repeatable. However, the practice of repeating the ‡c is not widely used. Multiple dates, such as for date of production and copyright, may be included in the 260 field, ‡c.

Consult the chief and/or prescribed sources of information first. Record publication date, or distribution date if publication date is not available. In the absence of either dates, record copyright date, which is preceded by a lower case "c". Information on date of publication, distribution, etc. is further outlined in Rule 1.4F, *AACR2R (1998)*.

example

Publication date
260   Media, Pa. :‡bEducational Clearinghouse,‡c1990.

Copyright date
260   Oxford :‡bIRL Press Ltd.,‡cc1986.

If information on publication, distribution, etc. date is not provided in either the chief or prescribed sources of information, approximate the date of publication. Approximated dates are bracketed.
example

Approximated date
260   [S.l.] :‡bT. Meyer Publishers,‡c[ca. 1997]

Probable date
260   Cherry Hill, N.J. :‡bAriel Press,‡[1990?]

Decade certain
260   Clifton, N.J. :‡bPiermatti Educational Resources,‡c[198-]

Probable decade
260   Chicago :‡bScholars Press,‡c[199-?]

Note: More information on dates is available in *AACR2R (1998)*, Chapter 1, "General Rules for Description."

Multipart items: Include a beginning date if the resource is not complete and/or is expected to continue indefinitely. An ending date may be included when a resource is complete. Rule 1.4F8, *AACR2R (1998)* notes that this practice is optional.
example

260   Palo Alto, Calif. :‡bDIALOG Information Services,‡c1965-
260   New Brunswick, N.J. :‡bRutgers University Libraries, ‡c1995-2000.

Unpublished items: Do not attempt to provide a place of publication, etc. or publisher, distributor, manufacturer, etc. name for unpublished items, as per Rule 1.4D9, *AACR2R (1998)*. Do not use the abbreviations "S.l." or "s.n." A date may be included for the item.

example

260	‡c1999.
260	‡c[2000?]

There are no indicators defined for the 260 field.

PHYSICAL DESCRIPTION

Includes extent (number and Specific Material Designation (SMD) of physical parts of an item), other physical details (color or sound characteristics, for example), dimensions, and information about accompanying materials.

The physical description is provided in the 300 field, **Physical Description**. The physical description field is repeatable, permitting a multilevel description, yet this option is not commonly applied.

Extent

Provide the number and SMD of the parts of an item, as per Rule 1.5B1, *AACR2R (1998)*. Format specific information is provided in subrule .5B in Chapters 3, 6-7, 9, and 11, *AACR2R (1998)*. The SMD is not identical to the GMD. It is used to specify material types, while the GMD describes the broad category of materials into which a resource may fall. Extent is provided in the ‡a, and is not repeatable.

example

300	1 film reel
300	2 videocassettes
300	1 sound disc
300	1 sound cassette
300	1 computer disk
300	4 computer optical discs
300	10 microfiches
300	50 microfilm reels

Serially issued resources that are not yet complete include a SMD preceded by three blank spaces, as per Rule 1.5B5, *AACR2R (1998)*. Serially issued resources are not limited to periodicals, and may include any resource that is intended to be published indefinitely.

example

300	computer optical discs
300	microfiche

Other Physical Details

Provide a description of characteristics other than extent or dimensions, as per Rule 1.5C, *AACR2R (1998)*. This information is provided in the ‡b, which is not repeatable. The format specific chapters provide greater detail on physical details as related to various resources.
example

Motion picture- silent, black and white
300   1 film reel (30 min.) :‡bsi., b&w

Videorecording- sound, color
300   2 videocassettes (180 min.) :‡bsd., col.

Sound recording- digital recording, stereophonic sound
300   1 sound disc (50 min.) :‡bdigital, stereo.

Electronic resource- sound, color
300   2 computer optical discs :‡bsd., col.

Dimensions

Provide information on size, width, etc. as appropriate, as per Rule 1.5D1, *AACR2R (1998)*. The format specific chapters provide more detail on dimensions. Dimensions are included in the ‡c, which is not repeatable.
example

300   2 film reels (180 min.) :‡bsd., col. with b&w sequences ;‡c16 mm.
300   2 computer optical discs :‡bsd., col. ;‡c4 3/4 in.
300   38 microfilm reels :‡bcol., ill. ;‡c35 mm.
300   2 fiche :‡bmaps ;‡c11 x 15 cm.

Accompanying Materials

Provide information describing accompanying materials in one of three ways, per Rule 1.5E1, *AACR2R (1998)*: (1) at the end of the physical description; (2) in a note separate from the physical description; or (3) as part of a multilevel description.
example

As part of the physical description:
300   2 film reels (180 min.) :‡bsd., col. ;‡c16 mm. +‡e1 teacher's guide (25 p. : ill. ; 28 cm.)

Note: If more than one item is included in the ‡e, 300, each item is preceded by a space and a plus sign.

300	1 computer disc :‡bsd., col. ;‡c4 3/4 in. +‡e 1 user's guide (30 p. : ill. ; 12 cm.) + 1 videocassette (20 min., VHS)

In a separate note:

300	2 film reels (180 min.) :‡bsd., col. ;‡c16 mm.
500	Accompanied by teacher's guide titled: Safety and your child.

Multilevel description:

300	2 film reels (180 min.) :‡bsd., col. ;‡c16 mm.
300	1 sound cassette (40 min.) :‡banalog
300	50 p. :‡bill. ;‡c28 cm.

SERIES

Provide series treatment if available in the chief and/or prescribed sources of information. General series information is presented in this text since the focus is on descriptive cataloging procedures. Series are represented in this text by the 440 field, **Series Statement/Added Entry—Title**, which is repeatable.

The following subfields are available for use in the 440 field: ‡a title; ‡n number of part/section; ‡p name of part/section; ‡v volume or numbering designation.

Provide series title in the 440, ‡a, which is not repeatable.

The first indicator value for the 440 field is undefined. The second indicator specifies number of nonfiling characters, with a range of 0-9 available.

Detailed information on series, including various types of treatment, is available on the USMARC Web page at http://lcweb.loc.gov/marc/bibliographic/ecbdsers.html.
example

440	0	Library of African cinema
440	0	BMG classics

Provide information on numbered parts in the ‡n Number of Part/Section of a Work.
example

440	0	Langues de l'Orient.‡nI,‡pManuals
440	0	Baseball.‡nVolume 7,‡pFourth inning

Provide the specific name of the part(s)/section(s) of a series in the ‡p Name of Part/Section of a Work.
example

| 440 | 0 | The Great explorers.‡pThe Columbus series |
| 440 | 0 | Janua linguarum.‡pSeries minor |

Provide numbering designation, such as "volume" or "part" in the ‡v.
example

| 440 | 0 | BMG classics ;‡vvol. 32 |
| 440 | 0 | Medicine at the crossroads ;‡vMECR108 |

NOTES

Notes provide a variety of information, including contents, names of individuals or corporate bodies responsible for creation or production of a resource, additional physical description, cast, language, etc. Format specific notes are covered in the other chapters of this text.

Notes of a very general nature are provided in the 500 field, **General Note**, which is repeatable. This type of note is more prevalent in nonprint cataloging than in cataloging for print resources since the bibliographic record must provide as much information as possible when a resource is noncirculating and not easily accessible to users. Internet resources are a little different in that bibliographic records often provide hyperlinks directly to the resource.

Nature, Scope, or Artistic Form

Rule 1.7B1, *AACR2R (1998)* instructs catalogers to provide a note on nature, scope, or artistic form of a resource. Provide this information in the 500 field, **General Note** only when it is not apparent from the description. The 500 field is repeatable.
This note is covered in more detail in the format specific chapters.
example

500	Interview.
500	Novel.
500	Dramatic re-enactment.

Language of the Item and/or Translation or Adaptation

Per rule 1.7B2, *AACR2R* (1998), indicate language of the nonprint resource when more than one language is present, or if the resource is in a language (or languages) other than the primary language of the cataloging agency. Provide this information in the 546 field, **Language Note,** which works in conjunction with the 041. This note also provides information on subtitles and accompanying printed material. The 546 field is repeatable.

This note is covered in more detail in the format specific chapters.

example

041	1	spa‡beng
546		In Spanish with English subtitles.
041	1	freeng‡beng
546		In French and English; subtitled in English.
041	0	engfrepordut
546		Search engine is available in English, French, Portuguese, or Dutch.

Source of Title Proper

Per Rule 1.7B3, *AACR2R (1998)* indicate source of title if not taken from chief or prescribed sources of information, or has been supplied by the cataloger. Provide this information in the 500 field, **General Note,** which is repeatable.

This note is covered in more detail in the format specific chapters.

example

500	Title supplied by cataloger.
500	Title taken from accompanying printed documentation.
500	Title from container.

Statements of Responsibility

Provide the names of individuals or corporate bodies not named in the statement of responsibility who have contributed to the production, as well as their function in the production. Provide this information in the 508 field, **Creation/Production Credits Note,** which is not repeatable.

This note is covered in more detail in the format specific chapters.

example

508	Written and directed by John Lapine ; musical direction by Paul Gemignani ; orchestration by Michael Starobin.
508	Writer/visual editor, Janice Mallin.

Edition and History

Per Rule 1.7B6, *AACR2R (1998)* provide additional information on the nonprint resource, or use to provide history of the nonprint resource. Provide this information in the 500 field, **General Note**, which is repeatable, and differs from what is provided in the 250 field, **Edition Statement**.

This note is covered in more detail in the format specific chapters.

example

500	Reissue of: Harmonia Mundi France HMC905149 (1985).
500	Transcribed from: The vision of William concerning Piers the Plowman : in three parallel texts together with Richard the Redeless / by William Langland ; edited from numerous manuscripts with preface, notes, and a glossary by Walter W. Skeat. Oxford : Clarendon Press, 1986.
500	This film is "...substantially as it was when it was first released in 1928."

Publication, Distribution, Etc. Information

Rule 1.7B9, *AACR2R (1998)* instructs catalogers to make notes on publication, distribution, etc., details not included in the publication, distribution, etc., area but which are considered to be important. Provide this information in the 500 field, **General Note**, which is repeatable.

This note is covered in more detail in the format specific chapters.

example

500	All selections previously released; recorded chiefly 1961-1963.
500	Previously released material.
500	Distributor information taken from label affixed to jewel case.

Physical Description

Rule 1.7B10, *AACR2R (1998)* instructs catalogers to provide additional physical description not represented in the 007 field, **Physical Description Fixed Field—General Information,** or the 300 field, **Physical Description.** This information is provided in the 500 field, **General Note**, which is repeatable.

Additional physical description includes notes on details that affect use, and other information deemed important by the cataloging agency.

This note is covered in more detail in the format specific chapters.

example

500	Printed on both sides of sheet, dissected and laminated.
500	Analog recording.
500	Automatic sequence.
500	Dolby surround sound.
500	Hand-painted in various colors.

Accompanying Materials

Rule 1.7B11, *AACR2R (1998)* instructs catalogers to provide details of accompanying materials in a note when they are not included in the physical description or a separate description. Provide additional information on accompanying materials in the 500 field, **General Note**, which is repeatable.

This note is covered in more detail in the format specific chapters.

example

500	Program notes by Charlotte Heth and bibliography and discography in container.
500	User's manual titled: Rx for pharmaceutical science research : a user's manual.
500	Accompanying materials housed in container (32 x 5 x 28 cm.)

Audience

Rule 1.7B14, *AACR2R (1998)* instructs catalogers to provide information on target audience. This information is provided in the 521 field, **Target Audience Note**, which is repeatable.

This note is covered in more detail in the format specific chapters.

example

521	2	Interest grade level: Grades 4-6.
521		Intended for high school students.
521		Available for teaching and research purposes.
521		For individuals doing pharmaceutical science library research.

Other Formats

Rule 1.7B16 *AACR2R (1998)* instructs catalogers to provide information on additional formats in which a resource is available. This information is provided in the 530 field, **Additional Physical Form Available Note**, which is repeatable.

This note is covered in more detail in the format specific chapters.

example

| 530 | Also available in print. |
| 530 | Also available on the World Wide Web. |

Summary

Rule 1.7B17, *AACR2R (1998)* instructs catalogers to provide a brief description of the contents of a resource. This information is provided in the 520 field, **Summary, Etc.,** which is repeatable.

This note is covered in more detail in the format specific chapters.

example

| 520 | Summary: Provides image and full-text online access to back issues. Consult the online table of contents for specific holdings. |
| 520 | Summary: Explores the system of juvenile justice in America today. Shows how the system's shortcomings often do damage to the children it intends to punish and rehabilitate. |

Contents Notes

Rule 1.7B18, *AACR2R (1998)* instructs catalogers to provide information detailing the contents of a resource. This information is provided in the 505 field, **Formatted Contents Note,** which is repeatable. It provides individual titles or parts contained in a resource, and may include statements of responsibility and durations (for sound recordings and visual materials, for example).

This note is covered in more detail in the format specific chapters.

example

| 505 | 0 | Introduction to Drug literature index - - Introduction to Index medicus - - Introduction to International pharmaceutical abstracts. |
| 505 | 0 | Currency exchanges (Metz) - - Currency exchanges (Mueller) - - Currency exchanges (Spufford) - - Prices (Metz) - - Prices (Posthumus). |

Descriptive or Library Specific Notes

Rule 1.7B20, *AACR2R (1998)* instructs catalogers to provide descriptive or copy specific information about nonprint resources. This information is provided in a 500 field, **General Note,** which is repeatable.

This note is covered in more detail in the format specific chapters.

example

500	Use restricted to Special Collections Reading Room.
500	Library's copy 1 lacks accompanying guide.
500	Library's copy imperfect.
500	Atlases are noncirculating.

"With" Notes

Rule 1.7B21, *AACR2R (1998)* instructs catalogers to provide notes for titles that are not the first in a collective title. This information is provided in the 500 field, **General Note**, which is repeatable.

This note is covered in more detail in the format specific chapters.

example

500	With: Mineral resources map of Mongolia.
500	With: Meinken, F. Wabash blues.
500	With: Baby Snooks.
500	With: Power Chinese.

SUBJECT ACCESS

Subject access to nonprint resources helps users to identify and locate resources, since the bibliographic record must provide as much information as possible when a resource is noncirculating and not easily accessible to users. Internet resources are a little different in that bibliographic records often provide hyperlinks directly to the resource. Subject headings are used to provide access to resources through *personal names*, *corporate names*, *topical terms*, or *geographic names*. Subject headings may be further subdivided by form division (format of material), general subdivisions, chronological subdivisions, and geographic subdivisions. Meeting names and subject added entries for uniform titles are not included in this text.

PERSONAL NAME

Provide subject access to personal names in the 600 field, **Subject Added Entry—Personal Name**, which is repeatable. Personal names are included in a bibliographic record when a resource is about an individual or individuals, or contains a significant portion of information about an individual or individuals.

The following subfields are available for use in the 600 field: ‡a personal name; ‡c titles associated with a name; ‡d dates associated with a name; ‡v form subdivision; ‡x general subdivision; ‡y chronological subdivision; ‡z geographic subdivision. There are additional subfields that may be used with the 600; this text focuses discussion and examples on those that are most predominantly used.

The initial indicator value indicates type of name. An initial article value of 0 indicates entry under forename; 1 indicates entry under single surname. The second indicator value provides source of name heading. A second indicator value of 0 indicates that a name is from the Library of Congress Name Authority file. Additional information is available on the USMARC Web page at http://lcweb.loc.gov/marc/bibliographic/ecbdsubj.html#mrcb600.

example

600	00	Cher,‡d1946-
600	10	Day-Lewis, Daniel.
600	10	Weinberg, Valerie Ann.
600	10	Irving, Henry,‡cSir,‡d1838-1905.
600	10	Ellington, Duke,‡d1899-1974.
600	10	King, Martin Luther,‡cJr.,‡d 1929-1968‡xAssassination.
600	10	Krupa, Gene,‡d1909-1973‡vBiography.
600	10	Shakespeare, William,‡d1564-1616‡xStage history ‡y1800-1950.
600	10	Gogh, Vincent van,‡d1853 1890‡xMuseums‡zNetherlands‡zAmsterdam.

CORPORATE NAME

Provide subject access to corporate names in the 610 field, **Subject Added Entry—Corporate Name**, which is repeatable. Corporate names are included in a bibliographic record when a resource is about a corporation or corporations, or contains a significant portion of information about a corporation or corporations.

The following subfields are available for use in the 610 field: ‡a corporate or jurisdiction names; ‡b subordinate units; ‡v form subdivision; ‡x general subdivision; ‡y chronological subdivision; ‡z geographic subdivision. There are additional subfields that may be used with the 610; this text focuses discussion and examples on those that are most predominantly used.

The initial indicator value indicates form of entry for names. An initial indicator value of 1 is for jurisdiction name; 2 is for a name presented in direct order. A second indicator value of 0 indicates that a name is from the Library of Congress Name Authority file. Additional information is available on the USMARC Web page at http://lcweb.loc.gov/marc/bibliographic/ecbdsubj.html#mrcb610 .

example

610	20	Lyceum Theatre (London, England)
610	10	United States.‡bDept. of the Interior.
610	20	Harvard University‡xFunds and scholarships‡vHandbooks, manuals, etc.
610	20	Microsoft Corporation‡xHistory.
610	20	Grand Central Terminal (New York, N.Y.)‡xHistory‡y20th century.
610	20	Salvation Army‡zEngland.

TOPICAL TERMS

Provide subject access to topical terms in the 650 field, **Subject Added Entry—Topical Term,** which is repeatable. Terms used in the 650 may describe form of the resource (Motion pictures, Spanish) or content (Jazz, Bicycle touring).

The following subfields are available for use in the 650 field: ‡a topical term or geographic name as entry element; ‡v form division; ‡x general subdivision; ‡y chronological subdivision; ‡z geographic subdivision. There are additional subfields that may be used with the 650; this text focuses discussion and examples on those that are most predominantly used.

The initial article value indicates level of subject; blank indicates that no information has been provided. Other first indicator values available are: 0 for no level specified; 1 for primary level of subject; and 2 for secondary level of subject. In many cases, subject headings supplied by catalogers or provided in records available through union databases have an initial indicator value of blank. A second indicator value of 0 indicates that a name is from the Library of Congress Name Authority file. Additional information is available on the USMARC Web page at http://lcweb.loc.gov/marc/bibliographic/ecbdsubj.html#mrcb650.

example

650	0	Violence in art.
650	0	Grandparents as parents‡xServices for‡zNew Jersey ‡vDirectories.
650	0	Crime prevention‡xCitizen participation.

| 650 | 0 | American prose literature‡y19th century. |
| 650 | 0 | Artists‡zUnited States. |

GEOGRAPHIC TERMS

Provide subject access to geographic terms in the 651 field, **Subject Added Entry—Geographic Name**, which is repeatable.

The following subfields are available for use in the 651 field: ‡a geographic name; ‡v form division; ‡x general subdivision; ‡y chronological subdivision; ‡z geographic subdivision. There are additional subfields that may be used with the 651; this text focuses discussion and examples on those that are most predominantly used.

The initial indicators are undefined for this field. A second indicator value of 0 indicates that a name is from the Library of Congress Name Authority file. Additional information is available on the USMARC Web page at http://lcweb.loc.gov/marc/bibliographic/ecbdsubj.html#mrcb651.

example

651	0	Brooklyn (New York, N.Y.)
651	0	Manhattan (New York, N.Y.)‡vTours‡vMaps.
651	0	United States‡xPopulation‡xStatistics.
651	0	United States‡xHistory‡yCivil War, 1861 1865.
651	0	United States‡xHistory‡zStudy and teaching (Higher) ‡zNew Jersey.

ADDED ENTRIES

Added entries provide access to personal and corporate names that are not main entries yet serve as important additional access points. Name added entries include directors, cast, editors, publishers, or production companies. Title added entries provide additional access for titles related to the main work.

PERSONAL NAME

Provide access to personal names in the 700 field, **Added Entry—Personal**, which is repeatable. Personal name added entries are used for individuals who have made significant contributions to the production of the resource being cataloged. Personal name added entries differ from personal names in the 600 in that they provide different types of information, and would be found in an online catalog using different types of searches (subject versus personal name).

The following subfields are available for use in the 700 field: ‡a personal name; ‡c titles or other words associated with a particular name; ‡d dates; ‡4 relator code. A list of relator codes is available on the USMARC Web page at http://lcweb.loc.gov/marc/relators/. There are additional subfields that may be used with the 700; this text focuses discussion and examples on those that are most predominantly used.

The initial indicator value indicates type of name. An initial article value of 0 indicates entry under forename; 1 indicates entry under single surname. The second indicator value indicates type of added entry. A second blank second indicator value indicates that no information is provided; a second indicator value of 2 indicates an analytical entry, and means the item in the bibliographic record contains the work represented by the added entry. Additional information is available on the USMARC Web page at http://lcweb.loc.gov/marc/bibliographic/ecbdadde.html#mrcb700. example

700	0	Liberace,‡d1919-
700	1	Glenn, Tyree.
700	1	Irving, Henry,‡cSir,‡d1838-1905.
700	1	Severinsen, Doc,‡d1927-
700	1	Fellini, Federico.‡4drt
700	1	Binoche, Juliette,‡d1964- ‡4prf

CORPORATE NAME

Provide access to corporate names in the 710 field, **Added Entry—Corporate Name,** which is repeatable. Corporate name added entries differ from corporate names in the 610 in that they provide different types of information, and would be found in an online catalog using different types of searches (subject versus corporate name).

The following subfields are available for use in the 710 field: ‡a corporate name or jurisdiction name; ‡b subordinate unit; and ‡4 relator code. There are additional subfields which may be used with the 710; this text focuses discussion and examples on those that are most predominantly used.

The initial indicator value indicates type of corporate name. An initial article value 1 indicates entry in jurisdiction order; a value of 2 indicates entry in direct order. The second indicator value indicates type of added entry. A blank second indicator value indicates that no information is provided; a second indicator value of 2 indicates an analytical entry, and means the item in the bibliographic record contains the work represented by the added entry. Additional information is available on the USMARC Web

page at http://lcweb.loc.gov/marc/bibliographic/ecbdadde.html#mrcb710.
example

710	1	United States.‡bArmy.
710	2	Warner Home Video.
710	2	United States.‡bBureau of the Census.
710	2	Beatles.‡4prf

UNIFORM TITLE

Provide access to a uniform title in the 730 field, **Added Entry—Uniform Title,** which is repeatable. Uniform titles provide a title related to the resource. Examples include radio, television programs, or motion pictures.

The following subfields are available for use in the 730 field: ‡a uniform title; ‡f date of a work; ‡h medium; ‡k form subheading; ‡l language. There are additional subfields that may be used with the 730; this text focuses discussion and examples on those that are most predominantly used.

The initial indicator value indicates number of nonfiling characters (0-9). The second indicator value indicates type of added entry. A blank second indicator value indicates that no information is provided; a second indicator value of 2 indicates an analytical entry, and means the item in the bibliographic record contains the work represented by the added entry. Additional information is available on the USMARC Web page at http://lcweb.loc.gov/marc/bibliographic/ecbdadde.html#mrcb730.
example

245	00	Organized crime‡h[videorecording].
730	0	Caucus New Jersey (Television program)
245	04	The collected works of Thomas Hobbes.
730	0	Thucydides.‡tHistory of the Peloponnesian War. ‡lEnglish.‡f1992.
245	00	Blade runner‡h[videorecording]
730	0	Blade runner.‡hMotion picture.
245	00	James Joyce reading "Anna Livia Plurabelle"‡h[sound recording].
730	0	Finnegan's wake.‡kSelections.
245	00	65 songs, for voice and piano.
730	0	Songs.‡lEnglish & German.‡kSelections.

RELATED TITLES

Provide access to titles related to the work described in the 245 field, **Title Statement** using the 740 field, **Added Entry—Uncontrolled Related/Analytical Title,** which is repeatable.

The following subfields are available for use in the 740 field: ‡a Uncontrolled related/analytical title; ‡h medium; ‡n number of part/section of a work; ‡p name of part/section of a work. There are additional subfields that may be used with the 740; this text focuses discussion and examples on those that are most predominantly used.

The initial indicator value indicates number of nonfiling characters (0-9). The second indicator value indicates type of added entry. A blank second indicator value indicates that no information is provided; a second indicator value of 2 indicates an analytical entry, and means the item in the bibliographic record contains the work represented by the added entry. Additional information is available on the USMARC Web page at http://lcweb.loc.gov/marc/bibliographic/ecbdadde.html#mrcb740.
example

245	00	Cape Fear‡h[motion picture].
500		Based on the novel "The Executioners" by John D. MacDonald.
740	0	Executioners.
245	00	Hail Mary‡h[videorecording]
500		Also includes a short film titled "The Book of Mary."
740	0	Book of Mary‡h[videorecording].
740	0	America by design.‡pThe workplace.
740	0	Against all odds : inside statistics ;‡vprogram 15-16.

CLASSIFICATION

Factors raised in regards to classification of nonprint resources include: book versus nonbook classification, catalog versus shelf access, separate versus integrated shelving, and browsing capabilities (Frost, 1989). Book versus nonbook classification raises the issue of what type of classification is most appropriate for describing nonprint resources. In many libraries, there is a variety of treatments used for nonprint collections. For example, microforms, maps, and electronic resources may be classified using Library of Congress Classification (LCC) or Dewey Decimal Classification (DDC). Governmental microforms and maps in the same library may be classified using Superintendent of Documents (SuDocs) Classification. And other resources, such as motion pictures, videorecordings, and sound recordings may be arranged according to an accession number scheme, alphabetically by title, arranged by genre, etc.

Catalog versus shelf access raises the issue of whether intellectual access to nonprint resources is provided by shelf arrangement or by the online catalog (Frost, 1989). Shelf arrangement offers limited access to a collection, while access through an online catalog offers a variety of means by which a resource can be searched and retrieved.

Separate versus integrated shelving raises the question of whether nonprint resources should be integrated with print resources, or should separate shelving/storage areas be provided? If separate shelving/storage areas are provided, there is also the issue of providing open or closed shelving. One could argue that integrated shelving promotes greater access since all materials in a given subject area are located together, which is more beneficial to users. Open shelving also makes materials more vulnerable to damage, wear and tear, and theft.

The issue of browsing capabilities raises the question of how easily nonprint resources lend themselves to browsing. Some materials, such as videorecordings, sound recordings, and computer files provide information on external containers that could be helpful to browsing users. Other materials, such as map and atlases lend themselves easily to browsing. However, other types of materials, such as microforms, do not lend themselves to browsing at all, and integrated shelving provides no benefits for users. Lastly, resources such as Internet resources are readily available in many online catalogs through hypertext links, eliminating the question of whether browsing is even needed.

REFERENCES

Frost, Carolyn O. 1989. *Media Access and Organization: A Cataloging and Reference Sources Guide for Nonbook Materials*. Englewood, Colo.: Libraries Unlimited.

Network Development and MARC Standards Office, Library of Congress in cooperation with Standards and Support, National Library of Canada. 1999. *MARC 21 Format for Bibiliographic Data Including Guidelines for Content Designation, 1999 Edition*. Washington, D.C.: Library of Congress Distribution Service.

2 CARTOGRAPHIC MATERIALS

OVERVIEW

Cartographic materials are an important part of the collections of many libraries. There are specialized libraries with collections that consist primarily of cartographic materials.

Level of description provided for cartographic materials depends on a library's collection, available staff, and the importance of these resources to their holdings. All examples included in this text use full level description.

The type of classification provided for cartographic materials varies with size and type of library as well as by kind of collection in which the resources are housed (restricted or freely available). Libraries may provide Library of Congress Classification numbers or Dewey Decimal numbers, accession numbers, may arrange cartographic materials alphabetically by title, geographic region or topic, etc. Arrangement and classification varies by library and how access is provided to these resources.

The glossary in *AACR2R (1998:616)* defines cartographic materials as "Any material representing the whole or part of the earth or any celestial body at any scale. Cartographic materials include two- and three-dimensional maps and plans (including maps of imaginary places); aeronautical, navigational, and celestial charts; atlases; globes; block diagrams; sections; aerial photographs with a cartographic purpose; bird's-eye views (map views), etc." The following categories of cartographic materials are covered in this text: maps and atlases. Globes are not covered in keeping with the aim of providing specific information for the broadest range of materials that are likely to be handled by the average cataloger.

ELEMENTS OF BIBLIOGRAPHIC RECORDS FOR CARTOGRAPHIC MATERIALS

The category of resources referred to as cartographic materials includes maps and atlases. This chapter does not include discussion and examples of globes or geospatial imaging. The discussion is limited to print maps and atlases in keeping with the focus of providing the broadest range of materials that are handled by the average cataloger.

The following information may be used to create bibliographic records for cartographic materials:

- **Chief Source of Information**
- **Prescribed Sources of Information**
- **Choice of Main Entry**
- **International Standard Book Number (ISBN)**
- **Coded Cartographic Mathematical Data**
- **Cataloging Source**
- **Language Code**
- **Geographic Information**
- **Library of Congress Call Number**
- **Geographic Classification**
- **Title**
- **Title Variations**
- **General Material Designation (GMD)**
- **Statement of Responsibility**
- **Edition**
- **Scale**
- **Projection**
- **Place of Publication and/or Distribution, or Manufacture, etc.**
- **Name of Publisher(s) and/or Distributor(s)**
- **Date of Publication, Distribution, Copyright, Manufacture, etc.**
- **Physical Description**
- **Series**
- **Notes**
- **Subject Access**
- **Added Entries (Personal and/or Corporate Names, Title Added Entries)**
- **Classification**

CHIEF SOURCE OF INFORMATION

The chief source of information for maps is the item itself. The entire item is considered as the chief source, and information may be taken from anywhere on a map, even when an item is issued in a number of parts, such as a map on several sheets. The title page of an atlas is the chief source of information.

If the chief source yields little or no useful information, consult accompanying printed matter.

PRESCRIBED SOURCES OF INFORMATION

Rule 3.0B2, *AACR2R (1998)* states that the following sources of information should be consulted when creating bibliographic information for cartographic materials:

- Title/statement of responsibility- Chief source of information
- Edition- Chief source of information, accompanying material
- Mathematical data- Chief source of information, accompanying material
- Publication, distribution, manufacture, etc.- Chief source of information, accompanying material
- Physical Description- Any source of information may be consulted
- Series- Chief source of information, accompanying material
- Notes- Any source of information may be consulted

CHOICE OF MAIN ENTRY

Main entry may be under personal authorship or corporate authorship, or title main entry may be chosen. Rule 21.1A1, *AACR2R (1998)* defines a personal author as the individual chiefly responsible for a resource's intellectual or artistic content. Rule 21.1B1, *AACR2R (1998)* defines a corporate author as an organization or group of persons with a particular name that functions as an entity. Lastly, Rule 21.1C1, *AACR2R (1998)* states that a resource should be entered under title proper (or uniform title if appropriate) when: personal authorship is unknown or shared by a large number of individuals, and authorship can not be attributed to one particular individual or when a resource is not issued by a corporate body; or when a resource is a collection of works by different individuals or corporate bodies.

In some cases, title main entry is the most logical choice since the cartographic material is the result of the work of many individuals and/or corporate bodies, and it is not possible to attribute authorship to a particular individual or corporate body. A cartographer must provide more than a drawing to be given main entry; a corporate body must be a map making body to be given main entry. Lack of a statement of responsibility is another reason why title main entry is chosen for maps or atlases. Rule 21.1B2f, *AACR2R (1998)* instructs catalogers to enter a work emanating from one or more corporate bodies under the appropriate corporate body if it falls into one of six categories. Category f applies to cartographic materials, and states that corporate main entry is appropriate for materials that emanate from a corporate body other than one responsible only for publication or distribution. For this reason, it is not uncommon for the publisher and main entry to be the same.

example

Corporate body main entry

110	2	Hagstrom Map Company.
245	10	Hagstrom Middlesex County atlas.
260		Maspeth, N.Y. :‡bHagstrom Map Co.,‡c1998.
110	2	Franklin Maps (Firm)
245	10	Metro street map of Burlington County, New Jersey ‡h[map].
260		King of Prussia, Pa. :‡bFranklin Maps,‡c1999.

Title main entry

| 245 | 00 | Bathymetric map of the Franz Josef Land area‡h[map] / ‡ccompiled by Gennady G. Matishov ... [et al.]. |
| 260 | | Boulder, Co. :‡bGeological Society of America ;‡aCapitol Heights, Md. :‡bWilliams & Neintz Map Corporation, ‡c1995. |

PHYSICAL DESCRIPTION

Physical description is provided both in fixed fields and the 300 field, **Physical Description.** The 007 field, **Physical Description Fixed Field—General Information** provides information on physical description in alphabetic coded form. Some bibliographic utilities and cataloging modules display the 007 field at the top of the bibliographic record with other fixed fields; other utilities and modules provide this information in the bibliographic record with the variable fields. In this text, the 007 field is displayed with the variable fields in examples of bibliographic records.

There are no subfields or indicators defined for the 007 field.

The 007 for cartographic materials (maps and atlases) begins with an s (globes are coded with a d) and has eight characters defined for use. Selected values are provided in the following text.

Position 00- Category of material; is always **a** for "map"

Position 01- SMD; **d** (atlas); **j** (map); **y** (view); **z** (other)

Position 02- Undefined; leave blank

Position 03- Color; **a** (one color); **c** (multicolored)

Position 04- Physical medium; **a** (paper); **g** (textile); **u** (unknown); **z** (other)

Position 05- Type of reproduction; **f** (facsimile); **n** (not applicable); **u** (unknown); **z** (other)

Position 06- Production/reproduction details; **b** (photocopy); **d** (film); **u** (unknown); **z** (other)

Position 07- Positive/negative aspects; **a** (positive); **b** (negative); **m** (mixed polarity); **n** (not applicable)

example

```
007  ad aanzn
     a = map
     d = atlas
     blank
     a = one color
     a = paper
     n = type of reproduction not applicable
     z = other production/reproduction details
     n = positive/negative aspect not applicable

     aj cgnzn
     a = map
     j = map
     blank
     c = multicolored
     g = textile
     n = type of reproduction not applicable
     z = other production/reproduction details
     n = positive/negative aspect not applicable
```

A full list of values for the 007 field is available on the USMARC Web page at http://lcweb.loc.gov/marc/bibliographic/ecbd007s.html#mrcb007s.

INTERNATIONAL STANDARD BOOK NUMBER (ISBN)

Monographic resources are often assigned ISBNs. Provide this information in the 020 field, **International Standard Book Number**, which is repeatable. This information can be helpful in identifying specific versions of a resource.

The following subfields are used in the 020: ‡a ISBN; ‡c terms of availability (price).

There are no indicators defined for the 020 field.

example

| 020 | 9211198208 |
| 020 | 1877911925 |

CODED CARTOGRAPHIC MATHEMATIC DATA

Information on cartographic mathematical data, which includes scale, projection, and/or coordinates, is provided in coded form in the 034 field, **Coded Cartographic Mathematic Data**, which is repeatable.

The following subfields are available for use in the 034 field: ‡a category of scale, with three code values: a- linear scale, b- angular scale, and z- other type of scale; ‡b constant ratio linear horizontal scale; ‡c constant ratio linear vertical scale; ‡d coordinates- westernmost longitude; ‡e coordinates- easternmost longitude; ‡f coordinates- northernmost latitude; ‡g coordinates- southernmost latitude; ‡h angular scale; ‡j declination- northern limit; ‡k declination- southern limit; ‡m right ascension- eastern limit; ‡n right ascension- western limit; ‡p equinox; ‡s G-ring latitude; ‡t G-ring longitude.

The first indicator value specifies type of scale. An initial indicator value of 0 indicates that scale is indeterminable or no scale information is recorded; a value of 1 indicates the presence of a single horizontal scale; a value of 3 indicates that there is a range of scales. The second indicator value specifies type of ring for digital cartographic materials. A second indicator value of blank indicates that information on type of ring is not applicable (meaning that the item is not a digital cartographic resource).

Additional information on the 034 field and indicator values is available on the USMARC Web page at http://lcweb.loc.gov/marc/bibliographic/ecbdnot1.html#mrcb034.

example

| 034 | 1 | a‡b425000 |
| 034 | 1 | a‡b100000‡dE0154730‡eE0381000‡fS055510‡gS0352249 |

CATALOGING SOURCE

Information on the origin of a bibliographic record, plus any institutions that have modified a record, is provided in the 040 field, **Cataloging Source**, which is not repeatable.

The following subfields are available for use in the 040 field:

‡a original cataloging agency; ‡c transcribing agency (which is typically the institution in ‡a); and ‡d modifying agency. There are other subfields that may be used in the 040; this discussion is limited to those that are most predominantly used.

There are no indicators defined for the 040 field.

example

Original cataloging record created and transcribed by Rutgers University Libraries
040   NjR‡cNjR

Original cataloging record created and transcribed by Rutgers University Libraries, modified by Library X.
040   NjR‡NjR‡dXyZ

Original cataloging record created and transcribed by Rutgers University Libraries, modified at a later date by Rutgers University Libraries.
040   NjR‡NjR‡dNjR

LANGUAGE CODE

Provide information on language(s) present in a resource in the 041 field, **Language Code**, which is not repeatable. Information in the 041 is provided in alphabetic coded form. The 041 works in conjunction with the 546 field, **Language Note**.

Codes are provided according to their predominance in the resource (Network Development and MARC Standards Office, Library of Congress, 1999). The 041 field can provide codes for a maximum of six languages. If more than six languages are present in the resource, the language for the title is coded as "mul"(multiple) to represent all the languages.

The following subfields are used in the 041: ‡a language code for text, sound track, or separate title; ‡b language code for summary or subtitle; ‡g language code for accompanying materials other than librettos; ‡h language code for original and/or intermediate translations of text.

The initial indicator value indicates whether a resource is or includes a translation. An initial indicator of 0 indicates that the resource is a not a translation and does not include a translation; a value of 1 indicates that the item is a translation or includes a translation.

example

041   1   freita‡gengfreita
546   In French and Italian; summary notes in English, French, and Italian.

GEOGRAPHIC INFORMATION

Provide information on the geographic area presented, described, covered, etc. by the resource in the 043 field, **Geographic Area Code,** which is not repeatable. The 043 can accommodate one-three codes, which are represented in alphabetic coded form. Multiple geographic codes are separated by a ‡a.

Indicator values are not defined for the 043 field.

example

> *Resource contains information pertaining to New Jersey, in the United States*
> 043   n-us-nj

> *Resource contains information pertaining to the Great Plains region in the United States*
> 043   np- - - - -

> *Resource contains information pertaining to Japan*
> 043   a-ja- - -

> *Resource contains information pertaining to Spain and Mexico*
> 043   e-sp- - -‡an-mx- - -

A full list of geographic area codes is available on the USMARC Web page at http://lcweb.loc.gov/marc/geoareas/.

LIBRARY OF CONGRESS CALL NUMBER

Provide a Library of Congress Call Number (if applicable according to the cataloging agency's policies and procedures for nonprint resources) in the 050 field, **Library of Congress Call Number,** which is repeatable. Some institutions have policies governing whether an LC Call Number is included in the bibliographic portion of a record when their records are submitted to a national online bibliographic utility such as RLIN or OCLC.

The following subfields are available for use in the 050 field: ‡a classification number; ‡b item number.

The initial indicator value indicates whether the item is in Library of Congress's collection. An initial value of blank indicates that no information is provided, and is used when libraries other than the Library of Congress provide classification numbers. The second indicator value indicates source of call number. Classification numbers provided by Library of Congress have a second indicator value of zero; classification numbers provided by other libraries have a second indicator value of 4.

example

| 050 | 0 | G2165.H1‡bU5 1998 |
| 050 | 4 | G3813.M4 1999‡b.H3 |

Detailed instructions on how to classify maps using Library of Congress Classification (LCC) is provided in Library of Congress's *Map Cataloging Manual*. Maps classed according to LCC follow the G schedule, which covers geography, anthropology, and recreation. Numerical notations are provided to permit catalogers to classify maps by major geographical, political, or cultural units, which may be further subdivided according to major countries or geographic regions (Frost, 1989).

GEOGRAPHIC CLASSIFICATION

Provide information on geographic classification that represents the cartographic material's geographic area and (if appropriate) geographic subarea and populated place name covered by the resource. This information is provided in the 052 field, **Geographic Classification**, which is repeatable. The following subfields are available for use in the 052 field: ‡a geographic classification area code; ‡b geographic classification subarea code; ‡d populated place name.

The first indicator value provides information on source of code. A first indicator value of blank indicates that the source of the geographic code is the Library of Congress Classification; a value of zero indicates that the source of the code is the United States Department of Defense Classification. The second indicator is undefined.

example

052		2165
052		3814‡bM422‡bM85‡bM29
052		3813‡bO3

TITLE INFORMATION

Includes title, general material designation, remainder of title, and statement of responsibility.

Title

Consult the chief source of information first. If it is lacking or provides limited or no information, consult the prescribed sources of information. In the absence of chief or prescribed sources of information, a title may be supplied by the cataloger. The supplied title must be bracketed, and the source of title must be documented in a general note.

Some maps have insets with unique titles or additional maps on the verso. Additionally, envelopes or containers for cartographic materials will often bear a title that differs from that on the chief source of information. In such a case, make a note stating this difference, and include an added title entry for the variant title.

Title information is provided in the 245 field, **Title Statement**. The following subfields are available for use in the 245 field: ‡a title; ‡b remainder of title; ‡c statement of responsibility; ‡h GMD; ‡n number of part/section; ‡p name of part/section. One method of presenting subfields is to discuss them in the order in which they are used in bibliographic records, rather than alphabetically. However, the alphabetic approach is used in this text, and has been modeled after authoritative sources of information, such as *Concise MARC Format* and the RLIN and OCLC cataloging manuals. Placement of the subfields is illustrated in examples and illustrations. There are additional subfields that may be used in the 245; this text focuses discussion and examples on those that are most predominantly used.

Rule 1.1B1, *AACR2R (1998)*, instructs catalogers to transcribe the title proper exactly as to wording, order, and spelling, but not necessarily to capitalization and punctuation. Titles are provided in the 245 field, ‡a, which is not repeatable.

Indicator values in the 245 field indicates if a title added entry will be generated. Most nonprint items are cataloged using title main entry. Nonprint resources are rarely entered under an author (corporate or personal) main entry. (A discussion of choice of main entry for nonbook resources is provided in the following paragraph). For this reason, the majority of nonprint resources will have a first indicator value of 0. A first indicator value of 1 is used when a title added entry will be generated. The second indicator specifies number of nonfiling characters, with a range of 0-9 available.

example

Title from chief source of information:

245	00	Land of the Maya : a traveler's map

Title supplied by cataloger:

245	00	[Map of Douglass College, Rutgers University]
500		Title supplied by cataloger.

Rule 3.1B2, *AACR2R (1998)*, notes that statements of scale that appear as part of the title proper should be included in the transcription of the title statement.

Remainder of Title

The 245 field also provides the remainder of a title or other information, such as parallel titles. Provide this information in the ‡b, which is not repeatable.
example

245	00	Land of the Maya :‡ba traveler's map
246	3	Traveler's map

Title Variations

Provide title variations in the 246 field, **Varying Form of Title**, which is repeatable. The 246 provides other titles by which a resource may be known; this includes abbreviations or acronyms, parallel titles in another language, or when one title appears on external packaging and another title is given in the chief source of information. Providing access to title variations permits users to search for a resource in multiple ways.

The following subfields are available for use in the 246 field: ‡a title; ‡b remainder of title or parallel title; ‡h medium; ‡i display text; ‡n number of part/section of a work; ‡p name of a part/section of a work. There are additional subfields that may be used with the 246; this text focuses discussion and examples on those that are most predominantly used.

The initial indicator value indicates note or added entry. The second indicator value is used to provide information on type of title. A complete list of indicator values is available on the USMARC Web page at http://lcweb.loc.gov/marc/bibliographic/ecbdtils.html#mrcb246.
example

Title on chief source and external envelope differ

245	00	Land of the Maya :‡ba traveler's map
246	1	‡iTitle on envelope:‡aAncient Maya world

Portion of the main title

245	00	Metro road map of Philadelphia and vicinity
246	30	Metro road map of Philadelphia
246	30	Road map of Philadelphia and vicinity

GENERAL MATERIAL DESIGNATION (GMD)

Use of a GMD is deemed optional by Rule 1.1C, *AACR2R (1998)*. There are several reasons why a library may choose to use GMDs. It indicates to users the format of a resource when a search is done in an online catalog since all resources with a specific GMD will cluster together. Additionally, the resource described in an online catalog may not readily be apparent to users even when the bibliographic record includes a physical description that includes type of resource and characteristics. Use of a GMD helps users to distinguish between different formats in which a title is available. For example, *Midnight Express* is the title of a book, as well as a motion picture, a motion picture sound track, and is also available on videorecording. However, there is a growing sentiment that GMDs are no longer useful, particularly in a Web-based environment in which some libraries use one bibliographic record to represent multiple manifestations of a title (a paper and an electronic version of a serial title, for example).

The GMD is included in the 245 field, ‡h and is enclosed in brackets. It immediately follows the information provided in ‡a and precedes the ‡b. It is not repeatable.

Use the GMD "map" for all types of maps and atlases. However, some institutions may prefer not to use the GMD "map" for atlases. Do not confuse the GMD with the SMD, which specifies type of material. Provide the GMD in the 245 field, ‡h, which is not repeatable.

example

245	00	Land of the Maya ‡h[map] :‡ba traveler's map
245	00	World population atlas‡h[map]

STATEMENT OF RESPONSIBILITY

The statement of responsibility provides names of corporate bodies and/or individuals responsible for production, creation, manufacture, etc. of a nonprint resource. This information is taken from the chief or prescribed sources of information.

The statement of responsibility is included in the 245 field, ‡c, is preceded by a forward slash, and is not repeatable. Each corporate body or individual presented in the statement of responsibility is separated by semicolons. Per Rule 1.1F1, *AACR2R (1998)*, statements of responsibility are to be transcribed as they appear. Information taken from sources other than the chief source of information will be bracketed.

example

| 245 | 00 | Land of the Maya‡h [map] :‡btraveler's map /‡c produced by the Cartographic Division, National Geographic Society. |
| 245 | 00 | World population atlas‡h[map] /‡cproduced in the Cartographic Division, National Geographic Society ; John B. Garver, chief cartographer. |

EDITION

Provide edition information in the 250 field, **Edition Statement,** which is not repeatable. Edition information for nonprint resources is not limited to the term "edition," and includes "version," "revision," or other terms deemed appropriate by the cataloging agency. Rule 1.2B1, *AACR2R (1998),* instructs catalogers to transcribe edition statements in the form found on the item.

The following subfields are available for use in the 250 field: ‡a edition statement; ‡b remainder of edition statement. There are additional subfields that may be used with the 250; this text focuses discussion and examples on those that are most predominantly used.

There are no indicators defined for the 250 field.

example

250	4th large scale ed.
250	New census.
250	3rd rev. concise ed.

SCALE

Provide scale information in the 255 field, **Cartographic Mathematical Data,** which is repeatable. The following subfields are available for use in the 250 field: ‡a statement of scale; ‡b statement of projection; ‡c statement of coordinates; ‡d statement of zone; ‡e statement of equinox. There are additional subfields that may be used with the 255; this text focuses discussion and examples on those that are most predominantly used.

There are no indicators defined for the 255 field.

Consult the chief source of information and accompanying documentation for scale information. Record scale as a ratio of one to the given value (for example, 1:253,440). The statement of scale is preceded by the word "scale."

example

| 255 | Scale 1:253,440. |
| 255 | Scale 1:250,000‡c(W 6 30 - -E 10 15/N 28 00 - -N 17 45). |

If the statement of scale is not available from the chief source of information or accompanying materials, put the scale ratio in brackets and note the source of the scale.
example

255	Scale [1:253,440].
500	Statement of scale found on envelope.

Sometimes scale is given as a statement rather than as a ratio. Convert the information into numerical form. A rule of thumb is that there are 63,360 inches in a mile. If the cartographic material states "1 inch = 4 miles," multiply 63,360 x 4 = 253,440. Record as: Scale [1:253,440]. If the scale is approximated, use the abbreviation "ca." in the scale statement.
example

255	Scale [ca. 1:126,720]

If a resource contains more than one scale, or if a multipart item contains more than one scale, a separate statement may be provided for each scale. The *Amendments 2001* state in regard to Rule 3.3B5 that the note "Scales differ" may be provided when more than one scale is present, and catalogers are given the option of repeating the scale statement when details such as projection or coordinates are the same, or repeating the entire area if other details are different. Library of Congress's *Map Cataloging Manual* instructs catalogers to use the note "Scales differ" for a multipart item containing more than two scales. Form of note and number of scales present to determine its use will depend on how closely an institution follows *AACR2R (1998)* or Library of Congress policy.

Projection

Providing projection is optional. Consult any source of information. Give projection information only if available. Projection follows the statement of scale in the 255 field, **Cartographic Mathematical Data**. Abbreviate projection as "proj." Any information relating to projection may also be included. Library of Congress's *Map Cataloging Manual* instructs catalogers to transcribe projection statements in English regardless of language in which it may be given. Additionally, the *Manual* states that the first word and any proper names in a projection statement should be capitalized.

example

255	Scale 1:23,000,000 ;‡bAzimuthal equal-area proj.
255	Scale 1:1,609,000 ;‡bConic proj., standard parallels

Rule 3.3D1, *AACR2R (1998)* states that information on coordinates may also be included, that are expressed in degrees (°), minutes ('), and seconds ("). If appropriate, each coordinate may be preceded by W, E, N, or S.
example

255	Scale [ca. 1:2,025,000] ;‡bLambert conformal conic proj., standard parallels 47°55' and 59°35'.
255	Scale 1:1000,000lc(W 98°00' -- W 97°35'/N 19°45' -- N 19°20').

PUBLICATION INFORMATION

Consult the chief and/or prescribed sources of information to obtain information on where and when a resource was published, distributed, manufactured, etc. Publication, distribution, manufacture, etc. information is provided in the 260 field, **Publication, Distribution, etc. (Imprint)**, which is not repeatable.

PLACE OF PUBLICATION, DISTRIBUTION, COPYRIGHT, MANUFACTURE, ETC.

The place of publication, distribution, manufacture, etc. is provided in the 260 field, ‡a. It is repeatable if there is more than one place of publication, or if a resource is published in one location and distributed in another, for example.

Generally, the city and country or state of publication are given. If only a city name is given, and it is necessary to record the country, state, etc., for purposes of identification and clarification, record the supplied information in brackets, as per Rule 1.4C3, *AACR2R (1998)*.
example

260	Detroit, Mich.
260	Schmalkalden [Germany]

If a place of publication, distribution, manufacture, etc. is not provided, but may be ascertained, record in brackets with a question mark. Consult Rule 1.4C6, *AACR2R (1998)*, for further discussion of this topic.

example

260   [Denver?]

If no place of publication, distribution, manufacture, etc. is provided, and may not be ascertained, the abbreviation for the term "Sine loco, " [S.l.] is used per Rule 1.4C6, *AACR2R (1998)*. The abbreviation is always bracketed.
example

260   [S.l.] : National Map Co.

NAME OF PUBLISHER(S) AND/OR DISTRIBUTOR(S)

Consult the chief and/or prescribed sources of information first. Record the publisher's name following the place of publication as per Rule 1.4D1, *AACR2R (1998)*. If the distributor (or another body with a function related to the material being described) is included, transcribe the distributor, etc. name as it appears in the chief or prescribed sources of information. If the distributor's location differs from that of the publisher, record both locations.

Provide this information in the 260 field, ‡b, which is repeatable when there is more than one publisher, distributor, etc.
example

260   [S.l.] :‡bDyer Map Productions ;‡aChicago :‡bDistributed by Warwick Ltd.

The term "distributor" is added in brackets following distributor information only when this function (or other related functions) is not clear in the chief or prescribed sources of information, as per Rule 1.4E1, *AACR2R (1998)*. If distributor information is taken from a label affixed to the resource, external packaging, etc., this must be noted.
example

260   Detroit, Mich. :‡bNational Map Co. :‡bTraveler's Corp. [distributor]
260   Detroit, Mich. :‡bNational Map Co. ;‡aTrenton, N.J. :‡bSolely distributed by Maparama
500   Distributor information from external envelope.
500   Distributor information from accompanying printed pamphlet.

If there is no information provided for publisher, distributor, etc., and it may not be ascertained, use the abbreviation for the

term "sine nomine," [s.n.], as per Rule 1.4D7, *AACR2R (1998)*. The abbreviation is always bracketed.
example

260   Chicago :‡b[s.n.]

DATE OF PUBLICATION, DISTRIBUTION, COPYRIGHT, MANUFACTURE, ETC.

Provide this information in the 260 field, ‡c, which is repeatable. However, the practice of repeating the ‡c is not widely used. Multiple dates, such as for date of production and copyright, may be included in the 260 field, ‡c.

 Consult the chief and/or prescribed sources of information first. Record publication date, or distribution date if publication date is not available. In the absence of either dates, record copyright date, which is preceded by a lower case "c". Information on date of publication, distribution, etc. is further outlined in Rule 1.4F, *AACR2R (1998)*.
example

Publication date
260   New York :‡bUnited Nations,‡c1998.

Copyright date
260   King of Prussia, Pa. :‡bFranklin Maps,‡cc2000.

 If information on publication, distribution, etc. date is not provided in either the chief or prescribed sources of information, approximate the date of publication. Approximated dates are bracketed. The *Map Cataloging Manual* states that a date can be inferred from other dates appearing on a resource in the absence of a clearly stated publication, copyright, etc. date. A date may be inferred from a title (a date is included in the title statement), statement of responsibility, or an edition statement. Inferred dates must be bracketed.
example

Approximated date
260   [S.l.] :‡bT. Meyer Publishers,‡c[ca. 1997]

Probable date
260   Cherry Hill, N.J. :‡bAriel Press,‡[1990?]

Decade certain
260   Clifton, N.J. :‡bPiermatti Educational Resources,‡c[198-]

Probable decade

260   Chicago :‡bScholars Press,‡c[199-?]

Note: More information on dates is available in *AACR2R (1998)*, Chapter 1, "General Rules for Description."

Multipart items: Include a beginning date if the resource is not complete and/or is expected to continue indefinitely. An ending date may be included when a resource is complete. Rule 1.4F8, *AACR2R (1998)* notes that this practice is optional.
example

260   Chicago :‡bScholars Press,‡c1965-
260   King of Prussia, Pa. :‡bFranklin Maps,‡c1995-2000.

Unpublished items: Do not attempt to provide a place of publication, etc. or publisher, distributor, manufacturer, etc. name for unpublished items, as per Rule 1.4D9, *AACR2R (1998)*. Do not use the abbreviations "S.l." or "s.n." A date may be included for the item.
example

260   ‡c1999.
260   ‡c[2000?]

There are no indicators defined for the 260 field.

PHYSICAL DESCRIPTION

Includes extent (number and Specific Material Designation (SMD) of physical parts of an item), other physical details (color or sound characteristics, for example), dimensions, and information about accompanying materials.

The physical description is provided in the 300 field, **Physical Description**. The physical description field is repeatable, permitting a multilevel description, yet this option is not commonly applied.

EXTENT

Provide the number and SMD of the parts of an item, as per Rule 3.5B1, *AACR2R (1998)*. The SMD is not identical to the GMD. It is used to specify material types, while the GMD describes the broad category of materials into which a resource may fall. Ex-

tent is provided in the 300 field, **Physical Description**, ‡a, and is not repeatable.
example

300	1 atlas
300	1 map

If the resource consists of more than one map, or if the map is available on more than one sheet, specify number of maps or sheets.
example

300	1 map on four sheets
300	2 maps on one sheet

Include pagination or number of volumes for atlases as per Rule 2.5B, *AACR2R (1998)*.
example

300	1 atlas (ix, 153 p.)
300	1 atlas (61 p.)

Serially issued resources that are not yet complete include a SMD preceded by three blank spaces, as per Rule 1.5B5, *AACR2R (1998)*. Serially issued resources are not limited to periodicals, and may include any resource that is intended to be published indefinitely.
example

300	atlases
300	maps

OTHER PHYSICAL DETAILS

Provide a description of characteristics other than extent or dimensions, as per Rule 3.5C1, *AACR2R (1998)*. This information is provided in the ‡b, which is not repeatable. The rule instructs catalogers to provide the following information as appropriate, in this order: number of maps in an atlas, color, material, and mounting.

Number of Maps in Atlases

Provide this information in the 300 field, **Physical Description**, ‡b, which is not repeatable.

example

300	1 atlas (100 p.) :‡b100 maps
300	1 atlas (61 p.) :‡b20 maps

Color Characteristics

Record if the item is multicolored. Provide this information in the 300 field, **Physical Description**, ‡b, which is not repeatable.
example

300	1 atlas (100 p.) :‡b100 col. maps
300	1 map :‡bcol.

Material

Rule 3.5C4, *AACR2R (1998)* instructs catalogers to record material on which the item is available, if this is considered to be important. Provide this information in the 300 field, **Physical Description**, ‡b, which is not repeatable.
example

300	1 map :‡bvellum
300	1 map :‡bplastic

Mounting

Rule 3.5C5, *AACR2R (1998)* instructs catalogers to record type of mounting for maps if available. Provide this information in the 300 field, **Physical Description**, ‡b, which is not repeatable.
example

300	1 map :‡bcol., mounted on cloth

The *Amendments 2001* state that additional rules have been added to the Physical Description area for recording layout, medium, and production method. This information is forthcoming and more detail is not available at this time.

DIMENSIONS

Provide information on size, width, etc. as appropriate, as per Rule 3.5D1, *AACR2R (1998)*. Dimensions are included in the ‡c, which is not repeatable.

Record height times width for maps, and measure this information between the neat lines, which are the lines or borders that enclose a map. The dimensions of the sheet(s) are given if neat lines are lacking. If a map is in sheets of various sizes, record the different sizes. Rule 3.5D1, *AACR2R (1998:112)* instructs catalogers to record sheet size for maps when a map "...is printed with an outer cover within which it is intended to be folded or if the sheet itself contains a panel or section designed to appear on the outside when the sheet is folded...."

Record height in centimeters for atlases.

example

300	1 map on 7 sheets : ‡bcol. ;‡c140 x 196 cm., on sheets 82 x 108 cm.
300	1 atlas (100 p.) :‡b100 col. maps ;‡c29 cm.
300	1 map :‡bcol. ;‡con 2 sheets 85 x 108 cm., folded to 27 x 22 cm.

ACCOMPANYING MATERIALS

Provide information describing accompanying materials in one of three ways, per Rule 1.5E1, *AACR2R (1998)*: (1) at the end of the physical description; (2) in a note separate from the physical description; or (3) as part of a multilevel description.

example

As part of the physical description:

300	1 map :‡bcol. ;‡c137 x 203 cm. on 4 sheets 79 x 111 cm. +‡e1 text (109 p.)

Note: If more than one item is included in the ‡e, 300, each item is preceded by a space and a plus sign.

300	1 map :‡bcol. ;‡c137 x 203 cm. on 4 sheets 79 x 111 cm. +‡e1 text (109 p. ; 28 cm.) + 1 user guide (10 p. : col. ill. ; 28 cm.)

In a separate note:

300	1 map :‡bcol. ;‡c137 x 203 cm. on 4 sheets 79 x 111 cm.
500	Accompanied by user guide.

Multilevel description:

300	1 map :‡bcol. ;‡c137 x 203 cm. on 4 sheets 79 x 111 cm.
300	1 videocassette (35 min.) :‡bsd., col. ;‡c1/2 in.
300	1 computer optical disc :‡bcol. ;‡c4 3/4 in.

SERIES

Provide series treatment if available in the chief and/or prescribed sources of information. General series information is presented in this text since the focus is on descriptive cataloging procedures. Series are represented in this text by the 440 field, **Series Statement/Added Entry—Title,** which is repeatable.

The following subfields are available for use in the 440 field: ‡a title; ‡n number of part/section; ‡p name of part/section; ‡v volume or numbering designation.

Provide series title in the 440, ‡a, which is not repeatable.

The first indicator value for the 440 field is undefined. The second indicator specifies number of nonfiling characters, with a range of 0-9 available.

example

    440   0   Map and chart series (Geological Society of America)

Detailed information on series, including various types of treatment, is available on the USMARC Web page at http://lcweb.loc.gov/marc/bibliographic/ecbdhome.html#mrcb440.

Provide information on numbered parts in the ‡n Number of Part/Section of a Work.

example

    440   0   Map and chart series (Geological Society of
                America).‡nno. 40

Provide the specific name of the part(s)/section(s) of a series in the ‡p Name of Part/Section of a Work.

example

    440   0   Map and chart series (Geological Society of
                America).‡nno. 40,‡pSeries B

Provide numbering designation, such as "volume" or "part" in the ‡v.

example

    440   0   Map and chart series (Geological Society of America)
                ;‡vMC-33
    440   0   Publication of the North Carolina Biological Survey ;‡vno.
                1980-12

NOTES

Notes provide a variety of information, including contents, names of individuals or corporate bodies responsible for creation or production of a resource, additional physical description, language, etc.

NATURE AND SCOPE

As per Rule 3.7B1, *AACR2R (1998)* provide a note on nature or scope of the map or atlas in the 500 field, **General Note** only when it is not apparent from the description. This note is also used to record unusual features of the item. The 500 field is repeatable.
example

500	Shows plats, section by section, lot dimensions, named streets and railroad lines, surrounding areas and bodies of water, and restrictions contained in all deeds of conveyance.
500	Includes 3 inset maps, user information, legend, and note containing biodiversity priorities.
500	Plastic coated map is described as "easy to handle, easy to fold, durable- -won't tear, and write on-wipe off."

LANGUAGE

Provide information on language(s) if more than one language is present in the nonprint resource, or if the resource is in a language (or languages) other than the primary language of the cataloging agency. Use the 546 field, **Language Note**, which is repeatable. It is used in conjunction with the 041 field, **Language Code**, which is not repeatable.

The initial article value of 0 indicates that the resource is not a translation or does not include a translation; an initial article value of 1 indicates that the resource is a translation or includes a translation.
example

041	0	spa
546		In Spanish.
041	1	fre‡beng
546		In French with legend and accompanying printed matter in English.

A full list of language codes is available on the USMARC Web page at http://lcweb.loc.gov/marc/languages/.

SOURCE OF TITLE PROPER

Per Rule 3.7B3, *AACR2R (1998)* indicate source of title if not taken from chief or prescribed sources of information, or has been supplied by the cataloger.

Provide this information in the 500 field, **General Note**, which is repeatable.

example

500	Title from external envelope.
500	Title supplied by cataloger.

STATEMENTS OF RESPONSIBILITY

Provide information on individuals or corporate bodies not named in the statement of responsibility area who are considered to be important. Record this information in the 500 field, **General Note**, which is repeatable.

example

500	Engraving by Sanborn Map Company.
500	Reproduction details courtesy of Dyer Map Productions.

EDITION AND HISTORY

Provide additional information on the resource, or use to provide history of a map or atlas. This information is provided in the 500 field, **General Note**, which is repeatable, and differs from what is provided in the 250 field.

example

500	Originally published as the New York Times atlas of the world.
500	Reissued with corrections and new additions.

MATHEMATICAL AND OTHER CARTOGRAPHIC DATA

Per Rule 3.7B8, *AACR2R (1998)*, provide other mathematical and cartographic data in addition to, or which elaborate on, the information provided in the 255 field, **Cartographic Mathematical Data**. This information is provided in the 500 field, **General Note**, which is repeatable.

example

500	Depths and relief shown by hypsometric tints and contours (in uncorrected meters).
500	Relief shown by hachures and spot heights.

PUBLICATION, DISTRIBUTION, ETC. INFORMATION

Rule 3.7B9, *AACR2R (1998)* instructs catalogers to make notes on publication, distribution, etc., details not included in the publication, distribution, etc., area but which are considered to be important. Provide this information in the 500 field, **General Note**, which is repeatable.

example

500	Distributor information taken from label affixed to jacket.
500	Previously distributed by Maparama, Inc.

PHYSICAL DESCRIPTION

Rule 3.7B10, *AACR2R (1998)* instructs catalogers to provide additional physical description not represented in the 007 field, **Physical Description Fixed Field—General Information**, or the 300 field, **Physical Description**. This information is provided in the 500 field, **General Note**, which is repeatable.

Additional physical description includes notes on details that affect use, and other information deemed important by the cataloging agency.

example

500	Printed on both sides of sheet, dissected and laminated.
500	Relief indicated by shading and spot heights.

AUDIENCE

Provide information on target audience in the 521 field, **Target Audience Note**, which is repeatable.

The first indicator value provides an introductory phrase for the 521 field that describes audience or intellectual level of materials. A first indicator value of blank provides the display constant "Audience." The second indicator value is undefined. Additional information on indicator values for the 521 field is available on the USMARC Web page at http://lcweb.loc.gov/marc/bibliographic/ecbdnot1.html#mrcb521.

example

521	2	Interest grade level: Grades 4-6.

OTHER FORMATS

Provide information on additional formats in which a resource is available in the 530 field, **Additional Physical Form Available Note**, which is repeatable.

Indicator values are not defined for the 530 field.

example

530	Also available on CD-ROM.
530	Also issued on microfiche.

CONTENTS NOTES

Information detailing the contents of a resource is provided in the 505 field, **Formatted Contents Note,** which is repeatable. It provides individual titles or parts contained in a resource.

Contents notes in which the various parts of the note are coded are referred to as "enhanced." Enhanced contents notes contain a ‡t (title) and ‡r (statement of responsibility).

The first indicator value for the 505 field indicates completeness of the contents. A first indicator value of 0 indicates complete contents, a value of 1 is used for incomplete contents, and a value of 2 is used for partial contents. The second indicator value provides information on content designation. A second indicator value of 0 is used for enhanced contents. A second value of blank is used for nonenhanced contents notes. The indicators for an enhanced contents note are 00 (a nonenhanced contents has a single first indicator with a value from 0-2, or 8).

While not required, a contents note is useful to providing a description since the contents of a nonprint resource may not be browsed in the manner used for print resources.

example

505	0	Harrisburg-Palmyra-Brickerville - - Brickerville-Denver - - Bowmansville-Geigertown - - Geigertown-Evansburgh - - Evansburgh-Chamounix (Philadelphia) - - Chamounix (Philadelphia)-Dairview - - Fairview-Milmay - - Milmay-Ocean City - - Geigertown-Marsh Creek - - Marsh Creek-Ridley Creek - - Ridley Creek-Chamounix (Philadelphia) - - Valley Green (Philadelphia)-Newtown (Tyler) - - Ridley Creek-Evansburgh - - Evansburgh-Weisel - - Blue Bell-Newtown (Tyler) - - Trenton-Newtown (Tyler)-Furlong - - Furlong-Weisel-Gallows Hill - - Gallows Hill-Portland - - Portland-Old Mine Road - - Old Mine Road-La Anna - - La Anna-Portland.

Enhanced contents note

505	0	Sheet 1. ‡tOphiolitic terranes of part of the western United States /‡rcompiled by William P. Irwin. - - sheet 2. ‡tOphiolitic belts of the central Mediterranean / ‡rcompiled by Volker J. Dietrich - - sheet 3. ‡tOphiolitic

belt of the Urals /‡rcompiled by A. Knipper - - sheet 4. ‡tOphiolitic belts of the Himalayan and Tibetan region / ‡rcompiled by Augusto Gansser.

NUMBERS

Provide numbers other than the ISBN that are important for identification of a map or atlas. Provide this information in the 500 field, **General Note**, which is repeatable.
example

500	"HA-CC-CR-3299."
500	"S-CC-PR-3099" - - Cover.
500	"ST/ESCAP/1831" - - T.p. verso.
500	"United Nations publication sales no. E.99.II.F.4" - - T.p. verso.

DESCRIPTIVE OR LIBRARY SPECIFIC NOTES

Provide descriptive or copy specific information about maps or atlases in a 500 field, **General Note**, which is repeatable.
example

500	Use restricted to Special Collections Reading Room.
500	Library's copy 1 lacks accompanying guide.
500	Library's copy imperfect.
500	Atlases are noncirculating.

"WITH" NOTES

Provide notes for titles that are not the first in a collective title. This information is provided in the 500 field, **General Note**, which is repeatable. Additionally, information provided in this type of note may also be used as the basis for a 740 field, **Added Entry— Uncontrolled Related/Analytical Title**.
example

500		With: Mineral resources map of Mongolia.
740	0	Mineral resources map of Mongolia‡h[map].
500		With (on verso): Pictorial drive thru map of Six Flags Wild Safari Animal Park.

SUBJECT ACCESS

Subject access to nonprint resources helps users to identify and locate resources, since the bibliographic record must provide as much information as possible when a resource is noncirculating and not easily accessible to users. Subject headings are used to provide access to resources through *personal names, corporate names, topical terms,* or *geographic names.* Subject headings may be further subdivided by form division (format of material), general subdivisions, chronological subdivisions, and geographic subdivisions. Personal and corporate name subject headings are not included in this chapter since it is not likely that a map or atlas would be about an individual or corporate body. Meeting names and subject added entries for uniform titles are not included in this text.

Consult the *Library of Congress Subject Headings* (LCSH), the *Library of Congress Subject Cataloging Manual* (SCM), and the *Library of Congress Map Cataloging Manual* (MCM) for formulating subject headings for cartographic materials.

MCM states that the first subject heading provided in a bibliographic record should correspond most closely to the classification number used. *MCM* also states that, with the exception of the heading that most closely corresponds to the class number, there is no set order for presenting topics provided by the map or atlas.

Maps or atlases of an identifiable place must be assigned a subject heading for that area. However, peripheral areas may be ignored. For example, a map for one place may include small portions of surrounding states. In most cases, these areas can be disregarded.

Analyze the content of the map, and assign subject headings that are appropriate to what the item *is* rather than how the publisher describes the item. For example, a road map and tourist map are not the same thing, and the subject heading should accurately represent the content of the map.

In the case of atlases, map subject headings may be assigned to all atlases. The subject heading Atlases is used for world atlases published in the United States. For atlases published in other countries, use the subject heading Atlas, followed by the name of the country of publication.

example

650   0   Atlases, France.

TOPICAL TERMS

Provide subject access to topical terms in the 650 field, **Subject Added Entry—Topical Term,** which is repeatable. Terms used in the 650 may describe form of the resource (Motion pictures, Spanish) or content (Fishes, Freshwater, Bicycle touring).

The following subfields are available for use in the 650 field: ‡a topical term or geographic name as entry element; ‡v form division; ‡x general subdivision; ‡y chronological subdivision; ‡z geographic subdivision. There are additional subfields that may be used with the 650; this text focuses discussion and examples on those that are most predominantly used.

The initial article value indicates level of subject; blank indicates that no information has been provided. Other first indicator values available are: 0 for no level specified; 1 for primary level of subject; and 2 for secondary level of subject. In many cases, subject headings supplied by catalogers or provided in records available through union databases have an initial indicator value of blank. A second indicator value of 0 indicates that a name is from the Library of Congress Name Authority file. Additional information is available on the USMARC Web page at http://lcweb.loc.gov/marc/bibliographic/ecbdsubj.html#mrcb650. example

650	0	World maps.
650	0	Geology‡zMongolia‡vMaps.
650	0	Geography‡xStudy and teaching.
650	0	Geology‡zMongolia‡vMaps‡y2001-
650	0	Ophiolites‡zCalifornia‡vMaps.

GEOGRAPHIC TERMS

Provide subject access to geographic terms in the 651 field, **Subject Added Entry—Geographic Name**, which is repeatable.

The following subfields are available for use in the 651 field: ‡a geographic name; ‡v form division; ‡x general subdivision; ‡y chronological subdivision; ‡z geographic subdivision. There are additional subfields that may be used with the 651; this text focuses discussion and examples on those that are most predominantly used.

The initial indicators are undefined for this field. A second indicator value of 0 indicates that a name is from the Library of Congress Name Authority file. Additional information is available on the USMARC Web page at http://lcweb.loc.gov/marc/bibliographic/ecbdsubj.html#mrcb651. example

651	0	Brooklyn (New York, N.Y.)
651	0	Manhattan (New York, N.Y.)‡vTours‡vMaps.
651	0	United States‡xPopulation‡xStatistics.
651	0	United States‡xHistory‡yCivil War, 1861-1865.
651	0	United States‡xHistory‡xStudy and teaching (Higher) ‡zNew Jersey.

ADDED ENTRIES

Added entries provide access to personal and corporate names that are not main entries yet serve as important additional access points. Name added entries include directors, cast, editors, publishers, or production companies. Title added entries provide additional access for titles related to the main work.

PERSONAL NAME

Provide access to personal names in the 700 field, **Added Entry— Personal**, which is repeatable. It is used to include additional access points in the form of names taken from the 245, **Title Statement**, or other fields deemed appropriate by the cataloging agency. Personal name added entries differ from personal names in the 600 in that they provide different types of information, and would be found in an online catalog using different types of searches (subject versus personal name).

The following subfields are available for use in the 700 field: ‡a personal name; ‡c titles or other words associated with a particular name; ‡d dates, and ‡q fuller form of name. There are additional subfields that may be used with the 700; this text focuses discussion and examples on those that are most predominantly used.

The initial indicator value indicates type of name. An initial article value of 0 indicates entry under forename; 1 indicates entry under single surname. The second indicator value indicates type of added entry. A blank second indicator value indicates that no information is provided; a second indicator value of 2 indicates an analytical entry, and means the item in the bibliographic record contains the work represented by the added entry. Additional information is available on the USMARC Web page at http://lcweb.loc.gov/marc/bibliographic/ecbdadde.html#mrcb700. example

700	1	Thomas, Robert P.
700	1	Irving, Henry,‡cSir,‡d1838-1905.
700	1	Lee, David S.‡q(David Stephen),‡d1943-

CORPORATE NAME

Provide access to corporate names in the 710 field, **Added Entry—Corporate Name**, which is repeatable. Corporate name added entries differ from corporate names in the 610 in that they provide different types of information, and would be found in an online catalog using different types of searches (subject versus corporate name).

The following subfields are available for use in the 710 field: ‡a corporate name or jurisdiction name; and ‡b subordinate unit. There are additional subfields that may be used with the 710; this text focuses discussion and examples on those that are most predominantly used.

The initial indicator value indicates type of corporate name. An initial article value 1 indicates entry in jurisdiction order; a value of 2 indicates entry in direct order. The second indicator value indicates type of added entry. A blank second indicator value indicates that no information is provided; a second indicator value of 2 indicates an analytical entry, and means the item in the bibliographic record contains the work represented by the added entry. Additional information is available on the USMARC Web page at http://lcweb.loc.gov/marc/bibliographic/ecbdadde.html#mrcb710.
example

| 710 | 1 | Primary Educational Products. |
| 710 | 1 | International Geological Correlation Programme.‡bProject Ophiolites. |

UNIFORM TITLE

Provide access to a uniform title in the 730 field, **Added Entry— Uniform Title,** which is repeatable. Uniform titles provide a title related to the resource.

The following subfields are available for use in the 730 field: ‡a uniform title; ‡f date of a work; ‡h medium; ‡k form subheading; ‡l language. There are additional subfields that may be used with the 730; this text focuses discussion and examples on those that are most predominantly used.

The initial indicator value indicates number of nonfiling characters (0-9). The second indicator value indicates type of added entry. A blank second indicator value indicates that no information is provided; a second indicator value of 2 indicates an analytical entry, and means the item in the bibliographic record contains the work represented by the added entry. Additional information is available on the USMARC Web page at http://lcweb.loc.gov/marc/bibliographic/ecbdadde.html#mrcb730.
example

| 245 | 00 | Ophiolitic map of the world‡h[map]. |
| 505 | 0 | Sheet 1. ‡tOphiolitic terranes of part of the western United States /‡rcompiled by William P. Irwin. - - sheet 2. |

		‡tOphiolitic belts of the central Mediterranean / ‡rcompiled by Volker J. Dietrich - - sheet 3. ‡tOphiolitic belt of the Urals /‡rcompiled by A. Knipper - - sheet 4. ‡tOphiolitic belts of the Himalayan and Tibetan region / ‡rcompiled by Augusto Gansser.
730	02	Ophiolitic terranes of part of the western United States.
730	02	Ophiolitic belts of the central Mediterranean.
730	02	Ophiolitic belt of the Urals.
730	02	Ophiolitic belts of the Himalayan and Tibetan region.
245	04	The New York Times atlas of the world.
730	0	Times concise atlas of the world

RELATED TITLES

Provide access to titles related to the work described in the 245 field, **Title Statement** using the 740 field, **Added Entry—Uncontrolled Related/Analytical Title**, which is repeatable.

The following subfields are available for use in the 740 field: ‡a uncontrolled related/analytical title; ‡h medium; ‡n number of part/section of a work; ‡p name of part/section of a work. There are additional subfields that may be used with the 740; this text focuses discussion and examples on those that are most predominantly used.

The initial indicator value indicates number of nonfiling characters (0-9). The second indicator value indicates type of added entry. A blank second indicator value indicates that no information is provided; a second indicator value of 2 indicates an analytical entry, and means the item in the bibliographic record contains the work represented by the added entry. Additional information is available on the USMARC Web page at http://lcweb.loc.gov/marc/bibliographic/ecbdadde.html#mrcb740. example

245	00	Hagstrom street map of Ocean County, New Jersey‡h[map].
740	0	Map of Ocean County, New Jersey‡h[map].

CLASSIFICATION

If Library of Congress Classification is used for maps and atlases, the G schedule is used. Call number construction for atlases consist of three parts: area number (may be a major area or a sub-area atlas), Cutter number (may be for authority responsible for

the atlas or sub-area Cutter plus Cutter for authority responsible for the atlas), and date of publication. Call numbers for maps consist of three or four parts: area number (may be a major area or a sub-area map), date of map situation, sub-area Cutter, and Cutter for authority responsible for the map.
example

Atlas

050	4	G2165.H1‡bU5 1998
050	4	G1021‡b.N57 1994

Map

050	4	G3813.B8 2000‡b.F7
050	4	G3813.C3G46 1900‡b.R3

EXAMPLES OF BIBLIOGRAPHIC RECORDS

Examples follow on the next page.

Figure 2-1 Example of Atlas

| Control | **Bib** | MARC Hldgs | Vol/Copy |

Fixed Fields

Rec_Type: e	Bib_Lvt: m	Enc_Lvt:	Desc: a	TypeCtrl:
Entrd: 000504	Dat_Tp: s	Date1: 1999	Date2:	Ctry: nyu
Lang: eng	Mod_Rec:	Source: d	Relief:	Base:
Prim_Mer:	Rec_Grp: e	GovtPub: i	Indx: 0	Spec_Fmt:

Bibliographic Info

001			a1464724
007			ad aanzn
020			9211197929
034		0	a
040			NjR|cNjR
050		4	G2315.H1|bU5 1999
052			G2315
110		2	United Nations.|bEconomic and Social Commission for Asia and the Pacific.
245		10	Atlas of mineral resources of the ESCAP region.|nVol. 14, |pGeology and mineral resources of Mongolia / |cEconomic and Social Commission for Asia and the Pacific.
246		30	Geology and mineral resources of Mongolia
255			Scales differ.
260			New York :|bUnited Nations,|c1999.
300			1 atlas (xiii, 192 p.) :|bmap ;|c30 cm.
500			"ISSN 1014-5451."
500			"ST/ESCAP/1831"--T.p. verso.
500			"United Nations publication sales no. E.99.II.F.41"--T.p. verso.
500			One folded black-and-white "Mineral resources map of Mongolia" in pocket.
504			Includes bibliographical references (p. 186-188).
596		LSM	
650		0	Mines and mineral resources|zMongolia|vMaps.
650		0	Geology|zMongolia|vMaps.

Figure 2-2 Example of Atlas

| Control | **Bib** | MARC Hldgs | All Volumes |

Fixed Fields

Rec_Type: e	Bib_Lvt m	Enc_Lvl	Desc: a	TypeCtrl
Entrd: 991110	Dat_Tp: s	Date1: 1998	Date2	Ctry: nyu
Lang: eng	Mod_Rec:	Source: d	Relief:	Base:
Prim_Mer:	Rec_Grp:	GovtPub:	Indx: 1	Spec_Fmt:

TypeCode: e	Relief:	Base:	Prim_Mer:	Rec_Grp:
GovtPub:	Indx: 1	Spec_Fmt:		

Bibliographic Info

Tag	Ind1	Ind2	Data
001			a1414620
007			ad canzn
020			0880970073
034	0		a
040			NjR|cNjR|dNjR
043			n-us-nj
050		4	G1258.M5|bH34 1998
110	2		Hagstrom Map Company.
245	10		Hagstrom Middlesex county atlas.
246	30		Middlesex county atlas
250			4th large scale ed.
255			Scale differs.
260			Maspeth, N.Y. :|bHagstrom Map Co.,|c1998.
300			1 atlas (61 p.) :|bcol. maps ;|c33 cm.
500			Includes index.
500			Text, location map, publisher's map list, col. ill., and UPC barcode on cover.
500			"Middlesex County, New Jersey: fully street-indexed, U.S., state, interstate highways, N.J. Turnpike, Garden State Parkway, RR routes, hospitals, parks, golf courses, cemeteries, federal and state lands, zip codes"--Cover.
520			Includes a key map, brief county information, population statistics, main through routes, parks, points of interest, guides, indexes, street maps, zip codes and a legend.
596			DGLSS LSM
650		0	Zip codes|zNew Jersey|zMiddlesex County|vMaps.
651		0	Middlesex County (N.J.)|vMaps.

Figure 2-3 Example of Map

| Control | **Bib** | MARC Hldgs | Vol/Copy |

Fixed Fields

Rec_Type: e	Bib_Lvt m	Enc_Lvt	Desc: a	TypeCtrl
Entrd: 001002	Dat_Tp: s	Date1: 1999	Date2	Ctry: pau
Lang eng	Mod_Rec:	Source: d	Relief:	Base:
Prim_Mer.	Rec_Grp: a	GovtPub:	Indx 1	Spec_Fmt 0

Bibliographic Info

001			a1487729
007			aj canzn
020			1877911925
034	1		a|b63400
034	1		a|b42500
040			NjR|cNjR
043			n-us-nj
050	4		G3813.B8 2000|b.F7
052			3813|bB8
052			3814|bM422|bM85|bM29
110	2		Franklin Maps (Firm)
245	10		Metro street map of Burlington County, NJ|h[map] : |bincluding Medford, Mount Holly & Maple Shade.
246	30		Burlington County, NJ|h[map]
246	30		Street map of Burlington County, NJ|h[map]
255			Scale [ca. 1:63,400].
255			Scale [ca. 1:42,500].
260			King of Prussia, Pa. :|bFranklin Maps,|c1999.
300			1 map :|bboth sides, col. ;|con sheet 92 x 126 cm., folded to 12 x 26 cm.
500			"Industrial parks, shopping centers, schools, zip codes, golf courses, streets indexed with zip codes"--Cover.
500			Includes legend, notes, indexes, insets, col. ill. of postcards, zip codes and publishers advertisement.
596		SPCOL	
650	0		Zip codes|zNew Jersey|zBurlington County|vMaps.
651	0		Burlington County (N.J.)|vMaps.
651	0		Medford (N.J.)|vMaps.
651	0		Mount Holly (N.J.)|vMaps.
651	0		Maple Shade (N.J.)|vMaps.

Figure 2-4 Example of Map

| Control | **Bib** | MARC Hldgs | Vol/Copy |

Fixed Fields

Rec_Type: e	Bib_Lvt m	Enc_Lvt	Desc: a
TypeCtrl	Entrd 000620	Dat_Tp: q	Date1: 1900
Date2 1999	Ctry. pau	Lang eng	Mod_Rec:
Source d	Relief.	Base	Prim_Mer:
Rec_Grp:	GovtPub:	Indx 0	Spec_Fmt 0

Bibliographic Info

001			a1472688
007			aj cgnzn
034	0		a
040			NjR|cNjR
043			n-us-nj
050	4		G3813.C3G46 1900|b.R3
052			3813|bC3
100	1		R.A. Williams.
245	10		Plan of Anglesea|h[map] :|bon Five-Mile Beach, Cape May County, N.J.
246	30		Anglesea on Five-Mile Beach|h[map]
246	30		Five Mile Beach|h[map]
246	30		Anglesea|h[map]
246	3		Anglesea on 5 Mile Beach|h[map]
260			Philadelphia :|bR.A. Williams,|c[19??].
300			1 map :|bcol., mounted on cloth ;|c54 x 56 cm., on sheet 56 x 63 cm., folded to 11 x 14 cm.
500			Shows plats, section by section, lot dimensions, named streets and railroad line, surrounding areas and bodies of water, and restrictions contained in all deeds of conveyance.
596		SPCOL	
650	0		Real property|zNew Jersey|zCape May County|vMaps.
651	0		Cape May County (N.J.)|vMaps.

Figure 2-5 Example of Map

Control | **Bib** | MARC Hldgs | All Volumes

Fixed Fields

Rec_Type: e	Bib_Lvl: m	Enc_Lvl:	Desc: a
TypeCtrl:	Entrd: 000605	Dat_Tp: s	Date1: 2000
Date2:	Ctry: nju	Lang: eng	Mod_Rec:
Source: d	Relief:	Base:	Prim_Mer:
Rec_Grp:	GovtPub: s	Indx: 1	Spec_Fmt:

Bibliographic Info

Tag	Ind	Content
001		a1470219
007		aj canzn
034	1	a|b425000
035		(OCoLC)ocm44069715
040		NjR|cNjR
043		n-us-nj
050	4	G3810.E635 2000|b.N4
052		3810
245	00	New Jersey & you|h[map] :|bperfect together.
246	30	New Jersey and you|h[map]
246	1	|iPhrase:|aNew Jersey attractions map
255		Scale [ca. 1:425,000]. 1 in. = approx. 6.7 miles.
260		[Trenton] :|bNJ Commerce & Economic Growth Commission, Office of Travel & Tourism,|c[2000]
300		1 map :|bcol. ;|c35 x 62 cm., on sheet 56 x 90 cm., folded to 10 x 23 cm.
500		"To advertise in future editions ... cal Affinity Publishing."
500		Includes index to points of interest with telephone numbers and advertisements. Contains insets of Atlantic City, Newark, Trenton, Meadowlands, and passenger rail system.
500		Verso contains illustrations, list of "leading annual events", state parks, forests and marinas, Newark International Airport airlines and phone numbers, state facts, Atlantic City casinos and phone numbers, and advertisements
596		ALEX CAMDN DANA
651	0	New Jersey|vMaps, Tourist.
651	0	New Jersey|vMaps.
651	0	New Jersey|vGuidebooks.
710	1	New Jersey.|bOffice of Travel & Tourism.
710	2	Affinity Publishing.

Figure 2-6 Example of Map

| Control | **Bib** | MARC Hldgs | Vol/Copy |

Fixed Fields

Rec_Type: e	Bib_Lvt: m	Enc_Lvt:	Desc: a	TypeCtrl:
Entrd: 000523	Dat_Tp: s	Date1: 1999	Date2:	Ctry: nyu
Lang: eng	Mod_Rec:	Source: d	Relief:	Base:
Prim_Mer:	Rec_Grp:	GovtPub:	Indx: 1	Spec_Fmt:

Bibliographic Info

001			a1423008
007			aj canzn
020			0880973803
034		1	a|b745000
040			NjR|cNjR
050		4	G3811.P2 1999|b.H34
052			3811|bP2
110		2	Hagstrom Map Company.
245		10	StateSlicker New Jersey|h[map] :|bhighways, major roads, places to go /|cHagstrom Map Company ; manufactured by Laminating Services, Inc.
246		30	Hagstrom StateSlicker New Jersey|h[map]
246		3	State slicker New Jersey|h[map]
246		3	Hagstrom state slicker New Jersey|h[map]
255			Scale [ca. 1:745,000]. 1 in. = 11 3/4 miles.
260			Maspeth, N.Y. :|bHagstrom Map Co.,|cc1999.
300			1 map :|bboth sides, col., dissected, laminated ;|con sheet 26 x 52 cm., folded to 11 x 26 cm.
500			Panel title.
500			Includes New Jersey road map, portions of Pennsylvania and New York, and index to places. Verso contains descriptive points of interest, legend for map on reverse side, schematic of the Garden State Parkway interchanges, approaches to New York City, recreation areas and mileage chart.
500			"HA-CC-CR-3299."
596		SPCOL	
650		0	Roads|zNew Jersey|vMaps.
710		2	Laminating Services, Inc.

Figure 2-7 Example of Map

| Control | **Bib** | MARC Hldgs | Vol/Copy |

Fixed Fields

Rec_Type: e	Bib_Lvt: m	Enc_Lvt:	Desc: a	TypeCtrl:
Entrd: 000808	Dat_Tp: s	Date1: 1993	Date2:	Ctry: dcu
Lang: eng	Mod_Rec:	Source: d	Relief:	Base: bj
Prim_Mer:	Rec_Grp:	GovtPub: f	Indx: 0	Spec_Fmt:

Bibliographic Info

001			a1481194
007			aj canzn
034		1	a|b2500000
040			NjR|cNjR
050		4	G8161.D1 1993|b.C6
052			G8161|bD1
110		2	Conservation International.
245		10	Biodiversity priorities for Papua New Guinea|h[map] / |cproduced by Conservation International ; cartography [by] Andy Mitchell.
246		1	|iTitle from verso:|aMapping Papua New Guinea's biodiversity
255			Scale 1:2,500,000.
260			[Washington, D.C.] :|bConservation International, Biodiversity Support Program ;|a[Boroko, Papua New Guinea] :|bGovernment of Papua New Guinea, Dept. of Environment and Conservation,|c1993.
300			1 map :|bcol. ;|c51 x 68 cm., on sheet 62 x 93 cm., folded to 21 x 30 cm.
500			Includes 3 inset maps, user information, legend, and note containing biodiversity priorities.
500			Verso contains 3 inset maps, descriptive text and list of CNA participants.
500			"This map ... attempts to identify areas richest in biodiversity based on available knowledge."
596		LSM	
650		0	Biological diversity conservation|zPapua New Guinea.
650		0	Nature conservation|zPapua New Guinea.
650		0	Environmental policy|zPapua New Guinea.
710		2	Biodiversity Support Program.
710		1	Papua New Guinea.|bDept. of Environment and Conservation.

REFERENCES

Frost, Carolyn O. 1989. *Media Access and Organization: A Cataloging and Reference Sources Guide for Nonbook Materials.* Englewood, Colo.: Libraries Unlimited.

Joint Steering Committee for the Revision of AACR2. 1998. *Anglo-American Cataloguing Rules, Second Edition, 1998 Revision.* Chicago: American Library Association.

Network Development and MARC Standards Office, Library of Congress in cooperation with Standards and Support, National Library of Canada. 1999. *MARC 21 Format for Bibliographic Data Including Guidelines for Content Designation, 1999 Edition.* Washington, D.C.: Library of Congress Distribution Service.

3 SOUND RECORDINGS

OVERVIEW

Sound recordings have become an important part of the collections of many libraries. Once relegated to uncataloged and sometimes recreational collections, they are now recognized as a valuable resource. There are specialized music libraries consisting primarily of sound recordings, or in which sound recordings make up a substantial portion of the collection.

Level of description provided for sound recordings depends on a library's collection, available staff, and the importance of these resources to their holdings. All examples included in this text use full level description.

The type of classification provided for sound recordings varies with type and size of library as well as by kind of collection in which the resources are housed (restricted or freely available). Libraries may provide Library of Congress Classification numbers or Dewey Decimal numbers, accession numbers, may arrange sound recordings alphabetically by title, performer, conductor, etc. or according to genre (classical, jazz, folk, rap, ethnic, etc.). Arrangement and classification varies by library and how access is provided to these resources.

The glossary in *AACR2R (1998:623)* defines sound recordings as "A recording on which sound vibrations have been registered by mechanical or electrical means so that the sound may be reproduced." The following categories of sound recording are covered in this text: vinyl discs, sound cassettes, and compact discs.

ELEMENTS OF BIBLIOGRAPHIC RECORDS FOR SOUND RECORDINGS

The category of resources referred to as sound recordings includes discs, both 12 inch (vinyl, commonly referred to as "LPs") and 4 3/4 inch (compact discs), and sound cassettes (commonly referred to as "tapes"). This chapter does not include discussion and examples for sound cartridges, sound tape reels, sound track film, or rolls (such as piano rolls). This text includes a discussion of both musical and nonmusical sound recordings.

The following information may be used to create bibliographic records for sound recordings:

- Chief Source of Information
- Prescribed Sources of Information
- Choice of Main Entry
- Other Standard Identifier
- Publisher Number
- Cataloging Source
- Language Code
- Geographic Information
- Form of Musical Composition
- Number of Musical Instruments or Voices
- Library of Congress Call Number
- Title
- Title Variations
- General Material Designation (GMD)
- Statement of Responsibility
- Edition
- Place of Publication and/or Distribution, or Manufacture, etc.
- Name of Publisher(s) and/or Distributor(s)
- Date of Publication, Distribution, Copyright, Manufacture, etc.
- Physical Description
- Playing Time
- Series
- Notes
- Subject Access
- Added Entries (Personal and/or Corporate Names, Title Added Entries)
- Classification

CHIEF SOURCE OF INFORMATION

The chief source of information for sound recordings is the physical item and any label(s) on the item. It typically includes title information and credits, and publication/distribution information. If the item or labels yield little or no useful information, consult accompanying printed material or external container(s).

PRESCRIBED SOURCES OF INFORMATION

Rule 6.0B2, *AACR2R (1998)* states that the following sources of information should be consulted when creating bibliographic records for sound recordings:

- Title/statement of responsibility- Chief source of information
- Edition- Chief source of information, accompanying material, or container
- Publication, distribution, manufacture, etc.- Chief source of information, accompanying material, or container
- Physical description- Any source of information may be consulted
- Series- Chief source of information, accompanying material, or container
- Notes- Any source of information may be consulted

CHOICE OF MAIN ENTRY

Main entry may be under personal authorship or corporate authorship, or title main entry may be chosen. Rule 21.1A1, *AACR2R (1998)* defines a personal author as the individual chiefly responsible for a resource's intellectual or artistic content. Rule 21.1B1, *AACR2R (1998)* defines a corporate author as an organization or group of persons with a particular name that functions as an entity. Lastly, Rule 21.1C1, *AACR2R (1998)* states that a resource should be entered under title proper (or uniform title if appropriate) when: personal authorship is unknown or shared by a large number of individuals, and authorship can not be attributed to one particular individual or when a resource is not issued by a corporate body; or when a resource is a collection of works by different individuals or corporate bodies.

In some cases, title main entry is the most logical choice since the nonprint resource is the result of the work of many individuals and/or corporate bodies, and it is not possible to attribute authorship to a particular individual or corporate body. Lack of a statement of responsibility is another reason why title main entry is chosen for some nonprint resources.

Maxwell's Handbook for AACR2R: Explaining and Illustrating the Anglo-American Cataloging Rules and the 1993 Amendments (hereafter referred to as *"Maxwell's"*) explains that main entry for sound recordings is based on the same principles of authorship used for other materials, meaning that entry is under the person chiefly responsible for intellectual or artistic content.

In many cases, this is the composer. Main entry may also be under performer or musical group.

Chapter 21, *AACR2R (1998)* contains rules that pertain specifically to choice of main entry for sound recordings. Rule 21.23A1 instructs catalogers to enter sound recordings of one work under the heading appropriate for that work. Provide added entries for principal performers (which *AACR2R (1998)* cites as singers, readers, or orchestras) unless there are more than three. If there are more than three principal performers, provide an added entry for the first named.

example

245	00	Rock for babies‡h[sound recordings] /‡cperformed by Jerry Garcia, David Grisman, Mickey Hart, and Phish.
700	1	Garcia, Jerry,‡d1942-

100	1	Plath, Sylvia.
245	10	Sylvia Plath reads her poetry‡h[sound recording] / ‡cSylvia Plath.
511	0	Commentary by Ted Hughes, Linda Anderson.
700	1	Hughes, Ted,‡d1930-
700	1	Anderson, Linda R.,‡d1950-

Rule 21.23B1, *AACR2R (1998)* applies to a situation in which there are two or more works by the same person(s) or body (or bodies). In such a case, the work is entered under the heading appropriate to all those works. Added entries are provided for principal performers unless there are more than three. If so, provide an added entry only for the first individual or body named.

example

100	1	Cash, Johnny.
245	00	Tribute to Johnny Cash‡h[sound recording] /‡cJohnny Cash.
511	0	Performed by Willie Nelson, Waylon Jennings, Garth Brooks, Roseanne Cash, and Wyclef Jean.
700	1	Nelson, Willie,‡d1933-

Rule 21.3C1, *AACR2R (1998)* applies to situations in which a sound recording contains different works by different persons or bodies that is given a collective title. The main entry is provided for the individual or corporate body named as principal performer.

example

110	1	Chieftains (Musical group)
245	14	The long black veil‡h[sound recording] /‡csongs written

by various artists ; performed by the Chieftains.

If two or three persons or bodies are principal performers, the Rule instructs catalogers to provide main entry under the heading for the first named, and provide added entries for the other performers.
example

100	1	Morrison, Toni.
245	10	Women writers speak out‡h[sound recording].
511	0	Lectures by Toni Morrison, Alice Walker, and Margaret Atwood.
700	1	Walker, Alice,‡d1944-
700	1	Atwood, Margaret,‡d1939-

If four or more persons or bodies are cited as principal performers, or if there is no principal performer, the Rule instructs catalogers to provide title main entry.
example

245	00	New Jersey High School Marching Bands Competition‡h[sound recording.
511	0	Featuring various high school marching bands from around the state.

245	00	Ladies of rock‡h[sound recording] :‡ba benefit concert.
511	0	Performances by Pat Benatar, Heart, Cheryl Crow, Natalie Merchant, Stevie Nicks, and Cher.

Rule 21.23D1, *AACR2R (1998)* applies to situations in which a sound recording contains different works by different persons or bodies that lacks a collective title and is intended to be cataloged as a unit. The rule offers catalogers two options, a and b. Option a applies if the item contains works in which the participation of the performer(s) extends beyond that of performance, execution, or interpretation, which is typical for popular, rock, or jazz music. In such cases, main entry is under person or corporate body cited as principal performer.
example

100	1	Jackson, Janet.
245	00	Love songs /‡cJimmy Jam and Terry Lewis ; sung by Janet Jackson. Woman's world /‡cBabyface and Eric Clapton ; sung by Janet Jackson.

If two or three persons or bodies are cited as principal performers, main entry is under the first named, and added entries are provided for the others.
example

110	2	Time Capsule (Musical group)
245	10	New Jersey battle of the bands‡h[sound recording] :‡blocal bands perform.
511	0	Performances by Time Capsule, Soul What?, and Blues Generation.
710	2	Soul What? (Musical group)
710	2	Blues Generation (Musical group)

If four or more persons or bodies are cited as principal performers or if there is no principal performer, main entry is provided in relation to the first work named.
example

100	1	Alden, Tor.
245	10	Butterflies /‡cAlden and Kacherian ; Lawrence Welk and his Orchestra . La la /‡cKing, Stern ; Brian Setzer Orchestra. Irish eyes /‡cDolan and Dolan ; Chris Alberti and his Orchestra. Race days/‡cKapp, Zazzara ; the Solitares with Susanna Evans.

Option b, Rule 21.23D1 applies if the item contains works in which the participation of the performer(s) does not extend beyond that of performance, execution, or interpretation, which is typical for classical and what *AACR2R (1998)* describes as "other serious music." In such cases, main entry is provided in relation to the first work and added entries are provided for the other works. Added entries are provided for the principal performers of each work, as per Rule 21.23A1.
example

100	1	Schubert, Franz,‡d1797-1828.
245	10	Piano sonata in C minor, Opus posth., D. 958 / ‡cSchubert. Fantasia in C, op. 17 : 3rd mvt. /‡cSchumann.
511	0	Leonard Shure, piano.
700	10	Shure, Leonard.‡4prf
700	12	Schumann, Robert,‡d1810-1856.
100	1	Beethoven, Ludwig van,‡d1770-1827.
245	1	Mengelberg conducts Beethoven‡h[sound recording] / ‡cBeethoven.

511	0	Concertgebouw Orchestra of Amsterdam ; Willem Mengelberg, conductor.
700	1	Mengelberg, Willem,‡d1871-1951.‡4cnd
710	2	Concergebouworkest.‡4prf

Physical Description

Physical description is provided both in fixed fields and the 300 field, **Physical Description**. The 007 field, **Physical Description Fixed Field—General Information** provides information on physical description in alphabetic coded form. Some bibliographic utilities and cataloging modules display the 007 field at the top of the bibliographic record with other fixed fields; other utilities and modules provide this information in the bibliographic record with the variable fields. In this text, the 007 field is displayed with the variable fields in examples of bibliographic records.

There are no subfields or indicators defined for the 007 field.

The 007 field for sound recordings (sound cassettes, vinyl discs, CDs) begins with an s and has 14 characters defined for use. Selected values are provided in the following text.

Position 00- Category of material; is always **s** for "sound recording"

Position 01- SMD; **d** (disc); **s** (cassette); discussion in this text is limited to discs and cassettes.

Position 02- Undefined; leave blank

Position 03- Speed; **a** (16 rpm); **b** (33 1/3 rpm); **l** (1 7/8 ips)

Position 04- Configuration of playback channels; **m** (mono.); **q** (quadraphonic); **s** (stereo.)

Position 05- Groove width/groove pitch; **m** (microgroove)

Position 06- Dimensions; **e** (12 in.); **g** (4 3/4 in. or 12 cm.)

Position 07- Tape width; **l** (1/8 in.); **m** (1/4 in.)

Position 08- Tape configuration; **a** (full track); **b** (half track)

Position 09- Kind of disc, cylinder or tape; **a** (master tape); **m** (mass produced); **t** (test pressing)

Position 10- Kind of material; **m** (plastic and metal); **p** (plastic); **u** (unknown)

Position 11- Kind of cutting; **h** (hill and dale); **l** (lateral or combined); **n** (not applicable)

Position 12- Special playback characteristics; **a** (NAB standard); **c** (Dolby-B encoded); **e** (digital recording); **h** (CX encoded)

Position 13- Capture and storage technique; **a** (acoustical capture, direct storage); **d** (digital storage); **e** (analog electrical storage)

example

```
007                    sd fsngnnmmned
```
s = sound recording
d = sound disc
blank
f = 1.4 mps
s = stereophonic
n = groove width/groove pitch not applicable
g = 4 3/4 in. or 12 in.
n = tape width not applicable
n = tape configuration not applicable
m = mass produced
m = metal and plastic
n = kind of cutting not applicable
e = digital recording
d = digital storage

```
007                    ss lsnjlbmnnue
```
s = sound recording
s = sound cassette
blank
l = 1 7/8 ips
s = stereophonic
n = groove width/groove pitch not applicable
j = 3 7/8 x 2 1/2 in.
l = 1/8 in.
b = half (2) track
m = mass produced
n = kind of material not applicable
n = kind of cutting not applicable
u = special playback characteristics unknown
e = analog electrical storage

A full list of values for the 007 field is available on the USMARC Web page at http://lcweb.loc.gov/marc/bibliographic/ecbd007s.html#mrcb007s.

Other Standard Identifier

Provide information on a standard number or code appearing on an item that is not applicable for inclusion in another field. Record the International Standard Music Number for sound recordings in the 024 field, **Other Standard Identifier**, which is repeatable.

The following subfields are defined for use in the 024 field when used for sound recordings: ‡a standard number or code; ‡c terms of availability; ‡d additional codes to follow the standard number or code; ‡z canceled/invalid standard number or code.

The first indicator value indicates type of standard number or code. In the case of sound recordings, the following first indicator values are applicable: 0 = International Standard Recording Code; 2 = International Standard Music Number. The second indicator value indicates if there is a difference between a scanned number or code and the same information if provided in eye-readable form. A second indicator value of blank indicates that no information is provided; a value of 0 indicates no difference; a value of 1 indicates that there is a difference.
example

024	2	GM270310072
024	0	3185900008515

Publisher Number

Provide information on a formatted publisher number in the 028 field, **Publisher Number**, which is repeatable. Rule 6.7B19, *AACR2R (1998)* instructs catalogers to provide the publisher's stock number (typically an alphabetic and/or numeric symbol), preceded by the brand or trade name provided on the label or container. When two or more numbers are given, and one applies to a set as a whole, it must be provided first and its significance should be noted. The LCRI for Rule 6.7B19 states that matrix numbers should be provided when they are the only numbers available on an item. Each matrix number should be followed by the word "matrix," provided in parentheses. Publisher numbers may also be provided in the 500 field, **General Note**, in an unformatted form.

The following subfields are available for use in the 028 field for sound recordings: ‡a publisher number; ‡b source.

Publisher numbers for sound recordings have first indicator values ranging from 0-3 (0 = issue number; 1 = matrix number; 2 = plate number; 3 = other music number). The second indicator value for the 028 field may be used to generate a note and/or added entry. A second indicator value of 0 indicates that no note or added entry is generated from the 028 field; all examples in this text have a second indicator value of 0.
example

028	00	BLS 5560‡bBellaphon
028	02	8034-2‡bNew World Records
500		LRC: EJ-1005.
500		Bellaphon: BLS 5560; Bellaphon: LC 1421.

Cataloging Source

Information on the origin of a bibliographic record, plus any institutions that have modified a record, is provided in the 040 field, **Cataloging Source**, which is not repeatable.

The following subfields are available for use in the 040 field: ‡a original cataloging agency; ‡c transcribing agency (which is typically the institution in ‡a); and ‡d modifying agency. There are other subfields that may be used in the 040; this discussion is limited to those that are most predominantly used.

There are no indicators defined for the 040 field.

example

Original cataloging record created and transcribed by Rutgers University Libraries
040   NjR‡cNjR

Original cataloging record created and transcribed by Rutgers University Libraries, modified by Library X.
040   NjR‡NjR‡dXyZ

Original cataloging record created and transcribed by Rutgers University Libraries, modified at a later date by Rutgers University Libraries.
040   NjR‡NjR‡dNjR

Language Code

Provide information on language(s) present in a resource in the 041 field, **Language Code**, which is not repeatable. Information in the 041 is provided in alphabetic coded form. The 041 works in conjunction with the 546 field, **Language Note**.

Codes are provided according to their predominance in the resource (Network Development and MARC Standards Office, Library of Congress, 1999). The 041 field can provide codes for a maximum of six languages. If more than six languages are present in the resource, the language for the title is coded as "mul"(multiple) to represent all the languages.

The following subfields are used in the 041: ‡a language code for text, sound track, or separate title; ‡b language code for summary or subtitle; ‡d language code for sung or spoken text; ‡e language code for librettos; ‡g language code for accompanying materials other than librettos; ‡h language code for original and/or intermediate translations of text.

The initial indicator value indicates whether a resource is or includes a translation. An initial indicator of 0 indicates that the resource is not a translation and does not include a translation; a

value of 1 indicates that the item is a translation or includes a translation.
example

041	1	freita‡gengfreita
546		In French and Italian; program notes in English, French, and Italian.
041	1	‡dgerita‡egeritaengfre‡hgerita‡genggerfreitas pa‡henggerfre
546		Program notes by Alan Newcombe, Richard Osborne, Klaus Bennert, and Francis Drêsel, in English, German and French, with Italian and Spanish translations, and texts of the vocal works, in German and Italian, with English and French translations (16 p. : ill.) included.

Geographic Information

Provide information on the geographic area presented, described, covered, etc. by the resource in the 043 field, **Geographic Area Code,** which is not repeatable. The 043 can accommodate 1-3 codes, which are represented in alphabetic coded form. Multiple geographic codes are separated by a ‡a.

Indicator values are not defined for the 043 field.

A full list of geographic codes is available on the USMARC Web page at http://lcweb.loc.gov/marc/geoareas/.
example

Resource contains information pertaining to New Jersey, in the United States
043　　　n-us-nj

Resource contains information pertaining to the Great Plains region in the United States
043　　　np- - - - -

Resource contains information pertaining to Japan
043　　　a-ja- - -

Resource contains information pertaining to Spain and Mexico
043　　　e-sp- - -‡an-mx- - -

Form of Musical Composition

Provide information on the form of musical composition contained on a sound recording in the 047 field, **Form of Musical Composition Code,** which is not repeatable. Form of composition is represented by a two character alphabetic code, and different forms of composition may be represented. There is a code to represent multiple composition types when a sound recording contains more than two types.

Indicator values are not defined for the 047 field.

A full list of musical composition codes is available on the USMARC Web page at http://lcweb.loc.gov/marc/bibliographic/ecbd008s.html#mrcb008m.

example

Concertos, symphonies
047   co‡asy

Choral preludes, requiems, other
047   cl‡arq‡azz

Number of Musical Instruments or Voices

Provide information on the number and type of musical instruments and/or number and type of voices represented in a sound recording in the 048 field, **Number of Musical Instruments or Voices Code,** which is repeatable.

The following subfields are available for use with the 048 field: ‡a performer or ensemble; ‡b soloist. The 048 can accommodate up to five codes.

Indicator values are not defined for the 048 field.

A full list of codes for musical instruments or voices is available on the USMARC Web page at http://lcweb.loc.gov/marc/bibliographic/ecbdnumb.html#mrcb048.

example

1 brass trumpet; 1 guitar; voices, unspecified; larger ensemble, unspecified
048   ‡bbb01‡btb01‡bvn01‡aon

1 drum; 1 saxophone; 1 trumpet; 1 piano; 1 double bass
048   ‡bpd01 ‡bwi01 ‡abb01 ‡aka01 ‡asd01

Library of Congress Call Number

Provide a Library of Congress Call Number (if applicable according to the cataloging agency's policies and procedures for nonprint resources) in the 050 field, **Library of Congress Call Number,** which is repeatable. Some institutions have policies governing whether an LC Call Number is included in the bibliographic portion of a record when their records are submitted to a national online bibliographic utility such as RLIN or OCLC.

The following subfields are available for use in the 050 field:

‡a classification number; ‡b item number.

The initial indicator value indicates whether the item is in Library of Congress's collection. An initial value of blank indicates that no information is provided, and is used when libraries other than the Library of Congress provide classification numbers. The second indicator value indicates source of call number. Classification numbers provided by Library of Congress have a second indicator value of zero; classification numbers provided by other libraries have a second indicator value of 4.

example

| 050 | 0 | HB1335‡b.M84 |
| 050 | 4 | GB1399.4.N5‡bF566 1971 |

TITLE INFORMATION

Includes title, general material designation, remainder of title, and statement of responsibility.

Title

Consult the chief source of information first. If it is lacking or provides limited or no information, consult the prescribed sources of information. In the absence of chief or prescribed sources of information, a title may be supplied by the cataloger. The supplied title must be bracketed, and the source of title must be documented in a general note.

Title information is provided in the 245 field, **Title Statement** as per Rule 5.1B, *AACR2R (1998)*. The following subfields are available for use in the 245 field: ‡a title; ‡b remainder of title; ‡c statement of responsibility; ‡h GMD; ‡n number of part/section; ‡p name of part/section. One method of presenting subfields is to discuss them in the order in which they are used in bibliographic records, rather than alphabetically. However, the alphabetic approach is used in this text, and has been modeled after authoritative sources of information, such as *Concise MARC Format* and the RLIN and OCLC cataloging manuals. Placement of the subfields is illustrated in examples and illustrations. There are additional subfields that may be used in the 245; this text focuses discussion and examples on those that are most predominantly used.

Rule 1.1B1, *AACR2R (1998)* instructs catalogers to transcribe the title proper exactly as to wording, order, and spelling, but not necessarily to capitalization and punctuation. Titles are provided in the 245 field, ‡a, which is not repeatable.

Indicator values in the 245 field indicate if a title added entry

will be generated. Most nonprint items are cataloged using title main entry. Nonprint resources are rarely entered under an author (corporate or personal) main entry. (A discussion of choice of main entry for nonbook resources is provided in the following paragraph.) For this reason, the majority of nonprint resources will have a first indicator value of 0. A first indicator value of 1 is used when a title added entry will be generated. The second indicator specifies number of nonfiling characters, with a range of 0-9 available.
example

> *Title from chief source of information:*
> 245　　00　　　Kyushu-Okinawa Summit 2000 official guide
>
> *Title supplied by cataloger:*
> 245　　00　　　[Documentary on Douglass College, Rutgers University]
> 500　　　　　　　Title supplied by cataloger.

Provide title information in the 245 field, **Title Statement**, which is not repeatable.
example

> 245　　04　　　The Beatles live at the Star Club in Hamburg, Germany, 1962
> 245　　00　　　Powwow songs

Remainder of Title

The 245 field also provides the remainder of a title or other information, such as parallel titles. Provide this information in the ‡b, which is not repeatable.
example

> 245　　00　　　Powwow songs :‡bmusic of the Plains Indians

Title Variations

Provide title variations in the 246 field, **Varying Form of Title**, which is repeatable. The 246 provides other titles by which a resource may be known; this includes abbreviations or acronyms, parallel titles in another language, or when one title appears on external packaging and another title is given in the chief source of information. Providing access to title variations permits users to search for a resource in multiple ways.

The following subfields are available for use in the 246 field: ‡a title; ‡b remainder of title or parallel title; ‡h medium; ‡i display text; ‡n number of part/section of a work; ‡p name of a part/section of a work. There are additional subfields that may be used with the 246; this text focuses discussion and examples on those that are most predominantly used.

The initial indicator value indicates note or added entry. The second indicator value is used to provide information on type of title. A complete list of indicator values is available on the USMARC Web page at http://lcweb.loc.gov/marc/bibliographic/ecbdtils.html#mrcb246.

example

Portions of the main title

| 245 | 00 | Piano music of the unknown impressionists‡h[sound recording]. |
| 246 | 30 | Unknown impressionists‡h[sound recording] |

Remainder of title

| 245 | 00 | Riding with the king‡h[sound recording] :‡bB.B. King & Eric Clapton |
| 246 | 30 | B.B. King & Eric Clapton‡h[sound recording] |

Title on chief source and container differ

| 245 | 04 | The Beatles live at the Star Club in Hamburg, Germany, 1962‡h[sound recording]. |
| 246 | 1 | ‡iTitle on container:‡aLingasong Records presents the Beatles live at the Star Club in Hamburg, Germany, 1962 |

GENERAL MATERIAL DESIGNATION (GMD)

Use of a GMD is deemed optional by Rule 1.1C, *AACR2R (1998)*. There are several reasons why a library may choose to use GMDs. It indicates to users the format of a resource when a search is done in an online catalog since all resources with a specific GMD will cluster together. Additionally, the resource described in an online catalog may not readily be apparent to users even when the bibliographic record includes a physical description that includes type of resource and characteristics. Use of a GMD helps users to distinguish between different formats in which a title is available. For example, *Midnight Express* is the title of a book, as well as a motion picture, a motion picture sound track, and is also available on videorecording. However, there is a growing sentiment that GMDs are no longer useful, particularly in a Web-based environment in which some libraries use one bibliographic record to represent multiple manifestations of a title (a paper and an electronic version of a serial title, for example).

The GMD is included in the 245 field, ‡h and is enclosed in brackets. It immediately follows the information provided in ‡a and precedes the ‡b. It is not repeatable.

Use the GMD "sound recording" for all types of sound recordings. Do not confuse the GMD with the SMD, which specifies type of material. Provide the GMD in the 245 field, ‡h, which is not repeatable.

example

| 245 | 04 | The Beatles live at the Star Club in Hamburg, Germany, 1962‡h[sound recording]. |
| 245 | 00 | Powwow songs‡h[sound recording]. |

STATEMENT OF RESPONSIBILITY

The statement of responsibility for sound recordings includes the names of individuals (composers, lyricists, etc.) responsible for the content of the sound recording. Provide this information in the 245 field, ‡c. Rule 6.1F1, *AACR2R (1998)* states that the statement of responsibility for sound recordings should include individuals or corporate bodies with a major role in the intellectual content of the sound recording, such as writers of spoken words, composers of performed music, collectors of field material, or producers with artistic and/or intellectual responsibility. The rule further states that participation extending beyond performance, execution, or interpretation (common in rock and jazz music) is cited in the statement of responsibility. Additionally, the rule also states that participation confined to performance, execution, or intellectual interpretation (common in classical music or spoken word recordings) is cited in a note.

Performers are recorded in the 511 field, **Participant or Performer Note.**

example

| 245 | 04 | The Beatles live at the Star Club in Hamburg, Germany, 1962‡h[sound recording] /‡cthe Beatles. |
| 245 | 00 | Unity and diversity‡h[sound recording] /‡cthe Menninger Foundation. |

Edition

Provide information on an edition of a resource in the 250 field, **Edition Statement,** which is not repeatable. Edition information for nonprint resources is not limited to the term "edition," and also includes the terms "version," "release," "revision," or other terms deemed appropriate by the cataloging agency. Rule 6.2B1, *AACR2R (1998)* states that an edition statement should be provided when the item contains differences from other editions of the sound recording or a re-issue of the sound recording.

example

250	Complete edition.
250	Teacher edition.
250	First correct performing edition / edited by Roger Hellyer.

PUBLICATION INFORMATION

Consult the chief and/or prescribed sources of information to obtain information on where and when a resource was published, distributed, manufactured, etc. Publication, distribution, manufacture, etc. information is provided in the 260 field, **Publication, Distribution, etc. (Imprint)**, which is not repeatable.

PLACE OF PUBLICATION, DISTRIBUTION, MANUFACTURE, ETC.

The place of publication, distribution, manufacture, etc. is provided in the 260 field, ‡a. It is repeatable if there is more than one place of publication, or if a resource is published in one location and distributed in another, for example.

Generally, the city and country or state of publication are given. If only a city name is given, and it is necessary to record the country, state, etc., for purposes of identification and clarification, record the supplied information in brackets, as per Rule 1.4C3, *AACR2R (1998)*.
example

260	Detroit, Mich.
260	Schmalkalden [Germany]

If a place of publication, distribution, manufacture, etc. is not provided, but may be ascertained, record in brackets with a question mark. Consult Rule 1.4C6, *AACR2R (1998)*, for further discussion of this topic.
example

260	[Denver?]

If no place of publication, distribution, manufacture, etc. is provided, and may not be ascertained, the abbreviation for the term "Sine loco," [S.l.] is used per Rule 1.4C6, *AACR2R (1998)*. The abbreviation is always bracketed.

example

260	[S.l.] :‡bMedia Mix Productions

NAME OF PUBLISHER(S) AND/OR DISTRIBUTOR(S)

Provide name of publisher(s) and/or distributor(s) in the 260 field, **Publication, Distribution, etc. (Imprint)**, ‡b, which is repeatable.

A division, subsidiary, etc., of a recording company is sometimes given along with the name of the recording company. In such cases, record the division name, rather than the name of the recording company.

example

Label reads: Fresh Tunes, a division of Rim Records, New York, N.Y.

260	New York, N.Y. :‡bFresh Tunes,

DATE OF PUBLICATION, DISTRIBUTION, COPYRIGHT, MANUFACTURE, ETC.

Provide date of publication, distribution, manufacture, etc. in the 260 field, **Publication, Distribution, etc. (Imprint)**, ‡c, which is repeatable (although this option is not widely applied).

Consult the chief source of information first. If it yields no information, consult the prescribed sources of information. If no publication date is given, use the phonogram copyright date (date preceded by a lower case "p") or copyright date if given. The phonogram copyright date is the preferred type of copyright date for sound recordings. Additionally, if the recording date differs from the publication, distribution, etc., date(s), this difference may be stated in a 500 field, **General Note**.

example

Container indicates that music was recorded live at the Star Club, Hamburg, Germany, in 1962. The phonogram copyright date for the sound recording is 1977.

260	Germany :‡bBellaphon,‡cp1977.
500	Recorded at the Star Club in Hamburg, Germany in 1962.

PHYSICAL DESCRIPTION

Includes extent (number and Specific Material Designation (SMD) of physical parts of an item), other physical details (color or sound characteristics, for example), dimensions, and information about accompanying materials.

The physical description is provided in the 300 field, **Physical Description**. The physical description field is repeatable, permitting a multilevel description, yet this option is not commonly applied.

EXTENT

Provide information on extent (number and SMD of parts), duration, sound characteristics, dimensions, and accompanying materials.

The extent (number and SMD of parts) of a resource is provided in the 300 field, **Physical Description**, ‡a.
example

300	2 sound discs
300	1 sound cassette

Note: *AACR2R (1998)* states that the term "sound" can be omitted from the SMD if a GMD is used. This choice is at the discretion of the cataloging agency.

Duration

Record playing time as given on the item (1 hr., 35 min., for example). If playing time is not provided, use the necessary equipment to approximate the total playing time. When an approximated playing time is given, it is preceded by the abbreviation "ca." Provide duration in the 300 field, **Physical Description**, ‡a.
example

300	2 sound discs (90 min.)
300	1 sound cassette (ca. 40 min.)

SOUND CHARACTERISTICS

Indicate type of recording system and sound. Provide sound characteristics in the 300 field, **Physical Description**, ‡b. Additionally, Rule 6.5C2, *AACR2R (1998)* states that type of recording (analog or digital) should be provided for discs or cassettes. Rule 6.5C8 states that optional information relating to recording and reproduction characteristics (such as Dolby processing) may be included in this portion of the physical description.

example

300	2 sound discs (90 min.) :‡bdigital, stereo.
300	1 sound cassette (ca. 40 min.) :‡banalog, stereo., Dolby processed
300	1 sound disc (73 min.) :‡bdigital, mono.

DIMENSIONS

Record the size of discs in inches (in.). Since cassettes typically come in one standard size, dimensions are only recorded when there is a significant difference in size from that of the average cassette. Provide dimensions in the 300 field, **Physical Description, ‡c.**
example

300	2 sound discs (90 min.) :‡bdigital, stereo. ;‡c4 3/4 in.
300	1 sound cassette (ca. 40 min.) :‡banalog, stereo., Dolby processed

ACCOMPANYING MATERIALS

Provide information describing accompanying materials in one of three ways, per Rule 1.5E1, *AACR2R (1998)*: (1) at the end of the physical description; (2) in a note separate from the physical description; or (3) as part of a multilevel description.
example

As part of the physical description:
300	1 sound disc :‡bdigital ;‡c4 3/4 in. +‡eprogram notes (7 p.) inserted in container.

Note: If more than one item is included in the ‡e, 300, each item is preceded by a space and a plus sign.

300	1 sound disc :‡bdigital ;‡c4 3/4 in. +‡eprogram notes (7 p.) inserted in container + 1 sheet of lyrics.

In a separate note:
300	1 sound disc :‡bdigital ;‡c4 3/4 in.
500	Accompanied by one sheet of lyrics.

Multilevel description:
300	1 sound cassette (40 min.) :‡banalog
300	2 film reels (180 min.) :‡bsd., col. ;‡c16 mm.
300	50 p. :‡bill. ;‡c28 cm.

PLAYING TIME

Provide information on the total playing time in the 306 field, **Playing Time**, which is not repeatable. Playing time is provided in a numeric coded form; this information may be provided for both musical and non-musical sound recordings. This information is also provided in the 300 field, **Physical Description**.

Playing time is recorded in a six character numeric code representing hours, minutes, and seconds. Two positions are provided for each increment of time. The 306 field can accommodate up to six different playing times. The 306 field is not used when more than six playing times are provided.

Indicator values are not defined for the 306 field.

example

300	1 sound cassette (20 min.)
306	002000
300	1 sound disc (90 min., 20 sec.)
306	023020

SERIES

Provide series treatment if available in the chief and/or prescribed sources of information. General series information is presented in this text since the focus is on descriptive cataloging procedures. Series are represented in this text by the 440 field, **Series Statement/Added Entry—Title**, which is repeatable.

The following subfields are available for use in the 440 field: ‡a title; ‡n number of part/section; ‡p name of part/section; ‡v volume or numbering designation.

Provide series title in the 440, ‡a, which is not repeatable.

The first indicator value for the 440 field is undefined. The second indicator specifies number of nonfiling characters, with a range of 0-9 available.

Detailed information on series, including various types of treatment, is available on the USMARC Web page at http://lcweb.loc.gov/marc/bibliographic/ecbdhome.html#mrcb440.

example

440	0	Signature series
440	0	Music in America.‡nSeries 1
440	0	Music in America.‡nSeries 1,‡pChoral music
440	0	Signature series ;‡vno. C-233

NOTES

Notes used for sound recordings provide a variety of information, including edition, contents, language, or source of title. They are also used to describe characteristics of the sound recording or to note features unique to a library's copy of an item.

The notes in this section are provided in the order in which they appear in MARC records. Notes are not arranged in numeric order by MARC tag number.

Notes of a very general nature are provided in the 500 field, **General Note**, which is repeatable. This type of note is more prevalent in nonprint cataloging than in cataloging for print resources since the bibliographic record must provide as much information as possible when a resource is noncirculating and not easily accessible to users.

NATURE AND FORM

Rule 6.7B1, *AACR2R (1998)* states that a note may be provided on nature and form of the sound recording in the 500 field, **General Note** only when it is not apparent from the description. The 500 field is repeatable.
example

500	Whale sounds.
500	Poetry reading.
500	Motivational tape.
500	Nature sounds recorded digitally on PCM/DAT system.

LANGUAGE

Indicate language of the sound recording when more than one language is present, or if the language is other than the primary language of the cataloging agency. Provide this information in the 546 field, **Language Note**, which works in conjunction with the 041 field, **Language Code**. This note also provides information on accompanying printed documentation.
example

041	1	eng‡bengger
546		Songs performed in English; program notes in English and German.
041	0	‡gengjpn
546		Credits on container in English and Japanese.

SOURCE OF TITLE PROPER

Per Rule 6.7B3, *AACR2R (1998)* indicate source of title if not taken from chief or prescribed sources of information, or has been supplied by the cataloger.

Provide this information in the 500 field, **General Note**, which is repeatable.
example

500	Title from container.
500	Title supplied by cataloger.

CREDITS

Per Rule 6.7B6, *AACR2R (1998)* provide the names of individuals or corporate bodies not named in the statement of responsibility who have contributed to the production of the sound recording if their contributions are considered to be necessary and significant. This information is provided in the 508 field, **Creation/Production Credits Note**, which is not repeatable.
example

508	All songs written by John Lennon.
508	Written and directed by John Lapine ; musical direction by Paul Gemignani ; orchestration by Michael Starobin.

The LCRI for Rule 6.7B6 states that individuals or corporate bodies provided in this type of note (when used for nonmusical sound recordings) should be preceded with the display constant "Cast." In such cases, this information would be provided in a 511 field, **Participant or Performer Note**, rather than a 508 field.
example

511	1	Cast: Voices provided by Mary Lou Pratt and Mila C. Su.
511	1	Cast: Sylvia Plath reads her poetry.

EDITION AND HISTORY

Provide additional information on the resource, or use to provide history of the sound recording. This information is provided in the 500 field, **General Note**, which is repeatable, and differs from what is provided in the 250 field.
example

500	Eds. recorded: G. Schirmer (Judith); Merion Music (Night journey In sweet music).
500	The last work recorded during the Bang on a Can Festival at the Society for Ethical Culture, May 1992; the remainder

recorded at the Brooklyn Anchorage, Aug. 1997 and June 1998.

500   "Remastered and transferred to digital" - - Container.

500   Reissue of: Harmonia Mundi France HMC905149 (1985).

PUBLICATION, DISTRIBUTION, ETC., AND DATE INFORMATION

Rule 6.7B9, *AACR2R (1998)* instructs catalogers to make notes on publication, distribution, etc., details not included in the publication, distribution, etc., area but which are considered to be important. Provide this information in the 500 field, **General Note,** which is repeatable.

example

500   Recorded Aug. 1975 at the sixth annual Kihekah Steh Pow-wow, Okla., and elsewhere in Oct. 1975 at an informal performance.

500   All selections previously released; recorded chiefly 1961-1963.

500   Previously released material.

PHYSICAL DESCRIPTION

Rule 6.7B10, *AACR2R (1998)* instructs catalogers to provide additional physical description not represented in the 007 field, **Physical Description Fixed Field—General Information,** or the 300 field, **Physical Description.** This information is provided in the 500 field, **General Note,** or 538 field, **System Details Note** (depending on criteria described); both are repeatable.

Additional physical description includes notes on details that affect use, and other information deemed important by the cataloging agency. There are other criteria outlined in *AACR2R (1998)*; this discussion concentrates those criteria most applicable to the types of sound recordings covered in this chapter.

example

500   Analog recording.

500   Automatic sequence.

500   Compact disc.

500   Acoustic recording.

ACCOMPANYING MATERIALS

Provide additional information on accompanying materials in the 500 field, **General Note,** which is repeatable. Rule 6.7B11, *AACR2R (1998)* states that details of accompanying materials may be provided in a note when they are not included in the physical description or a separate description.

example

500	Program notes by Charlotte Heth and bibliography and discography in container.
500	Accompanied by lyrics ([5] p. ; 12 cm.)

AUDIENCE

Provide information on the intended audience or intellectual level of sound recordings. Take this information from chief or prescribed sources of information. This information is provided in the 521 field, **Target Audience Note**, which is repeatable.
example

521	Grades 1-4.
521	Intended for high school students.

OTHER FORMATS

Provide information on other formats in which a sound recording has been issued. This information is provided in the 530 field, **Additional Physical Form Available Note**, which is repeatable.
example

530	Also issued as a compact disc.
530	Also available on cassette.

SUMMARY

Provide a brief description of the contents of the sound recording. Since users may not browse for nonprint resources in the manner used for print resources, the summary should provide specific information to accurately describe the resource. Information taken from the container, external sources of information, or other sources should be noted. Generally, summaries should be limited to two-three sentences unless more information is warranted; this is determined by individual cataloging agencies. Summaries are typically provided for nonmusical sound recordings.

This information is provided in the 520 field, **Summary, Etc.**, which is repeatable.

The first indicator value provides an introductory phrase for the 520 field. A blank first indicator value generates the display "Summary." The second indicator value is undefined. Additional information on indicator values for the 520 field is available on the USMARC Web page at http://lcweb.loc.gov/marc/bibliographic/ecbdnot1.html#mrcb520.

example

| 520 | Summary: Selections from the last 6 years of her life—recordings from the Poetry Room at Harvard, in which she reads from her first book, The Colossus, as well as readings for the B.B.C. recorded before she wrote her controversial novel, The Bell jar. |
| 520 | Summary: The poet reads selections from his poems. Compiled from various recordings from different sources. |

CONTENTS

Provide information on the contents of a sound recording in the 505 field, **Formatted Contents Note**, which is repeatable. Per Rule 6.7B18, *AACR2R (1998)* statements of responsibility and durations may be included to provide additional information to users.

Contents notes in which the various parts of the note are coded are referred to as "enhanced." Enhanced contents notes contain a ‡t (title) and ‡r (statement of responsibility).

The first indicator value for the 505 field indicates completeness of the contents. A first indicator value of 0 indicates complete contents, a value of 1 is used for incomplete contents, and a value of 2 is used for partial contents. The second indicator value provides information on content designation. A second indicator value of 0 is used for enhanced contents. A second value of blank is used for nonenhanced contents notes. The indicators for an enhanced contents note are 00 (a nonenhanced contents has a single first indicator with a value from 0-2, or 8).

While not required, a contents note is useful to providing a description since the contents of a nonprint resource may not be browsed in the manner used for print resources.
example

| 505 | 0 | I saw her standing there / Lennon, McCartney (2:22) - - Roll over Beethoven / Chuck Berry (2:15) - - Lend me your comb / Carl Perkins (1:44) - - To know her is to love her / P. Spector (3:02). |
| 505 | 0 | The waste land (25:35) - - The hollow men (4:20) - - Journey of the Magi from the Ariel poems (2:27) - - La figlia che piange (1:22) - - Landscapes: New Hampshire, Virginia, Usk, Rannoch by Glencoe, Cape Ann (3:50) - - Morning at the window (:37) - - Difficulties of a statesman from Coriolan (3:20) - - Sweeney among the night- |

ingales (1:54) - - Whispers of immortality (1:42) - - Macavity: the mystery cat (5:25).

Enhanced contents note

505 00 ‡tBalcony rock /‡rD. Brubeck, P. Desmond - - ‡tOut of nowhere /‡r Heyman, J.W. Green - - ‡tLe souk /‡rD. Brubeck, P. Desmond - - ‡t Take the "A" train /‡rStrayhorn - - ‡tThe song is you /‡rHammerstein II, Kern - - ‡tDon't worry 'bout me /‡rKoehler, Bloom - - ‡tI want to be happy /‡rCaesar, Youmans.

DATE, TIME, AND PLACE OF AN EVENT

Provide information on the date and time and/or place of creation, capture, or broadcast associated with an event in the 518 field, **Date/Time and Place of An Event Note,** which is repeatable (Network Development and MARC Standards Office, Library of Congress, 1999).
example

518 Recorded at the Star Club in Hamburg, Germany, 1962.

518 Recorded Aug. 1975 at the sixth annual Kihekah Steh Pow-wow, Skiatook, Okla., and elsewhere in Oct. 1975 at an informal performance.

DESCRIPTIVE OR LIBRARY SPECIFIC NOTES

Provide descriptive or copy specific information regarding a sound recording in a 500 field, **General Note,** which is repeatable.
example

500 Container signed by various performers.

500 Reproduction of instantaneous acetate airchecks custom-produced at Gui de Buire studios (England), Hollick & Taylor Recording (England), Nola Recording Studios (New York), and Rockhill Recording Studios (New York).

500 Program notes by F. Driggs, bibliography, and discography bound in container.

"WITH" NOTES

Provide notes for titles that are not the first in a collective title. This information is provided in the 500 field, **General Note,** which is repeatable. Additionally, information provided in this type of note may also be used as the basis for a 740 field, **Added Entry— Uncontrolled Related/Analytical Title.**

example

500	With: Meinken, F. Wabash blues.
500	With: Baby Snooks.

SUBJECT ACCESS

Subject access to nonprint resources helps users to identify and locate resources, particularly when resources are maintained in a closed collection or are not available in a physical format, as is the case for Internet resources. Subject headings are used to provide access to resources through *personal names, corporate names, topical terms,* or *geographic names.* Subject headings may be further subdivided by form division (format of material), general subdivisions, chronological subdivisions, and geographic subdivisions. Meeting names and subject added entries for uniform titles are not included in this text.

Consult the *Library of Congress Subject Headings* (LCSH) and the *Library of Congress Subject Cataloging Manual* (SCM) (1996:1) for formulating subject headings for sound recordings. *SCM* instructs catalogers to assign the heading that represents the most predominant topic first. If the predominant topic can not be represented by one subject heading, *SCM* instructs catalogers to "...assign as the first and second headings the two headings that, taken together, express the predominant topic." If a sound recording has two major topics of equal importance, the first and second subject headings assigned will express these topics. These subject headings are assigned before headings for secondary topics. Secondary topics may be provided in any order following the major topics.

PERSONAL NAME

Provide subject access to personal names in the 600 field, **Subject Added Entry—Personal Name,** which is repeatable. Personal names are included in a bibliographic record when a resource is about an individual or individuals, or contains a significant portion of information about an individual or individuals.

The following subfields are available for use in the 600 field: ‡a personal name; ‡c titles associated with a name; ‡d dates associated with a name; ‡v form subdivision; ‡x general subdivision; ‡y chronological subdivision; ‡z geographic subdivision. There are additional subfields that may be used with the 600;

this text focuses discussion and examples on those that are most predominantly used.

The initial indicator value indicates type of name. An initial article value of 0 indicates entry under forename; 1 indicates entry under single surname. The second indicator value provides source of name heading. A second indicator value of 0 indicates that a name is from the Library of Congress Name Authority file. Additional information is available on the USMARC Web page at http://lcweb.loc.gov/marc/bibliographic/ecbdsubj.html#mrcb600. example

600	10	Weinberg, Valerie Ann.
600	10	Irving, Henry,‡cSir,‡d1838-1905.
600	10	Ellington, Duke,‡d1899-1974.
600	10	Krupa, Gene,‡d1909-1973‡vBiography.
600	10	King, Martin Luther,‡cJr.,‡d 1929-1968‡xAssassination.
600	10	Shakespeare, William,‡d1564 1616‡xStage history ‡y1800-1950.
600	10	Gogh, Vincent van,‡d1853-1890‡xMuseums‡zNetherlands‡zAmsterdam.

CORPORATE NAME

Provide subject access to corporate names in the 610 field, **Subject Added Entry—Corporate Name**, which is repeatable. Corporate names are included in a bibliographic record when a resource is about a corporation or corporations, or contains a significant portion of information about a corporation or corporations.

The following subfields are available for use in the 610 field: ‡a corporate or jurisdiction names; ‡b subordinate units; ‡v form subdivision; ‡x general subdivision; ‡y chronological subdivision; ‡z geographic subdivision. There are additional subfields that may be used with the 610; this text focuses discussion and examples on those that are most predominantly used.

The initial indicator value indicates form of entry for names. An initial indicator value of 1 is for jurisdiction name; 2 is for a name presented in direct order. A second indicator value of 0 indicates that a name is from the Library of Congress Name Authority file. Additional information is available on the USMARC Web page at http://lcweb.loc.gov/marc/bibliographic/ecbdsubj.html#mrcb610.
example

| 610 | 20 | Lyceum Theatre (London, England) |
| 610 | 10 | United States.‡bDept. of the Interior. |

610	20	Harvard University‡xFunds and scholarships‡vHandbooks, manuals, etc.
610	20	Microsoft Corporation‡xHistory.
610	20	Grand Central Terminal (New York, N.Y.)‡xHistory‡y20th century.
610	20	Salvation Army‡zEngland.

TOPICAL TERMS

Provide subject access to topical terms in the 650 field, **Subject Added Entry—Topical Term,** which is repeatable. Terms used in the 650 may describe form of the resource (Motion pictures, Spanish) or content (Jazz, Bicycle touring).

The following subfields are available for use in the 650 field: ‡a topical term or geographic name as entry element; ‡v form division; ‡x general subdivision; ‡y chronological subdivision; ‡z geographic subdivision. There are additional subfields that may be used with the 650; this text focuses discussion and examples on those that are most predominantly used.

The initial article value indicates level of subject; blank indicates that no information has been provided. In most cases, subject headings supplied by catalogers or provided in records available through union databases will have an initial indicator value of blank. A second indicator value of 0 indicates that a name is from the Library of Congress Name Authority file. Additional information is available on the USMARC Web page at http://lcweb.loc.gov/marc/bibliographic/ecbdsubj.html#mrcb650. example

650	0	Aleatory music.
650	0	Ballets‡vExcerpts.
650	0	Crime prevention‡xCitizen participation.
650	0	Jazz‡y2001-
650	0	Blues (Songs, etc.)‡zUnited States.

GEOGRAPHIC TERMS

Provide subject access to geographic terms in the 651 field, **Subject Added Entry—Geographic Name,** which is repeatable.

The following subfields are available for use in the 651 field: ‡a geographic name; ‡v form division; ‡x general subdivision; ‡y chronological subdivision; ‡z geographic subdivision. There are additional subfields that may be used with the 651; this text focuses discussion and examples on those that are most predominantly used.

The initial indicators are undefined for this field. A second indicator value of 0 indicates that a name is from the Library of

Congress Name Authority file. Additional information is available on the USMARC Web page at http://lcweb.loc.gov/marc/bibliographic/ecbdsubj.html#mrcb651.

The following examples provide limited information since it is not likely that a sound recording would be about a geographic place.

example

651	0	Brooklyn (New York, N.Y.)
651	0	United States‡xHistory‡yCivil War, 1861-1865.

ADDED ENTRIES

Added entries provide access to personal and corporate names that are not main entries yet serve as important additional access points. Name added entries include composers (if there is more than one), performers, conductors, etc. Title added entries provide additional access for titles related to the main work.

PERSONAL NAME

Provide access to personal names in the 700 field, **Added Entry—Personal**, which is repeatable. It is used to include additional access points in the form of names taken from the 245, **Title Statement**, and 511, **Participant or Performer Note** fields, or other fields deemed appropriate by the cataloging agency. Personal name added entries differ from personal names in the 600 in that they provide different types of information, and would be found in an online catalog using different types of searches (subject versus personal name).

The following subfields are available for use in the 700 field: ‡a personal name; ‡c titles or other words associated with a particular name; ‡d dates; ‡4 relator code. A list of relator codes is available on the USMARC Web page at http://lcweb.loc.gov/marc/relators/. There are additional subfields that may be used with the 700; this text focuses discussion and examples on those that are most predominantly used.

The initial indicator value indicates type of name. An initial article value of 0 indicates entry under forename; 1 indicates entry under single surname. The second indicator value indicates type of added entry. A second blank second indicator value indicates that no information is provided; a second indicator value of 2 indicates an analytical entry, and means the item in the bibliographic record contains the work represented by the added entry. Additional information is available on the USMARC Web page at http://lcweb.loc.gov/marc/bibliographic/ecbdadde.html#mrcb700. example

700	0	Liberace,‡d1919-
700	1	Glenn, Tyree.
700	1	Irving, Henry,‡cSir,‡d1838-1905.
700	1	Severinsen, Doc,‡d1927-
700	1	Fellini, Federico.‡4drt
700	1	Binoche, Juliette,‡d1964- ‡4prf

CORPORATE NAME

Provide access to corporate names in the 710 field, **Added Entry—Corporate Name**, which is repeatable. It is used to include additional access points in the form of names taken from the 245, **Title Statement**, 511, **Participant or Performer Note** fields, or other fields deemed appropriate by the cataloging agency. Corporate name added entries differ from corporate names in the 610 in that they provide different types of information, and would be found in an online catalog using different types of searches (subject versus corporate name).

The following subfields are available for use in the 710 field: ‡a corporate name or jurisdiction name; ‡b subordinate unit; and ‡4 relator code. There are additional subfields that may be used with the 710; this text focuses discussion and examples on those that are most predominantly used.

The initial indicator value indicates type of corporate name. An initial article value 1 indicates entry in jurisdiction order; a value of 2 indicates entry in direct order. The second indicator value indicates type of added entry. A blank second indicator value indicates that no information is provided; a second indicator value of 2 indicates an analytical entry, and means the item in the bibliographic record contains the work represented by the added entry. Additional information is available on the USMARC Web page at http://lcweb.loc.gov/marc/bibliographic/ecbdadde.html#mrcb710.
example

710	2	Beatles.‡4prf
710	2	University of Utah.‡bChorus.
710	2	Philadelphia Singers Chorale.‡4prf

UNIFORM TITLE

Provide access to uniform titles in the 730 field, **Added Entry—Uniform Title**, which is repeatable. Uniform titles provide a title related to the resource. Examples include radio or television programs.

The following subfields are available for use in the 730 field: ‡a uniform title; ‡f date of a work; ‡h medium; ‡k form subheading; ‡l language. There are additional subfields that may be used with the 730; this text focuses discussion and examples on those that are most predominantly used.

The initial indicator value indicates number of nonfiling characters (0-9). The second indicator value indicates type of added entry. A blank second indicator value indicates that no information is provided; a second indicator value of 2 indicates an analytical entry, and means the item in the bibliographic record contains the work represented by the added entry. Additional information is available on the USMARC Web page at http://lcweb.loc.gov/marc/bibliographic/ecbdadde.html#mrcb730.
example

| 245 | 00 | James Joyce reading "Anna Livia Plurabelle"‡h[sound recording]. |
| 730 | 0 | Finnegan's wake.‡kSelections. |

245	00	65 songs, for voice and piano.
730	0	Songs.‡lEnglish & German.‡kSelections.
730	0	Lum and Abner (Radio program)

RELATED TITLES

Provide access to titles related to the work described in the 245 field, **Title Statement** using the 740 field, **Added Entry—Uncontrolled Related/Analytical Title**, which is repeatable. The 740 field is created using information taken from 500, **General Note**, or 505, **Formatted Contents Note** fields, or other fields deemed appropriate by the cataloging agency.

The following subfields are available for use in the 740 field: ‡a uncontrolled related/analytical title; ‡h medium; ‡n number of part/section of a work; ‡p name of part/section of a work. There are additional subfields that may be used with the 740; this text focuses discussion and examples on those that are most predominantly used.

The initial indicator value indicates number of nonfiling characters (0-9). The second indicator value indicates type of added entry. A blank second indicator value indicates that no informa-

tion is provided; a second indicator value of 2 indicates an analytical entry, and means the item in the bibliographic record contains the work represented by the added entry. Additional information is available on the USMARC Web page at http://lcweb.loc.gov/marc/bibliographic/ecbdadde.html#mrcb740.
example

245	00	Nature sounds‡h[sound recording].
505	0	Vol. 1. Water sounds - - v. 2. Animal sounds.
740	0	Water sounds‡h[sound recording].
740	0	Animal sounds‡h[sound recording].

CLASSIFICATION

Classification schemes such as LCC and DDC are limited in their usefulness for classifying sound recordings. Both schemes are more oriented towards books on music and musical scores than sound recordings. As a result, libraries may use accession numbers or some type of local arrangement for their sound recordings, such as alphabetical by artist or composer, alphabetical by title, grouping by genre, and so on.

EXAMPLES OF BIBLIOGRAPHIC RECORDS

Examples follow on the next page.

Figure 3-1 Analog Sound Cassette

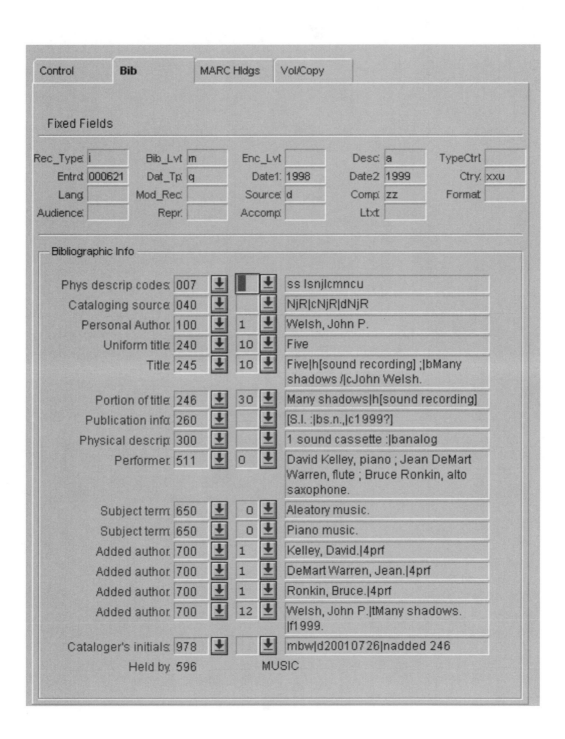

Figure 3-2 Analog Sound Cassette

| Control | **Bib** | MARC Hldgs | Vol/Copy |

Fixed Fields

Rec_Type: i		Bib_Lvt m		Enc_Lvt		Desc: a		TypeCtrl
Entrd 000000		Dat_Tp: p		Date1: 1984		Date2 1979		Ctry: nyu
Lang eng		Mod_Rec:		Source: d		Comp: zz		Format
Audience:		Repr:		Accomp: dez		Ltxt:		

Bibliographic Info

Phys descrip codes	007	⬇	▮	⬇	ss ulsnnlcmnnce
Publisher #	028	⬇	02	⬇	8442A|bNew Wilderness Audiographics
Event capture data	033	⬇	0	⬇	1983----|b3804|cA2
Event capture data	033	⬇	0	⬇	1980----
Event capture data	033	⬇	0	⬇	1979----|b3804|cP6
Cataloging source	040	⬇		⬇	NjR|cNjR
Personal Author	100	⬇	1	⬇	Benary, Barbara.
Uniform title	240	⬇	10	⬇	Selections
Title	245	⬇	00	⬇	Pieces for Gamelan Son of Lion |h[sound recording] /|c Barbara Benary.
Publication info	260	⬇		⬇	New York :|bNew Wilderness Audiographics,|c1984.
Physical descrip	300	⬇		⬇	1 sound cassette :|banalog.
Duration	306	⬇		⬇	000404|a001024|a000840 |a000420|a001815|a000639
Performer	511	⬇	0	⬇	Gamelan Son of Lion.
Date/place captured	518	⬇		⬇	Recorded in 1983 at Stoneface Recording Studio in Accord, NY (works 1-4) ; 5th work was recorded in 1980 at Livingston College Electronic Studio ; 6th work was recorded in 1979 in performance at Mid-Hudson Museum, Poughkeepsie, NY.

Figure 3-2 *Continued*

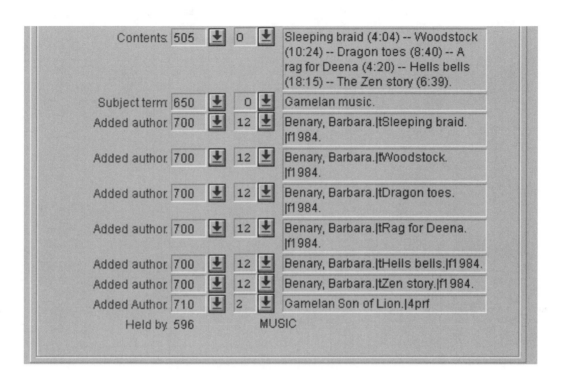

Figure 3-3 Analog Sound Disc

Control	**Bib**	MARC Hldgs	Vol/Copy

Fixed Fields

Rec_Type:	1	Bib_Lvt: m	Enc_Lvl:	Desc: a	TypeCtrl:
Entrd: 870203		Dat_Tp: s	Date1: 1984	Date2:	Ctry: flu
Lang:		Mod_Rec:	Source: d	Comp: mu	Format:
Audience:		Repr:	Accomp:	Ltxt:	

Bibliographic Info

Old Geac BCN: 980			00696809
Phys descrip codes: 007			sd bsmennmpln
LCCN: 010			84743022
Publisher #: 028		02	2015|bAudiofon
Local system #: 035			(CStRLIN)NJRG87-R123
Cataloging source: 040			NjR|cNjR|dNjR
Content time period: 045		2	|bd1828|bd1838
Form of composition: 047			sn|aft
Instrum/voices code: 048			ka01
Local LC call number: 090			|i02/25/87 CT
Local call number: 099			13031
Personal Author: 100		1	Schubert, Franz,|d1797-1828.
Uniform title: 240		10	Sonatas,|mpiano,|nD. 958,|rC minor
Title: 245		10	Piano sonata in C minor, Opus posth., D. 958 /|cSchubert. |bFantasia in C, op. 17 : 3rd mvt. / Schumann|h[sound recording].
Publication info: 260			Miami, Fla. :|bAudiofon,|cp1984.
Physical descrip: 300			1 sound disc :|banalog, 33 1/3 rpm, stereo. ;|c12 in
Duration: 306			003108|a001015
General Note: 500			Durations: 31:08 ; 10:15.
Performer: 511		0	Leonard Shure, piano.
Subject term: 650		0	Sonatas (Piano)
Subject term: 650		0	Piano music.
Added author: 700		10	Shure, Leonard.|4prf
Added author: 700		12	Schumann, Robert,|d1810-1856. |tFantasie,|mpiano,|nop. 17,|rC major.|pLangsam getragen.|f1984.
RLIN holdings: 950			|lMUSIC|a13031|d\DISC|p4 |i02/25/87 C
RLIN copy: 955			|lMUSIC|c1|aDISC|i02/25/87 C
Held by: 596			MUSIC

Figure 3-4 Stereophonic Sound Disc

| Control | **Bib** | MARC Hldgs | All Volumes |

Fixed Fields

Rec_Type:	Bib_Lvl: m	Enc_Lvl:	Desc: i	TypeCtrl:
Entrd: 840831	Dat_Tp: s	Date1: 1978	Date2:	Ctry: ilu
Lang: eng	Mod_Rec:	Source: d	Comp: mu	Format:
Audience:	Repr:	Accomp: f	Ltxt:	

Bibliographic Info

Old Geac BCN: 980			00478995
Phys descrip codes: 007			sd bsmennmpln
Publisher #: 028		02	AL 4713|bAlligator
Event capture data: 033		0	197805--|b4104|cC6
Local system #: 035			(CStRLIN)NJRG84-R685
Cataloging source: 040			NJR|cNJR|dNjR
Geographic area code: 043			n-us---
Content time period: 045		2	|bd1958|bd1978
Form of composition: 047			bl|ajz
Instrum/voices code: 048			vn01|atb02|awi02|aka01|asd01 |apd01
Local LC call number: 090			M1630.18|i07/27/88 T|h07/29/85 CT |h06/10/85 T
Local call number: 099			M1630.18
Personal Author: 100		1	Collins, Albert,|d1932-|4prf
Title: 245		10	Ice pickin'|h[sound recording] / |c[performed by] Albert Collins [with others]
Variant title: 246		3	Ice picking|h[sound recording]
Publication info: 260		0	Chicago, Ill. :|bAlligator,|cp1978.
Physical descrip: 300			1 sound disc (38 min., 1 sec.) :|b33 1/3 rpm, stereo. ;|c12 in.
Duration: 306			003801
General Note: 500			Program notes by Bruce Iglauer and Lee Hildebrand on container.

Figure 3-4 *Continued*

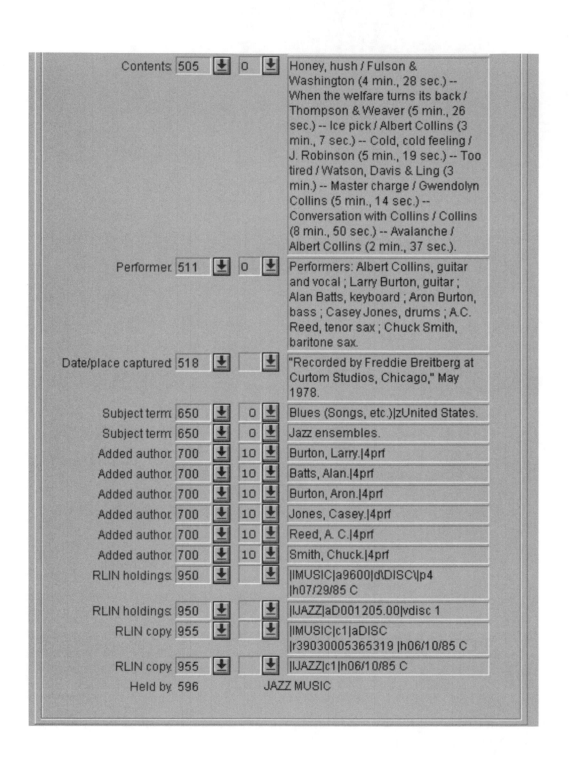

Figure 3-5 Digital Sound Disc

| Control | **Bib** | MARC Hldgs | Vol/Copy |

Fixed Fields

Rec_Type:	i	Bib_Lvt:	m	Enc_Lvt:		Desc:	a	TypeCtrl:	
Entrd:	010619	Dat_Tp:	s	Date1:	2000	Date2:		Ctry:	nyu
Lang:		Mod_Rec:		Source:	d	Comp:	mu	Format:	
Audience:		Repr:		Accomp:		Ltxt:			

Bibliographic Info

Phys descrip codes:	007				sd fsngnnmmned
Publisher #:	028		02		FDS 57939|bFleur De Son Classics
Event capture data:	033				|b3804|cN4
Cataloging source:	040				NjR|cNjR|dNjR
Personal Author:	100		1		Reeves, David.|4prf
Title:	245		10		Piano music of the unknown impressionists|h[sound recording].
Portion of title:	246		30		Unknown impressionists|h[sound recording]
Publication info:	260				Buffalo, NY :|bFleur De Son Classics,|cp2000.
Physical descrip:	300				1 sound disc :|bdigital ;|c4 3/4 in.
Performer:	511		0		David Reeves, piano.
Date/place captured:	518				Recorded Town Hall, NY.
General Note:	500				Compact disc.
Contents:	505		0		Three tone pictures, op. 5. The lake at evening (3:28) ; The vale of dreams (3:35) ; The night winds (2:28) ; Roman sketches, op. 7. The white peacock (6:01) ; Nightfall (6:56) ; The fountain of the Acqua Paola (3:56) ; Clouds (4:25) / Charles T. Griffes -- Moonlight through the cedar tree / Hilda Dederich (5:44) -- Cradle song (3:09) ; Improvisation, op. 67, no. 5 (2:18) ; May night, op. 27, no. 4 (3:18) ; The sea, op. 17, no. 12 (2:01) / Selim Palmgren -- Berceuse / Alfred Bachelet (6:18) -- Cielo di Settembre (4:23) ; Cipressi (8:03) ; I naviganti (5:51) / Mario Castelnuovo-Tedesco.

Figure 3-5 *Continued*

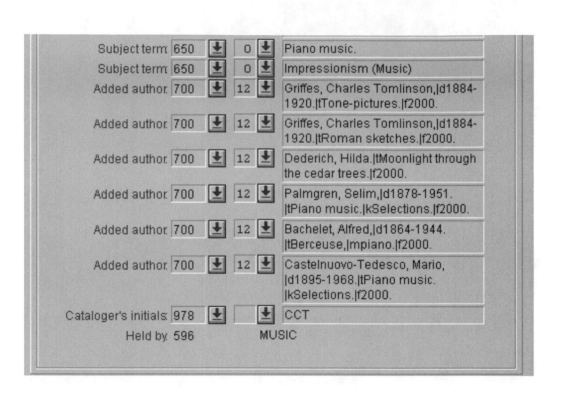

Figure 3-6 Digital Sound Discs

| Control | **Bib** | MARC Hldgs | Vol/Copy |

Fixed Fields

Rec_Type: j	Bib_Lvt: m	Enc_Lvt:	Desc: a
TypeCtrl:	Entrd: 010515	Dat_Tp: p	Date1: 2000
Date2: 1937	Ctry: enk	Lang:	Mod_Rec:
Source: d	Comp: mu	Format:	Audience:
Repr:	Accomp:	Ltxt:	

Bibliographic Info

001			a1498654
007			sd fmngnnmmned
024		1	2703100742
028		02	GEMS 0074|bPearl
033		2	19370404|a19421101
040			NjR|cNjR
100		1	Beethoven, Ludwig van,|d1770-1827.
240		10	Symphonies.|kSelections
245		10	Mengelberg conducts Beethoven|h[sound recording].
260			Wadhurst, E. Sussex, England :|b Pearl,|cp1999.
300			3 sound discs :|bdigital, mono. ;|c4 3/4 in.
500			Compact discs.
505		0	Symphony no. 1 in C major, op. 21 (21:51) -- Symphony no. 3 in E flat major, op. 55 (Eroica) (45:06) -- Symphony no. 4 in B flat, op. 60 (32:52) -- Symphony no. 5 in C minor, op. 67 (30:43) -- Symphony no. 6 in F major, op. 68 (Pastoral) (37:12) -- Symphony no. 8 in F major, op. 93 (24:54) -- Creatures of Prometheus, ballet music, op. 43 (9:23).
511		0	Concertgebouw Orchestra of Amsterdam ; Willem Mengelberg, conductor.
518			Recorded between Apr. 4, 1937 and Nov. 1, 1942.
596			MUSIC
650		0	Symphonies.
650		0	Ballets|vExcerpts.
700		1	Mengelberg, Willem,|d1871-1951.|4cnd
700		12	Beethoven, Ludwig van,|d1770-1827.|tGeschèopfe des Prometheus.|kSelections.|f2000.
710		2	Concertgebouworkest.|4prf
978			CCT

Figure 3-7 Spoken Word Sound Cassette

| Control | **Bib** | MARC Hldgs | Vol/Copy |

Fixed Fields

Rec_Type:	Bib_Lvl: m	Enc_Lvl:	Desc: a	TypeCtrl:
Entrd: 910301	Dat_Tp: s	Date1: 1989	Date2:	Ctry: dcu
Lang: eng	Mod_Rec:	Source: d	Comp: nn	Format:
Audience:	Repr:	Accomp:	Ltxt: p	

Bibliographic Info

Old Geac BCN:	980		01019327	
Date/time stamp:	005			19910409113127.0
Phys descrip codes:	007			ss?lsnjlnnnnce
Event capture data:	033	0		19880326|b3844|cL4:2M6
Event capture data:	033	0		19880325|b3852|cW32:2H6
Event capture data:	033	0		19880831|b3852|cW32:2J4
Local system #:	035			(CStRLIN)NJRG91-R173
Local LC call number:	090			|i04/09/91 CT
Local call number:	099			407
Personal Author:	100	10		Ostriker, Alicia.
Title:	245	10		Move|h[sound recording] /|cAlicia Ostriker.
Publication info:	260	0		Washington, DC :|bWatershed Tapes,|cp1989.
Physical descrip:	300			1 sound cassette (62 min.) : |banalog, stereo., Dolby processed
Series Title:	440	0		Signature series ;|vno. C-223
General Note:	500			Production of this tape was made possible in part by a grant from the Literature Program of the National Endowment for the Arts.
Contents:	505	0		The exchange -- Dream: The disclosure -- The runner -- His speed and strength -- Listen -- A question of time -- Cat -- Beer -- The pure products of America -- From "Lilith to Eve": House/garden -- The man -- Where trees come from -- A new song -- Excerpts from "Mother/Child" -- Mother/Child: Coda -- The leaf pile -- To kill the dove -- Stream -- Homecoming --

Figure 3-7 *Continued*

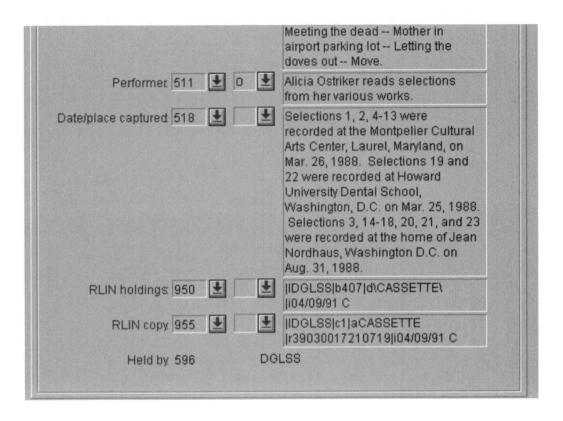

REFERENCES

Cataloging Policy and Support Office, Library of Congress. 1996. "Order of Subject Headings," from *Subject Cataloging Manual: Subject Headings*. Washington, D.C.: Library of Congress, Cataloging Distribution Service.

Maxwell, Robert L., and Margaret F. Maxwell. 1997. *Maxwell's Handbook for AACR2R: Explaining and Illustrating the Anglo-American Cataloging Rules and the 1993 Amendments*. Chicago: American Library Association.

Network Development and MARC Standards Office, Library of Congress in cooperation with Standards and Support, National Library of Canada. 1999. *MARC 21 Format for Bibliographic Data including Guidelines for Content Designation, 1999 Edition*. Washington, D.C.: Library of Congress Distribution Service.

4 MOTION PICTURES AND VIDEORECORDINGS

OVERVIEW

Motion pictures and videorecordings are an established part of the collections of many libraries. Once relegated to uncataloged and sometimes recreational collections, they are recognized as a powerful medium for communication and education. A new material type, the digital video disc (DVD), has emerged. This format is one area where cataloging of motion pictures and videorecordings continues to evolve.

The level of description provided for motion pictures and videorecordings depends on a library's collection, available staff, and the importance of motion pictures and videorecordings to their holdings. All examples included in this chapter use full level description (second level of description).

The type of classification provided for motion pictures and videorecordings varies with type and size of library and kind of collection in which the resources are housed (restricted or freely available). Libraries may provide Library of Congress Classification numbers or Dewey Decimal numbers, accession numbers, may arrange motion pictures and videorecordings alphabetically by title or director, or according to genre (documentary films, feature films, comedy films, etc.). Arrangement and classification varies by library and how access is provided to these resources.

The glossary in *AACR2R (1998:620)* defines motion pictures as "A length of film, with or without recorded sound, bearing a sequence of images that create the illusion of movement when projected in rapid succession." The glossary (1998:624) defines videorecordings as "A recording on which visual images, usually in motion and accompanied by sound, have been registered; designed for playback by means of a television set." The following categories of materials are covered in this chapter: motion pictures, videorecordings, laser videodiscs, and DVDs.

ELEMENTS OF BIBLIOGRAPHIC RECORDS FOR MOTION PICTURES AND VIDEORECORDINGS

The category of resources referred to as motion pictures includes 8, 16, and 35 millimeter (mm) films. This text limits discussion and examples to film reels. The category of resources referred to as videorecordings covers 1/2 inch VHS cassettes, 12 inch videodiscs, and 4 3/4 inch DVDs; discussion and examples are likewise limited.

The following information is necessary to create bibliographic records for motion pictures and videorecordings:

- **Chief Source of Information**
- **Prescribed Sources of Information**
- **Choice of Main Entry**
- **International Standard Book Number (ISBN)**
- **Cataloging Source**
- **Language Code**
- **Geographic Information**
- **Library of Congress Call Number**
- **Title**
- **Title Variations**
- **General Material Designation (GMD)**
- **Statement of Responsibility**
- **Edition**
- **Place of Publication and/or Distribution, or Manufacture, etc.**
- **Name of Publisher(s) and/or Distributor(s)**
- **Date of Publication, Distribution, Copyright, Manufacture, etc.**
- **Physical Description**
- **Series**
- **Notes**
- **Subject Access**
- **Added Entries (Personal and/or Corporate Names, Title Added Entries)**
- **Classification**

CHIEF SOURCE OF INFORMATION

The chief source of information for motion pictures and videorecordings are title and credit frames. The chief source of information typically includes title information and credits (director, screenwriter, production company, cast), and publication/distribution information. If title and credit frames yield little or no useful information, the container and external labels may also serve as chief sources of information. If neither of these sources yield information, accompanying printed materials or other sources may be consulted.

PRESCRIBED SOURCES OF INFORMATION

Rule 7.0B2, *AACR2R (1998)* states that the following sources of information should be consulted when creating bibliographic records for motion pictures and videorecordings:

- Title/statement of responsibility- Chief source of information
- Edition- Chief source of information, accompanying material, or container
- Publication, distribution, manufacture, etc.- Chief source of information, accompanying material, or container
- Physical Description- Any source of information may be consulted
- Series- Chief source of information, accompanying material, or container
- Notes- Any source of information may be consulted

CHOICE OF MAIN ENTRY

Main entry may be under personal authorship or corporate authorship, or title main entry may be chosen. Rule 21.1A1, *AACR2R (1998)* defines a personal author as the individual chiefly responsible for a resource's intellectual or artistic content. Rule 21.1B1, *AACR2R (1998)* defines a corporate author as an organization or group of persons with a particular name that functions as an entity. Lastly, Rule 21.1C1, *AACR2R (1998)* states that a resource should be entered under title proper (or uniform title if appropriate) when: personal authorship is unknown or shared by a large number of individuals, and authorship can not be attributed to one particular individual or when a resource is not issued by a corporate body; or when a resource is a collection of works by different individuals or corporate bodies.

In some cases, title main entry is the most logical choice since the nonprint resource is the result of the work of many individuals and/or corporate bodies, and it is not possible to attribute authorship to a particular individual or corporate body. Lack of a statement of responsibility is another reason why title main entry is chosen for some nonprint resources.

Rule 21.1B2, *AACR2R (1998:313)* instructs catalogers to provide corporate main entry for the appropriate corporate body when a work results from one or more corporate bodies. Option e of this rule states that "...those that result from the collective activity of a performing group as a whole where the responsibility of the group goes beyond that of mere performance, execution, etc. Publications resulting from such activity include sound recordings, films, videorecordings...." Many motion pictures and videorecordings are assigned title main entry due to the fact that authorship is shared by a large number of individuals and corporate bodies, and can not be attributed to one particular individual or corporate body.

example

245	03	L'Homme sur les quais‡h[videorecording] =‡bThe man by the shore /‡ca co-production of Frouma Films International, Blue Films, Les Productions Du Regard, Velvet Film GmbH Berlin ; director, Raoul Peck ; producer, Pascal Verroust ; screenplay, Andre Graill and Raoul Peck.

However, a motion picture or videorecording may be given author main entry when responsibility can easily be attributed to a single individual or corporate body. Rule 21.1A2, *AACR2R (1998)* instructs catalogers to provide author main entry for works by one or more individuals.

example

100	1	Nigrin, Albert Gabriel.
245	14	The films of Al Nigrin‡h[motion picture] /‡cconceived, written, and directed by Al Nigrin.

Physical Description

Physical description is provided both in fixed fields and the 300 field, **Physical Description**. The 007 field, **Physical Description Fixed Field—General Information** provides information on physical description in alphabetic coded form.

Motion pictures: The 007 field for motion pictures has 23 characters defined for use. The first eight positions are those which are most frequently used; discussion in this text is limited to those eight positions. Selected values are provided in the following text.

Position 00- Category of material; is always **m** for "motion picture"

Position 01- SMD; **r** for "film reel" (discussion is limited to reels)

Position 02- Undefined; leave blank

Position 03- Color characteristics; **b** (black and white); **c** (multicolored); **m**(mixed)

Position 04- Format of presentation; **a** (standard sound aperture); **c** (3D); **f** (standard silent aperture, full frame)

Position 05- Sound on medium or separate; **blank** (silent); **a** (sound on medium); **b** (sound separate from medium)

Position 06- Medium for sound; **blank** (silent); **a** (optical sound track on motion picture); **b** (magnetic sound track on motion picture)

Position 07- Dimensions; **a** (standard 8); **d** (16 mm.); **f** (35 mm.)

Position 08- Configuration of playback channels; **m** (mono.); **q** (quadraphonic, multichannel, or surround); **s** (stereo.)
example

```
007          mr baaadm
m = motion picture
r = reel
blank
b = black and white
a = standard sound aperature
a = sound on medium
a = optical sound track on motion picture
d = 16 mm.
m = mono. sound
```

Videorecordings: The 007 field for videorecordings has nine characters defined for use. Selected values are provided in the following text.

Position 00- Category of material; is always **v** for "videorecording"

Position 01- SMD; **d** (videodisc); **f** (videocassette)

Position 02- Undefined; leave blank

Position 03- Color; **b** (black and white); **c** (multicolored); **m** (mixed)

Position 04- Videorecording format; **b** (VHS); **g** (laser optical videodisc); **h** (videotape)

Position 05- Sound on medium or separate; **blank** (silent); **a** (sound on medium)

Position 06- Medium for sound; **blank** (silent); **b** (magnetic sound track on film)

Position 07- Dimensions; **a** (8 mm.); **o** (1/2 in.)

Position 08- Configuration of playback channels; **m** (mono.); **q** (quadraphonic, multichannel, or surround); **s** (stereo.)
example

```
007              vf cbahos
v = videorecording
f = videocassette
blank
c = multicolored
b = VHS
a = sound on medium
h = videotape (medium for sound)
o =  1/2 in.
s = stereo.
```

Video discs: The 007 for videodiscs has nine characters defined for use. Selected values are provided in the following text.

Position 00- Category of material; is always **v** for "video-recording"

Position 01- SMD; **d** (videodisc)

Position 02- Undefined; leave blank

Position 03- Color; **b** (black and white); **c** (multicolored); m (mixed)

Position 04- Videorecording format; **g** (laser optical videodisc)

Position 05- Sound on medium or separate; **blank** (silent); **a** (sound on medium)

Position 06- Medium for sound; **i** (videodisc)

Position 07- Dimensions; **z** (other)

Position 08- Configuration of playback channels; **m** (mono.); **q** (quadraphonic, multichannel, or surround); **s** (stereo.)
example

```
007 vd cgaizs
v = videorecording
d = videodisc
blank
c = multicolored
g = laser optical
a = sound on medium
i = videodisc (medium for sound)
```

z = other (coding not available for 12 in.)
s = stereo.

A full list of values for the 007 field is available on the USMARC Web page at http://lcweb.loc.gov/marc/bibliographic/ecbd007s.html.

International Standard Book Number (ISBN)

Monographic resources are often assigned ISBNs. Provide this information in the 020 field, **International Standard Book Number**, which is repeatable. This information can be helpful in identifying specific versions of a resource.

The following subfields are used in the 020: ‡a ISBN; ‡c terms of availability (price).

There are no indicators defined for the 020 field.
example

    020   0774701919

Cataloging Source

Information on the origin of a bibliographic record, plus any institutions that have modified a record, is provided in the 040 field, **Cataloging Source**, which is not repeatable.

The following subfields are available for use in the 040 field: ‡a original cataloging agency; ‡c transcribing agency (which is typically the institution in ‡a); and ‡d modifying agency. There are other subfields that may be used in the 040; this discussion is limited to those that are most predominantly used.

There are no indicators defined for the 040 field.
example

Original cataloging record created and transcribed by Rutgers University Libraries
040   NjR‡cNjR

Original cataloging record created and transcribed by Rutgers University Libraries, modified by Library X.
040   NjR‡NjR‡dXyZ

Original cataloging record created and transcribed by Rutgers University Libraries, modified at a later date by Rutgers University Libraries.
040   NjR‡NjR‡dNjR

Language Code

Provide information on language(s) present in a resource in the 041 field, **Language Code**, which is not repeatable. Information in the 041 is provided in alphabetic coded form. The 041 works in conjunction with the 546 field, **Language Note**.

Codes are provided according to their predominance in the resource (Network Development and MARC Standards Office, Library of Congress, 1999). The 041 field can provide codes for a maximum of six languages. If more than six languages are present in the resource, the language for the title is coded as "mul"(multiple) to represent all the languages.

The following subfields are used in the 041: ‡a language code for text, sound track, or separate title; ‡b language code for summary or subtitle; ‡d language code for sung or spoken text; ‡e language code for librettos; ‡g language code for accompanying materials other than librettos; ‡h language code for original and/or intermediate translations of text.

The initial indicator value indicates whether a resource is or includes a translation. An initial indicator of 0 indicates that the resource is a not a translation and does not include a translation; a value of 1 indicates that the item is a translation or includes a translation.

example

041	0	‡beng
546		Silent with captions in English.
041	1	freita‡gengfreita
546		In French and Italian; program notes in English, French, and Italian.
041	1	‡dgerita‡egeritaengfre‡hgerita‡genggerfreitaspa‡henggerfre
546		Program notes by Alan Newcombe, Richard Osborne, Klaus Bennert, and Francis Drêsel, in English, German and French, with Italian and Spanish translations.

Geographic Information

Provide information on the geographic area presented, described, covered, etc. by the resource in the 043 field, **Geographic Area Code**, which is not repeatable. The 043 can accommodate 1-3 codes, which are represented in alphabetic coded form. Multiple geographic codes are separated by a ‡a.

Indicator values are not defined for the 043 field.

example

Resource contains information pertaining to New Jersey, in the United States
043   n-us-nj

Resource contains information pertaining to the Great Plains region in the United States
043   np- - - - -

Resource contains information pertaining to Japan
043   a-ja- - -

Resource contains information pertaining to Spain and Mexico
043   e-sp- - -‡an-mx- - -

A full list of geographic area codes is available on the USMARC Web page at http://lcweb.loc.gov/marc/geoareas/.

Library of Congress Call Number

Provide a Library of Congress Call Number (if applicable according to the cataloging agency's policies and procedures for nonprint resources) in the 050 field, **Library of Congress Call Number**, which is repeatable. Some institutions have policies governing whether an LC Call Number is included in the bibliographic portion of a record when their records are submitted to a national online bibliographic utility such as RLIN or OCLC.

The following subfields are available for use in the 050 field: ‡a classification number; ‡b item number.

The initial indicator value indicates whether the item is in Library of Congress's collection. An initial value of blank indicates that no information is provided, and is used when libraries other than the Library of Congress provide classification numbers. The second indicator value indicates source of call number. Classification numbers provided by Library of Congress have a second indicator value of zero; classification numbers provided by other libraries have a second indicator value of 4.
example

050   0   HB1335‡b.M84
050   4   GB1399.4.N5‡bF566 1971

TITLE INFORMATION

Includes title, general material designation, remainder of title, and statement of responsibility.

Title

Consult the chief source of information first. If it is lacking or provides limited or no information, consult the prescribed sources of information. In the absence of chief or prescribed sources of information, a title may be supplied by the cataloger. The supplied title must be bracketed, and the source of title must be documented in a general note.

Title information is provided in the 245 field, **Title Statement.** The following subfields are available for use in the 245 field: ‡a title; ‡b remainder of title; ‡c statement of responsibility; ‡h GMD; ‡n number of part/section; ‡p name of part/section. One method of presenting subfields is to discuss them in the order in which they are used in bibliographic records, rather than alphabetically. However, the alphabetic approach is used in this text, and has been modeled after authoritative sources of information, such as *Concise MARC Format* and the RLIN and OCLC cataloging manuals. Placement of the subfields is illustrated in examples and illustrations. There are additional subfields that may be used in the 245; this text focuses discussion and examples on those that are most predominantly used.

Rule 1.1B1, *AACR2R (1998)*, instructs catalogers to transcribe the title proper exactly as to wording, order, and spelling, but not necessarily to capitalization and punctuation. Titles are provided in the 245 field, ‡a, which is not repeatable.

Indicator values in the 245 field indicates if a title added entry will be generated. Most nonprint items are cataloged using title main entry. Nonprint resources are rarely entered under an author (corporate or personal) main entry. (A discussion of choice of main entry for nonbook resources is provided in the following paragraph). For this reason, the majority of nonprint resources will have a first indicator value of 0. A first indicator value of 1 is used when a title added entry will be generated. The second indicator specifies number of nonfiling characters, with a range of 0-9 available.

Provide title information in the 245 field, **Title Statement**, which is not repeatable.

GENERAL MATERIAL DESIGNATION (GMD)

Use the GMD "motion picture" for films and "videorecording" for videocassettes, laser videodiscs, and DVDs. Do not confuse the GMD with the SMD, which specifies type of material. Provide the GMD in the 245 field, ‡h.

example

245	00	Xala‡h[motion picture]
245	00	Batman‡h[videorecording]

STATEMENT OF RESPONSIBILITY

The statement of responsibility for motion pictures and videorecordings includes the names of individuals (directors, producers, screenwriters), production companies, and other corporate bodies responsible for producing the motion picture or videorecording. Rule 7.1F1, *AACR2R (1998)* instructs catalogers to include in the statement of responsibility individuals or corporate bodies with a major role in creating a film. Additionally, the Library of Congress Rule Interpretation (hereafter referred to as "LCRI") for Rule 7.1F1 states that catalogers generally should include those names with some degree of overall responsibility in the statement of responsibility.

Provide this information in the 245 field, ‡c. Names provided in the 245 field, ‡c are typically used to create name added entries in 7XX personal and corporate name added entry fields. example

245	00	Windwalker‡h[motion picture] /‡cSanta Fe International Productions ; Windwalker Productions ; directed by Keith Merrill ; produced by Thomas E. Ballard, Arthur R. Dubs.
245	00	Zero hour‡h[videorecording] /‡ca production of WGBH/Boston and Central Independent Television/England in association with NHK/Japan ; written and produced by Ben Shephard.

Title Variations

Provide title variations in the 246 field, **Varying Form of Title**, which is repeatable. The 246 provides other titles by which a resource may be known; this includes abbreviations or acronyms, parallel titles in another language, or when one title appears on external packaging and another title is given in the chief source of information. Providing access to title variations permits users to search for a resource in multiple ways.

The following subfields are available for use in the 246 field: ‡a title; ‡b remainder of title or parallel title; ‡h medium; ‡i display text; ‡n number of part/section of a work; ‡p name of a part/section of a work. There are additional subfields that may be used with the 246; this text focuses discussion and examples on those that are most predominantly used.

The initial indicator value indicates note or added entry. The second indicator value is used to provide information on type of title. A complete list of indicator values is available on the USMARC Web page at http://lcweb.loc.gov/marc/bibliographic/ecbdtils.html#mrcb246.
example

Remainder of title

| 245 | 00 | To steal or not to steal‡h[videorecording] :‡bthat is the copyright question. |
| 246 | 30 | That is the copyright question‡h[videorecording] |

Title on chief source and container differ

| 245 | 00 | White trash‡h[videorecording] |
| 246 | 1 | ‡iTitle on container:‡aAndy Warhol's White trash |

| 245 | 00 | Luisa Capetillo‡h[videorecording] |
| 246 | 1 | ‡iTitle on external container:‡aLuisa Capitillo |

Portion of the main title

| 245 | 00 | Excavating the Bible.‡nVolume two,‡pMarine archaeology ‡h[videorecording]. |
| 246 | 30 | Marine archaeology‡h[videorecording] |

Edition

Provide edition information in the 250 field, **Edition Statement**, which is not repeatable. Edition information for nonprint resources is not limited to the term "edition," and includes "version," "release," "revision," or other terms deemed appropriate by the cataloging agency. Rule 1.2B1, *AACR2R (1998)*, instructs catalogers to transcribe edition statements in the form found on the item.

Edition statements for motion pictures and videorecordings are often format related. Rule 7.2B1, *AACR2R (1998)* states that an edition statement should be provided when the item in hand contains differences from other editions of the film or from a reissue of the film.

The following subfields are available for use in the 250 field: ‡a edition statement; ‡b remainder of edition statement. There are additional subfields that may be used with the 250; this text focuses discussion and examples on those that are most predominantly used.

There are no indicators defined for the 250 field.

example

250	Collector's edition.
250	Widescreen edition.
250	Letterboxed edition.
250	1988 commemorative edition.
250	Director's cut.

PUBLICATION INFORMATION

Consult the chief and/or prescribed sources of information to obtain information on where and when a resource was published, distributed, manufactured, etc. Publication, distribution, manufacture, etc. information is provided in the 260 field, **Publication, Distribution, etc. (Imprint)**, which is not repeatable.

PLACE OF PUBLICATION, DISTRIBUTION, MANUFACTURE, ETC.

The place of publication, distribution, manufacture, etc. is provided in the 260 field, ‡a. It is repeatable if there is more than one place of publication, or if a resource is published in one location and distributed in another, for example.

Generally, the city and country or state of publication are given. If only a city name is given, and it is necessary to record the country, state, etc., for purposes of identification and clarification, record the supplied information in brackets, as per Rule 1.4C3, *AACR2R (1998)*.
example

260	Detroit, Mich.
260	Schmalkalden [Germany]

If a place of publication, distribution, manufacture, etc. is not provided, but may be ascertained, record in brackets with a question mark. Consult Rule 1.4C6, *AACR2R (1998)*, for further discussion of this topic.
example

260	[Denver?]

If no place of publication, distribution, manufacture, etc. is provided, and may not be ascertained, the abbreviation for the term

"Sine loco," [S.l.], is used per Rule 1.4C6, *AACR2R (1998)*. The abbreviation is always bracketed.
example

260	[S.l.] :‡bMedia Mix Productions

NAME OF PUBLISHER(S) AND/OR DISTRIBUTOR(S)

Consult the chief and/or prescribed sources of information first. Record the publisher's name following the place of publication as per Rule 1.4D1, *AACR2R (1998)*. If the distributor (or another body with a function related to the material being described) is included, transcribe the distributor, etc. name as it appears in the chief or prescribed sources of information. If the distributor's location differs from that of the publisher, record both locations.

Provide this information in the 260 field, ‡b, which is repeatable when there is more than one publisher, distributor, etc.
example

260	[S.l.] :‡bMedia Mix Productions ;‡aChicago :‡bDistributed by Light Pharmacy Films

The term "distributor" is added in brackets following distributor information only when this function (or other related functions) is not clear in the chief or prescribed sources of information, as per Rule 1.4E1, *AACR2R (1998)*. If distributor information is taken from a label affixed to the resource, external packaging, etc., this must be noted.
example

260	New Brunswick, N.J. :‡bT. Meyer Publishers ;‡aRobinson Media Group [distributor]
260	San Francisco, CA :‡bNan Hai Co., Inc. [distributor], ‡cc1988.
500	Distributor information from label affixed to external container.
500	Distributor information from cassette label.

If there is no information provided for publisher, distributor, etc., and it may not be ascertained, use the abbreviation for the term "sine nomine" [s.n.], as per Rule 1.4D7, *AACR2R (1998)*. The abbreviation is always bracketed.
example

260	Chicago :‡b[s.n.]

DATE OF PUBLICATION, DISTRIBUTION, COPYRIGHT, MANUFACTURE, ETC.

Provide this information in the 260 field, ‡c, which is repeatable. However, the practice of repeating the ‡c is not widely used. Multiple dates, such as for date of production and copyright, may be included in the 260 field, ‡c.

Consult the chief and/or prescribed sources of information first. Record publication date, or distribution date if publication date is not available. In the absence of either date, record copyright date, which is preceded by a lower case "c." Information on date of publication, distribution, etc. is further outlined in Rule 1.4F, *AACR2R (1998)*.

example

Publication date
260   Media, Pa. :‡bEducational Clearinghouse,‡c1990.

Copyright date
260   Oxford :‡bIRL Press Ltd.,‡cc1986.

If information on publication, distribution, etc. date is not provided in either the chief or prescribed sources of information, approximate the date of publication. Approximated dates are bracketed.

example

Approximated date
260   [S.l.] :‡bT. Meyer Publishers,‡c[ca. 1997]

Probable date
260   Cherry Hill, N.J. :‡bAriel Press,‡[1990?]

Decade certain
260   Clifton, N.J. :‡bPiermatti Educational Resources,‡c[198-]

Probable decade
260   Chicago :‡bScholars Press,‡c[199-?]

Note: More information on dates is available in *AACR2R (1998)*, Chapter 1, "General Rules for Description."

Multipart items: Include a beginning date if the resource is not complete and/or is expected to continue indefinitely. An ending date may be included when a resource is complete. Rule 1.4F8, *AACR2R (1998)* notes that this practice is optional.

example

260	Palo Alto, Calif. :‡bDIALOG Information Services,‡c1965-
260	New Brunswick, N.J. :‡bRutgers University Libraries, ‡c1995-2000.

Unpublished items: Do not attempt to provide a place of publication, etc. or publisher, distributor, manufacturer, etc. name for unpublished items, as per Rule 1.4D9, *AACR2R (1998)*. Do not use the abbreviations "S.l." or "s.n." A date may be included for the item.
example

260	‡c1999.
260	‡c[2000?]

There are no indicators defined for the 260 field.

PHYSICAL DESCRIPTION

Provide information on extent (number and SMD of parts), duration, sound characteristics, color characteristics, dimensions, and accompanying materials.

Physical description is provided in the 300 field, **Physical Description**, which may be repeated (this option is not commonly applied, however).

EXTENT

Provide the number and SMD of the parts of an item, as per Rule 7.5B1, *AACR2R (1998)*. The SMD is not identical to the GMD. It is used to specify material types, while the GMD describes the broad category of materials into which a resource may fall. Extent is provided in the ‡a, and is not repeatable.

Provide extent in the 300 field, ‡a.
example

300	1 film reel
300	2 videocassettes
300	1 videodisc

Note: Rule 7.5B1, AACR2R (1998) states that the terms "film" and "video" can be omitted from the SMD if a GMD is used.

This choice is at the discretion of the cataloging agency.

DURATION: Record playing time as given on the item (1 hr., 35 min., for example). If playing time is not provided, use the necessary equipment to approximate the total playing time. When an approximated playing time is given, it is preceded by the abbreviation "ca." Provide duration in the 300 field, ‡a.

example

300	1 film reel (30 min.)
300	2 videocassettes (ca. 180 min.)
300	1 videodisc (52 min.)

SOUND CHARACTERISTICS

Indicate whether the motion picture or videorecording is silent (si.) or has sound (sd.). If a silent film includes background music, indicate this in a note. Provide sound characteristics in the 300 field, ‡b.

example

300	1 film reel (30 min.) :‡bsi.
500	Silent film with musical score.

300	2 videocassettes (ca. 180 min.) :‡bsd.
300	1 videodisc (52 min.) :‡bsd.

COLOR CHARACTERISTICS

Indicate if the motion picture or videorecording is in black and white (b&w), color (col.), or some combination of both. Provide color characteristics in the 300 field, ‡b.

example

300	1 film reel (30 min.) :‡bsi., b&w
300	2 videocassettes (ca. 180 min.) :‡bsd., col.
300	1 videocassette (45 min.) :‡bcol. with b&w sequences

DIMENSIONS

Record the width of motion picture films in millimeters (mm.). Record the width of videocassettes in inches (in.). Although there are 3/4 inch videocassettes, the majority of videocassettes are 1/2 inch. This text limits discussion and examples to 1/2 inch videocassettes. Record the diameter of videodiscs in inches (in.). Provide dimensions in the 300 field, ‡c. Further detail on dimensions for motion pictures and videorecordings is provided in Rules 7.5D1-7.5D4, *AACR2R (1998)*.

example

300	1 film reel (30 min.) :‡bsi., b&w ;‡c16 mm.
300	2 videocassettes (ca. 180 min.) :‡bsd., col. ;‡c1/2 in.
300	1 videodisc (52 min.) :‡bsd. col. ;‡c12 in.

ACCOMPANYING MATERIALS

Provide information describing accompanying materials in one of three ways, per Rule 7.5E1, *AACR2R (1998)*: (1) at the end of the physical description; (2) in a note separate from the physical description; or (3) as part of a multilevel description.
example

300	1 videocassette (75 min.) :‡bsd., b&w, tinted ;‡c1/2 in. +‡e1 guide (12 p. : ill. ; 18 cm.)
300	1 videocassette (90 min.) :‡bsd., col. ;‡c1/2 in. +‡evarious instructional and information sheets.
300	1 videodisc (ca. 162 min.) :‡bsd., col. ;‡c4 3/4 in.
300	2 film reels (43 min.) :‡bsd., col. ;‡c16 mm.

SERIES

Provide series treatment if available in the chief and/or prescribed sources of information. General series information is presented in this text since the focus is on descriptive cataloging procedures. Series are represented in this text by the 440 field, **Series Statement/Added Entry—Title**, which is repeatable.

The following subfields are available for use in the 440 field: ‡a title; ‡n number of part/section; ‡p name of part/section; ‡v volume or numbering designation.

Provide series title in the 440, ‡a, which is not repeatable.

The first indicator value for the 440 field is undefined. The second indicator specifies number of nonfiling characters, with a range of 0-9 available.

Detailed information on series, including various types of treatment, is available on the USMARC Web page at http://lcweb.loc.gov/marc/bibliographic/ecbdhome.html#mrcb440.
example

440	0	Standard Deviants tech series
440	0	Films of Al Nigrin.‡nSeries One
440	0	Films of Al Nigrin.‡nSeries One,‡pFantasia suite
440	0	Against all odds : inside statistics ;‡vprogram 15-16

NOTES

Notes for motion pictures and videorecordings provide a variety of information, including edition, contents, language, source of title, credits, cast, and summary. They are also used to describe characteristics of the motion picture or videorecording or to note features unique to a library's copy of an item. The notes in this section are provided in the order which they appear in MARC records. Notes are not arranged in numeric order by MARC tag number. However, some online catalogs may arrange MARC tags numerically by default.

Notes of a very general nature are provided in the 500 field, **General Note**, which is repeatable. This type of note is more prevalent in nonprint cataloging than in cataloging for print resources since the bibliographic record must provide as much information as possible when a resource is noncirculating and not easily accessible to users.

NATURE AND FORM

As per Rule 7.7B1, *AACR2R (1998)* provide a note on nature and form of the motion picture or videorecording in the 500 field, **General Note** only when it is not apparent from the description. The 500 field is repeatable.
example

500	Opera in three acts.
500	Panel discussion with moderator.
500	Interview.

LANGUAGE

Indicate language of the motion picture or videorecording when more than one language is present, or if the resource is in a language (or languages) other than the primary language of the cataloging agency. Provide this information in the 546 field, **Language Note**, which works in conjunction with the 041. This note also provides information on subtitles and accompanying printed material.

The 546 field, **Language Note** may also be used to indicate when a motion picture or videorecording is closed-captioned for the hearing impaired. In 1997, OCLC advised catalogers contributing to their database to provide separate bibliographic records for both uncaptioned and captioned versions of titles. Previously, such differences were attributed to a lack of uniform standards

used by publishers and/or catalogers not knowledgeable in the motion pictures and videorecordings format. Information on closed-captioning is available from the National Captioning Institute at www.ncicap.org/.
example

| 041 | 1 | spa‡beng |
| 546 | | Spanish dialogue with English subtitles. |

| 041 | 0 | engfrespa |
| 546 | | Dialogue in English, French, and Spanish. |

| 546 | | Closed-captioned for the hearing impaired. |
| 546 | | Program contains essay by Wolfgang Stèahr and synopsis, in English, German, French, Italian, and Spanish. |

SOURCE OF TITLE PROPER

Per Rule 7.7B3, *AACR2R (1998)* indicate source of title if not taken from chief or prescribed sources of information, or has been supplied by the cataloger.

Provide this information in the 500 field, **General Note,** which is repeatable.
example

500	Title supplied by cataloger.
500	Title taken from accompanying printed documentation.
500	Title from container.

CAST

Provide the names of individuals or groups that participate or perform in the production. This field is not limited to performers or actors, and may include hosts, narrators, interviewees, etc. The names of characters portrayed by performers may be included in this field. Provide this information in the 511 field, **Participant or Performer Note,** which is repeatable.

The initial indicator value of 0 does not provide a display constant, the name(s) provided in the 511 field are preceded with a word or phrase indicating the role of those individuals cited. The initial indicator value of 1 is reserved for the display constant "Cast."
example

| 511 | 0 | Narrator, Howard James. |

| 511 | 1 | Kim Basinger, Alec Baldwin, Michael Madsen, Jennifer Tilly. |
| 511 | 0 | Hosted by Bill Moyers. |

In cases where more than one title is available on a motion picture or videorecording, cast information may be provided in one 511 field, or a separate 511 may be provided for each title.

Information for a motion picture containing more than one film.

| 511 | 0 | Narration, Paul Sullivan (Paradise precarious) ; narration, James Ward (Waste not, want not) ; narration, Paul Sullivan (Seeing is believing) ; narration, Josephine Mbeo-Oduoul (A livelihood from waste). |

Alternate approach for a videorecording containing more than one title.

| 511 | 0 | Narration, Paul Sullivan (Katowice). |
| 511 | 0 | Narration, Eleanor Cody (A tale of four cities). |

CREDITS

Provide the names of individuals or corporate bodies not named in the statement of responsibility who have contributed to the production, as well as their function in the production. Provide this information in the 508 field, **Creation/Production Credits Note,** which is not repeatable. The decision to create personal and corporate name added entries from names provided in the 508 field is subject to local practices. Rule 7.7B6, *AACR2R (1998)* instructs catalogers not to include assistants, associates, or others who have made minor contributions to the production. Additionally, the LCRI for Rule 7.7B6 instructs catalogers to provide individuals or corporate bodies in this order: photographers; camera; cameraman/men; cinematographer; animator(s); artist(s); illustrator(s); graphics; film editor(s); photo editor(s); narrator(s); voice(s); music; consultant(s); adviser(s). Furthermore, the LCRI for this rule stipulates that the following individuals or corporate bodies should not be provided in credits information: assistants or associates; production supervisors or coordinators; project or executive directors; technical advisers or consultants; audio or sound engineers; writers of discussion or program; others who have made minor or purely technical contributions.

Indicator values are undefined for the 508 field.

example

| 508 | | Script, Wayne Wang, Terrel Seltzer, Isaac Cronin ; cinematography, Michael Chin ; editor, Wayne Wang ; music, Robert Kikuchi. |

508	Screenplay, Ray Goldrup ; edited by Stephen L. Johnson, Janice Hampton, Peter McCrea ; music, Merrill Jensen.
508	Katowice: Produced by UNCHS (Habitat) ; director, Sharad Shankardass. A tale of four cities: Producers, Eleanor Cody, Sharad Shankardass ; director/script, Sharad Shankardass.

EDITION AND HISTORY

Per Rule 7.7B6, *AACR2R (1998)* provide additional information on the resource, or use to provide history of the motion picture or videorecording. Provide this information in the 500 field, **General Note**, which is repeatable, and differs from what is provided in the 250 field, **Edition Statement.**
example

500	This film is "...substantially as it was when it was first released in 1928."
500	Originally broadcast as a segment of the television program "Caucus New Jersey."
500	Originally released as a motion picture.
500	Based upon Batman characters created by Bob Kane and published by DC Comics.
500	Based on the novel Dog soldiers, by Robert Stone.

PUBLICATION, DISTRIBUTION, ETC., AND DATE INFORMATION

"Make notes on publication, distribution, etc., details that are not included in the publication, distribution, etc., area and are considered to be important" (Joint Steering Committee for the Revision of *AACR2R (1998)* : 196, Rule 7.7B9). The LCRI for Rule 7.7B9 states that when a foreign firm is given as emanator or originator of a film, it can not be assumed that the item was made or released in that country if it is not explicitly stated. In such cases, the type of note given in the second example below is provided.

Provide this information in the 500 field, **General Note**, which is repeatable.
example

500	Videocassette release of the 1978 motion picture.
500	A foreign film (France)

PHYSICAL DESCRIPTION

Rule 7.7B10, *AACR2R (1998)* instructs catalogers to provide additional physical description not represented in the 007 field, **Physical Description Fixed Field—General Information,** or the 300 field, **Physical Description.** This information is provided in the 500 field, **General Note,** or 538 field, **System Details Note** (depending on criteria described); both are repeatable. Additional physical description includes sound characteristics, color, videorecording system, and other information deemed important by the cataloging agency. There are other criteria outlined in *AACR2R (1998)*; this discussion is limited to those criteria applicable to the motion pictures and videorecordings covered in this chapter.

example

Sound characteristics

500	Hi-fi, stereo.
500	Digital sound.
500	Dolby surround sound.
500	Quadrophonic.

Color

500	Hand-painted in various colors.
500	Color tinted.

Videorecording system

538	VHS.
538	Laser Video CLV.
538	DVD.

Other

500	Extended play.
500	Full-frame presentation; prelude, overture, and exit music; teaser, trailers, and tags.
500	Includes trailers for Michael Porter on competitive strategy and competing through technology.

ACCOMPANYING MATERIALS

Provide additional information on accompanying materials. Rule 7.7B11, *AACR2R (1998)* states that details of accompanying materials may be provided in a note when they are not included in the physical description or in a separate description. This information is provided in the 500 field, **General Note,** which is repeatable.

example

500	Accompanying teacher's guide titled: Safety and your child.
500	Accompanying materials housed in container (32 x 5 x 28 cm.)

AUDIENCE

Provide information on the intended audience or intellectual level in the 521 field, **Target Audience Note,** which is repeatable. Take this information from chief or prescribed sources of information.

The first indicator value provides an introductory phrase for the 521 field that describes audience or intellectual level of materials. A first indicator value of blank provides the display constant "Audience." The second indicator value is undefined. Additional information on indicator values for the 521 field is available on the USMARC Web page at http://lcweb.loc.gov/marc/bibliographic/ecbdnot1.html#mrcb521.
example

521		Audience: PG-13.
521	2	Interest grade level: Appropriate for grades 1-4.
521		Audience: Not rated.

OTHER FORMATS

Provide information on other formats in which a motion picture or videorecording has been issued in the 530 field, **Additional Physical Form Available Note,** which is repeatable.

Indicator values are not defined for the 530 field.
example

| 530 | Also issued as a motion picture. |
| 530 | Also available on DVD. |

SUMMARY

Provide a brief description of the contents of the motion picture or videorecording in the 520 field, **Summary, Etc.,** which is repeatable. The summary should provide specific information to accurately describe the resource. Information taken from the container, external sources of information, or other sources should be noted. Generally, summaries should be limited to two-three sentences unless more information is warranted; this is determined by individual cataloging agencies.

The first indicator value provides an introductory phrase for the 520 field. A blank first indicator value generates the display "Summary," and is often used in bibliographic records for nonprint resources. The second indicator value is undefined. Additional information on indicator values for the 520 field is available on the USMARC Web page at http://lcweb.loc.gov/marc/bibliographic/ecbdnot1.html#mrcb520.

example

520		Summary: A comedy in which Laurel and Hardy portray two sailors on leave.
520		Summary: "Follows the true life story of a young Jewish woman growing up in Berlin whose secure home life is disrupted by Hitler's rise to power and her family's subsequent decision to leave Germany. This story is told through the use of home movies, special effects photography, and sound tracks." -- All-Movie Guide (http://allmovie.com/cgi-win/avg.exe)
520		Summary: "...a woman who has worked as a domestic for 12 years in the city comes home to her husband, children, and sister and to a terrible discovery. She realizes that the ruptures caused by apartheid can never be repaired." -- Container.

CONTENTS

Provide information on the contents of a motion picture or videorecording in the 505 field, **Formatted Contents Note**, which is repeatable. Per Rule 7.7B18, *AACR2R (1998)* statements of responsibility and durations may be included to provide additional information to users.

Contents notes in which the various parts of the note are coded are referred to as "enhanced." Enhanced contents notes contain a ‡t (title) and ‡r (statement of responsibility).

The first indicator value for the 505 field indicates completeness of the contents. A first indicator value of 0 indicates complete contents, a value of 1 is used for incomplete contents, and a value of 2 is used for partial contents. The second indicator value provides information on content designation. A second indicator value of 0 is used for enhanced contents. A second value of blank is used for nonenhanced contents notes. The indicators for an enhanced contents note are 00 (a nonenhanced contents note has a single first indicator with a value from 0-2, or 8).

While not required, a contents note is useful to providing a description since the contents of a nonprint resource may not be browsed in the manner used for print resources.

example

505	0	Vol. 1. The Bob Cummings show (30 min.) - - I love Lucy (25 min.) - - v. 2. Women in TV short (15 min.) - - Father knows best (25 min.).
505	0	Ch. 1. What is the Internet? - - ch. 2. How to use the Internet - - ch. 3. How the Internet works - - ch. 4. Internet functions and features - - ch. 5. Security on the Internet.

Enhanced contents note

505　00　‡tBalcony rock /‡rD. Brubeck, P. Desmond - - ‡tOut of nowhere /‡r Heyman, J.W. Green - - ‡tLe souk /‡rD. Brubeck, P. Desmond - - ‡t Take the "A" train /‡rStrayhorn - - ‡tThe song is you /‡rHammerstein II, Kern - - ‡tDon't worry 'bout me /‡rKoehler, Bloom - - ‡tI want to be happy /‡rCaesar, Youmans.

NUMBERS

Provide numbers other than the ISBN which are important for identification of the motion picture or videorecording. Provide information on a formatted publisher number in the 028 field, **Publisher Number**, which is repeatable. Publisher numbers may also be provided in the 500 field, **General Note**, in an unformatted form.

The following subfields are available for use in the 028 field: ‡a publisher number; ‡b source.

Publisher numbers for motion pictures and videorecordings have a first indicator value of 4. The second indicator value for the 028 field may be used to generate a note and/or added entry. A second indicator value of 0 indicates that no note or added entry is generated from the 028 field; all examples in this text have a second indicator value of 0. Publisher numbers are helpful when distinguishing different editions of a videorecording. They are searchable in RLIN and OCLC, and in some online catalogs.

Other numbers (or if a number can not be determined to be a publisher number) are provided in the 500 field, **General Note**, which is also repeatable.

example

028　4　LSP 2061‡bLOB
500　　"IMMW101 IMMW106"- -Container.

DESCRIPTIVE OR LIBRARY SPECIFIC NOTES

Provide descriptive or copy specific information about motion pictures and videorecordings in a 500 field, **General Note**, which is repeatable.

example

500　Noncirculating; on-site use only.
500　Does not include public performance rights.
500　Preview videocassette.

"WITH" NOTES

Provide notes for titles that are not the first in a collective title, or when a short film, trailer, etc. is included with the motion picture or videorecording. This information is provided in the 500 field, **General Note**, which is repeatable. Information provided in this type of note may also be used as the basis for a 740 field, **Added Entry—Uncontrolled Related/Analytical Title.**
example

245	00	Hail Mary‡h[videorecording].
500		With the short film "The Book of Mary."
740	0	Book of Mary‡h[videorecording].
500		With: Annabella dances.
740	0	Annabella dances‡h[videorecording].
500		With: Step by step : CEMIS in Ghana : improving living conditions in La ; Cities in common : a video pamphlet about our consuming passions ; Malindi : Mji safi (clean-up Malindi).
740	0	Step by step : CEMIS in Ghana : improving living conditions in La ‡h[videorecording].
740	0	Cities in common : a video pamphlet about our consuming passions ‡h[videorecording].
740	0	Malindi : Mji safi (clean-up Malindi)‡h[videorecording].
245	00	Katowice‡h[videorecording] :‡ba programme about the UNCHS (Habitat) Project on sustainable cities in the industrial heartland of the Upper Silesia, Poland ; A tale of four cities : a documentary about the Sustainable Cities Programme.
740	0	A tale of four cities : a documentary about the Sustainable Cities Programme‡h[videorecording].

Awards Note

External packaging will often indicate awards which a motion picture or videorecording has won. Include this information in the 586 field, **Award Note**, which is repeatable. This type of information may be important for libraries with collections that emphasize directors, film genres, cinema studies, etc.

The first indicator value for the 586 field may be used to generate the display constant "Awards." A first indicator value of blank generates the print display; a value of 8 generates no display. The second indicator value is undefined.

Additional information on indicator values for the 586 field is available on the USMARC Web page at http://lcweb.loc.gov/marc/bibliographic/ecbdnot2.html#mrcb586.
example

586	Awards: Academy Award: Best actress (Swank); Golden Globe: Best actress; Los Angeles Film Critics Association: Best actress; Best supporting actress (Sevigny).
586	Awards: Berlin Film Festival Silver Bear Award winner.
586	Awards: Academy Award Best Foreign Films nominee.

SUBJECT ACCESS

Subject access to nonprint resources helps users to identify and locate resources, since the bibliographic record must provide as much information as possible when a resource is noncirculating and not easily accessible to users. Subject headings are used to provide access to resources through *personal names*, *corporate names*, *topical terms*, or *geographic names*. Subject headings may be further subdivided by form division (format of material), general subdivisions, chronological subdivisions, and geographic subdivisions. Meeting names and subject added entries for uniform titles are not included in this text.

Consult the *Library of Congress Subject Headings* (LCSH) and the *Library of Congress Subject Cataloging Manual* (SCM) for formulating subject headings for motion pictures and videorecordings. *SCM* instructs catalogers to assign the heading that represents the most predominant topic first. If the predominant topic can not be represented by one subject heading, *SCM* (1996:1) instructs catalogers to "...assign as the first and second headings the two headings that, taken together, express the predominant topic." If a motion picture or videorecording has two major topics of equal importance, the first and second subject headings assigned will express these topics. These subject headings are assigned before headings for secondary topics. Secondary topics may be provided in any order following the major topics.

PERSONAL NAME

Provide subject access to personal names in the 600 field, **Subject Added Entry—Personal Name**, which is repeatable. Personal names are included in a bibliographic record when a resource is about an individual or individuals, or contains a significant portion of information about an individual or individuals.

The following subfields are available for use in the 600 field: ‡a personal name; ‡c titles associated with a name; ‡d dates associated with a name; ‡v form subdivision; ‡x general subdivision; ‡y chronological subdivision; ‡z geographic subdivision. There are additional subfields that may be used with the 600; this text focuses discussion and examples on those that are most predominantly used.

The initial indicator value indicates type of name. An initial article value of 0 indicates entry under forename; 1 indicates entry under single surname. The second indicator value provides source of name heading. A second indicator value of 0 indicates that a name is from the Library of Congress Name Authority file. Additional information is available on the USMARC Web page at http://lcweb.loc.gov/marc/bibliographic/ecbdsubj.html#mrcb600. example

600	00	Cher,‡d1946-
600	10	Day-Lewis, Daniel.
600	10	Weinberg, Valerie Ann.
600	10	Irving, Henry,‡cSir,‡d1838-1905.
600	10	Ellington, Duke,‡d1899-1974.
600	10	King, Martin Luther,‡cJr.,‡d 1929 1968‡xAssassination.
600	10	Krupa, Gene,‡d1909-1973‡vBiography.
600	10	Shakespeare, William,‡d1564-1616‡xStage history ‡y1800-1950.
600	10	Gogh, Vincent van,‡d1853 1890‡xMuseums‡zNetherlands‡zAmsterdam.

CORPORATE NAME

Provide subject access to corporate names in the 610 field, **Subject Added Entry—Corporate Name**, which is repeatable. Corporate names are included in a bibliographic record when a resource is about a corporation or corporations, or contains a significant portion of information about a corporation or corporations.

The following subfields are available for use in the 610 field: ‡a corporate or jurisdiction names; ‡b subordinate units; ‡v form subdivision; ‡x general subdivision; ‡y chronological subdivision; ‡z geographic subdivision. There are additional subfields that may be used with the 610; this text focuses discussion and examples on those that are most predominantly used.

The initial indicator value indicates form of entry for names. An initial indicator value of 1 is for jurisdiction name; 2 is for a name presented in direct order. A second indicator value of 0 indicates that a name is from the Library of Congress Name Authority file. Additional information is available on the USMARC Web page at http://lcweb.loc.gov/marc/bibliographic/ecbdsubj.html#mrcb610.

example

610	20	Lyceum Theatre (London, England)
610	10	United States.‡bDept. of the Interior.
610	20	Harvard University‡xFunds and scholarships‡vHandbooks, manuals, etc.
610	20	Microsoft Corporation‡xHistory.
610	20	Grand Central Terminal (New York, N.Y.)‡xHistory‡y20th century.
610	20	Salvation Army‡zEngland.

TOPICAL TERMS

Provide subject access to topical terms in the 650 field, **Subject Added Entry–Topical Term,** which is repeatable. Terms used in the 650 may describe form of the resource (Motion pictures, Spanish) or content (Jazz, Bicycle touring).

The following subfields are available for use in the 650 field: ‡a topical term or geographic name as entry element; ‡v form division; ‡x general subdivision; ‡y chronological subdivision; ‡z geographic subdivision. There are additional subfields that may be used with the 650; this text focuses discussion and examples on those that are most predominantly used.

The initial article value indicates level of subject; blank indicates that no information has been provided. Other first indicator values available are: 0 for no level specified; 1 for primary level of subject; and 2 for secondary level of subject. In many cases, subject headings supplied by catalogers or provided in records available through union databases have an initial indicator value of blank. A second indicator value of 0 indicates that a name is from the Library of Congress Name Authority file. Additional information is available on the USMARC Web page at http://lcweb.loc.gov/marc/bibliographic/ecbdsubj.html#mrcb650.

example

650	0	Violence in art.
650	0	Grandparents as parents‡xServices for‡zNew Jersey ‡vDirectories.
650	0	Crime prevention‡xCitizen participation.

650	0	American prose literature‡y19th century.
650	0	Artists‡zUnited States.

GEOGRAPHIC TERMS

Provide subject access to geographic terms in the 651 field, **Subject Added Entry—Geographic Name**, which is repeatable.

The following subfields are available for use in the 651 field: ‡a geographic name; ‡v form division; ‡x general subdivision; ‡y chronological subdivision; ‡z geographic subdivision. There are additional subfields which may be used with the 651; this text focuses discussion and examples on those which are most predominantly used.

The initial indicators are undefined for this field. A second indicator value of 0 indicates that a name is from the Library of Congress Name Authority file. Additional information is available on the USMARC Web page at http://lcweb.loc.gov/marc/bibliographic/ecbdsubj.html#mrcb651.
example

651	0	Brooklyn (New York, N.Y.)
651	0	Manhattan (New York, N.Y.)‡vTours‡vMaps.
651	0	United States‡xPopulation‡xStatistics.
651	0	United States‡xHistory‡yCivil War, 1861 1865.
651	0	United States‡xHistory‡zStudy and teaching (Higher) ‡zNew Jersey.

ADDED ENTRIES

Added entries provide access to personal and corporate names that are not main entries yet serve as important additional access points. Name added entries include directors, cast, editors, publishers, or production companies. Title added entries provide additional access for titles related to the main work. This information is provided in the 7XX fields, which are discussed in detail in the following paragraphs as they relate to motion pictures and videorecordings.

PERSONAL NAME

Provide access to personal names in the 700 field, **Added Entry—Personal**, which is repeatable. It is used to include additional access points from names taken from the 245, **Title Statement**, and 511, **Participant or Performer Note** fields, or other fields deemed appropriate by the cataloging agency. Personal name added entries differ from personal names in the 600 in that they provide different types of information, and would be found in an online catalog using different types of searches (subject versus personal name).

The following subfields are available for use in the 700 field: ‡a personal name; ‡c titles or other words associated with a particular name; ‡d dates; ‡4 relator code. A list of relator codes is available on the USMARC Web page at http://lcweb.loc.gov/marc/relators/. There are additional subfields that may be used with the 700; this text focuses discussion and examples on those that are most predominantly used.

The initial indicator value indicates type of name. An initial article value of 0 indicates entry under forename; 1 indicates entry under single surname. The second indicator value indicates type of added entry. A blank second indicator value indicates that no information is provided; a second indicator value of 2 indicates an analytical entry, and means the item in the bibliographic record contains the work represented by the added entry. Additional information is available on the USMARC Web page at http://lcweb.loc.gov/marc/bibliographic/ecbdadde.html #mrcb700.

example

245	00	Two tars‡h[motion picture] /‡cHal Roach Studios ; producer, Hal Roach ; director, James Parrott ; writer, Leo McCarey.
511	1	Stan Laurel, Oliver Hardy.
700	1	Roach, Hal,‡d1892-
700	1	Parrott, James,‡d1898-1939.‡4drt
700	1	Laurel, Stan.‡4prf
700	1	Hardy, Oliver,‡d1892-1957.‡4prf

CORPORATE NAME

Provide access to corporate names in the 710 field, **Added Entry—Corporate Name**, which is repeatable. It is used to include additional access points from names taken from the 245, **Title Statement**, 260, **Publication, Distribution, etc. (Imprint)**, or 511, **Participant or Performer Note** fields, or other fields deemed appropriate by the cataloging agency. Corporate name added entries differ from corporate names in the 610 in that they provide different types of information, and would be found in an online catalog using different types of searches (subject versus corporate name).

The following subfields are available for use in the 710 field:

‡a corporate name or jurisdiction name; ‡b subordinate unit; ‡4 relator code. There are additional subfields that may be used with the 710; this text focuses discussion and examples on those that are most predominantly used.

The initial indicator value indicates type of corporate name. An initial article value 1 indicates entry in jurisdiction order; a value of 2 indicates entry in direct order. The second indicator value indicates type of added entry. A blank second indicator value indicates that no information is provided; a second indicator value of 2 indicates an analytical entry, and means the item in the bibliographic record contains the work represented by the added entry. Additional information is available on the USMARC Web page at http://lcweb.loc.gov/marc/bibliographic/ecbdadde.html#mrcb710.

example

| 245 | 00 | Two tars‡h[motion picture] /‡cHal Roach Studios ; producer, Hal Roach ; director, James Parrott ; writer, Leo McCarey. |
| 710 | 2 | Hal Roach Studios. |

UNIFORM TITLE

Provide uniform titles in the 730 field, **Added Entry—Uniform Title,** which is repeatable. Uniform titles provide a title related to the resource being cataloged. Examples include radio or television programs, or motion pictures.

The following subfields are available for use in the 730 field: ‡a uniform title; ‡f date of a work; ‡h medium; ‡k form subheading; ‡l language. There are additional subfields that may be used with the 730; this text focuses discussion and examples on those that are most predominantly used.

The initial indicator value indicates number of nonfiling characters (0-9). The second indicator value indicates type of added entry. A blank second indicator value indicates that no information is provided; a second indicator value of 2 indicates an analytical entry, and means the item in the bibliographic record contains the work represented by the added entry. Additional information is available on the USMARC Web page at http://lcweb.loc.gov/marc/bibliographic/ecbdadde.html#mrcb730.

example

| 245 | 00 | [Images of women in American society in the twentieth century]‡h[videorecording]. |
| 505 | 0 | Vol. 1. The Bob Cummings show (30 min.) - - I love Lucy |

		(25 min.) - - - - v. 2. Father knows best (25 min.) - - The
		Mary Tyler Moore show (20 min.).
730	0	Bob Cummings Show (Television program)
730	0	I love Lucy (Television program)
730	0	Father knows best (Television program)
730	0	Mary Tyler Moore show (Television program)

RELATED TITLES

Provide access to titles related to the work described in the 245 field, **Title Statement**, in the 740 field, **Added Entry—Uncontrolled Related/Analytical Title**, which is repeatable. The 740 field is created using information taken from 500, **General Note**, or 505, **Formatted Contents Note** fields, or other fields deemed appropriate by the cataloging agency.

The following subfields are available for use in the 740 field: ‡a uncontrolled related/analytical title; ‡h medium; ‡n number of part/section of a work; ‡p name of part/section of a work. There are additional subfields that may be used with the 740; this text focuses discussion and examples on those that are most predominantly used.

The initial indicator value indicates number of nonfiling characters (0-9). The second indicator value indicates type of added entry. A blank second indicator value indicates that no information is provided; a second indicator value of 2 indicates an analytical entry, and means the item in the bibliographic record contains the work represented by the added entry. Additional information is available on the USMARC Web page at http://lcweb.loc.gov/marc/bibliographic/ecbdadde.html#mrcb740. example

245	00	Who'll stop the rain?‡h[videorecording].
500		Based on the novel Dog soldiers, by Robert Stone.
740	0	Dog soldiers.

CLASSIFICATION

Classification schemes such as LCC and DDC tend to be more oriented to subject matter represented in books and do not easily lend themselves to classification of motion pictures and videorecordings. As a result, libraries may arrange motion picture and videorecording collections by a local scheme such as accession numbers, alphabetically by title, by genre, etc.

EXAMPLES OF BIBLIOGRAPHIC RECORDS

Examples follow on the next page.

Figure 4-1 1/2-Inch Videorecording

Control	**Bib**	MARC Hldgs	Vol/Copy

Fixed Fields

Rec_Type:	Bib_Lvl: m	Enc_Lvl:	Desc: a	TypeCtrl:
Entrd: 001204	Dat_Tp: s	Date1: 1993	Date2:	Ctry: fr
Lang: fre	Mod_Rec:	Source: d	Time: 105	Audience:
Accomp:	GovtPub:	Type_Mat: v	Tech: l	

Bibliographic Info

Phys descrip codes:	007			vf cbahou
Cataloging source:	040			NjR|cNjR
Language codes:	041		0	fre|beng
Title:	245		03	L'Homme sur les quais |h[videorecording] =|bThe man by the shore /|ca co-production of Frouma Films International, Blue Films, Les Productions Du Regard, Velvet Film GmbH Berlin ; director, Raoul Peck ; producer, Pascal Verroust ; screenplay, Andre Graill and Raoul Peck.
Parallel title:	246		31	Man by the shore|h[videorecording]
Variant title:	246		1	|iAlso known as:|aMan on the shore
Publication info:	260			New York :|bKJM3 Entertainment Group [distributor],|c1993.
Physical descrip:	300			1 videocassette (105 min.) :|bsd., col. ;|c1/2 in.
Technical details:	538			VHS.
General Note:	500			A foreign film (France)
Audience:	521			Not rated.
Language:	546			In French with English subtitles.
Performer:	511		0	Jennifer Zubar, Toto Bissainthe, Jean-Michel Martial, Patrick Rameau.
Credits:	508			Cinematography, Armand Marco ; edited by Jacques Comets ; music by Amos Coulanges and Dominque Dejean.
Abstract:	520			Set in Haiti in the 1960's, 8-year-old Sarah and her two sisters are victims of Francois "Papa Doc" Duvalier's reign of terror.

Figure 4-1 *Continued*

Subject term	650	⬇	0 ⬇	Feature films.
Geographic term	651	⬇	0 ⬇	Haiti|xPolitics and government |y1934-1971|xIn motion pictures.
Geographic term	651	⬇	0 ⬇	Haiti|xHistory|y1934-1986|xIn motion pictures.
Subject term	650	⬇	0 ⬇	Haitians|xIn motion pictures.
Local subject	690	⬇	4 ⬇	French language.
Local subject	690	⬇	4 ⬇	Feature films.
Local subject	690	⬇	4 ⬇	Haiti.
Added author	700	⬇	1 ⬇	Peck, Raoul.|4drt
Added author	700	⬇	1 ⬇	Verroust, Pascal.
Added author	700	⬇	1 ⬇	Graille, Andre.
Added author	700	⬇	1 ⬇	Zubar, Jennifer.|4prf
Added author	700	⬇	1 ⬇	Bissainthe, Toto.|4prf
Added author	700	⬇	1 ⬇	Martial, Jean-Michel.|4prf
Added author	700	⬇	1 ⬇	Rameau, Patrick.|4prf
Added Author	710	⬇	2 ⬇	Frouma Films International.
Added Author	710	⬇	2 ⬇	Blue Films.
Added Author	710	⬇	2 ⬇	Productions du regard (Firm)
Added Author	710	⬇	2 ⬇	Velvet Film GmbH.
Added Author	710	⬇	2 ⬇	KJM3 Entertainment Group.
Held by	596		MEDIA	

Figure 4-2 1/2-Inch Videorecording

| Control | **Bib** | MARC Hldgs | Vol/Copy |

Fixed Fields

Rec_Type: g	Bib_Lvt m	Enc_Lvl	Desc: a	TypeCtrl
Entrd: 000315	Dat_Tp: s	Date1: 1999	Date2	Ctry: ne
Lang: mul	Mod_Rec:	Source: d	Time: 131	Audience: g
Accomp:	GovtPub:	Type_Mat: v	Tech: l	

Bibliographic Info

Field	Tag	Ind	Content
Phys descrip codes	007		vf mbahou
Cataloging source	040		NjR|cNjR
Language codes	041	0	enggerrus|bduteng
Title	245	00	Sotsgorod, steden voor de Heilstaat |h[videorecording] =|bCities for Utopia /|cregie, Anna Abrahams ; produktie, Renâe Scholten, Renâe Goossens.
Variant title	246	1	|iTitle on container:|aSotsgorod : cities for Utopia
Portion of title	246	30	Steden voor de Heilstaat |h[videorecording]
Portion of title	246	30	Cities for Utopia|h[videorecording]
Publication info	260		[Netherlands? :|bs.n.] ;|aNew York, N.Y. :|bdistributed by West Glen Communications,|cc1995.
Physical descrip	300		1 videocassette (ca. 131 min.) : |bsd., col. and b&w ;|c1/2 in.
Technical details	538		VHS.
General Note	500		Distributor information taken from label on container.
General Note	500		Duration on container given as 92 minutes; duration on cassette label given as 130 minutes, 50 seconds.
Language	546		Dialogue and voiceovers in Russian and German; subtitles in Dutch and English.
Abstract	520		"After the chaos of the Russian revolution and civil war, the desolate steppes, a seemingly limitless source of coal and iron, became a crucial part of the Communist Party's strategy for

Figure 4-2 *Continued*

financing the social utopia. Huge industrial cities had to be built to house hundreds of thousands of workers. The Soviet Union had no architects who could design cities such as these....in the late Twenties and early Thirties, well-known modern architects from Western Europe were invited to create the habitat for the workers' paradise."--Container. Tells the stories of the architects, and includes interviews with remaining survivors, Jan Rutgers, Magarete Schutte-Lihotzky, and Phillipp Tolziner.

General Note 500 | | "IC10716"--Cassette label.

Contents 505 | 0 | Ernst May, Moscow, 1930 -- Hannes Meyer, Dessau, 1930 -- Bauhaus Brigade -- Sotsgorod Kuznetsk, design: Ernst May, 1931; inhabitant: Sergei Kislitsin, 1995 -- Sotsgorod Magnitogorsk (infant school nr.74), 1930 -- Sotsgorod Orsk (canteen "Helios"), design: Schmidt Brigade, 1930; apprentice: Olga Suchova, 1995 -- Kemerovo (area Autonomous Industrial Colony), design: Van Loghem, 1926; inhabitant: Ivan Bykov, 1995 -- Magnitogorsk, 1930 -- Novokoeznetsk, 1995 -- Kemerovo, 1995 -- Magnitogorsk, 1995 -- Kemerovo, 1927 -- Mart Stam, Magnitogorsk, 1931 -- Kemerovo, 1995 -- Novokoeznetsk, 1995 -- Hannes Meyer, 1936 -- Hans Schmidt, 1934 -- Orsk, 1934 -- Phillipp Tolziner and Konrad Puschel -- Kemerovo.

General Note 500 | | "IC10716"--Cassette label.

Personal subject 600 | 10 | May, Ernst,|d1886-1970.

Personal subject 600 | 10 | Meyer, Hannes,|d1889-1954.

Personal subject 600 | 10 | Tolziner, Philipp.

Personal subject 600 | 10 | Pèuschel, Konrad,|d1907-

Personal subject 600 | 10 | Schutte-Lihotzky, Magarete.

Subject term 650 | 0 | Constructivism (Architecture) |zSoviet Union.

Figure 4-2 *Continued*

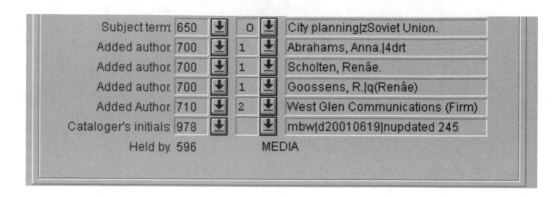

Figure 4-3 Videorecording Containing Two Titles with Separate Credits

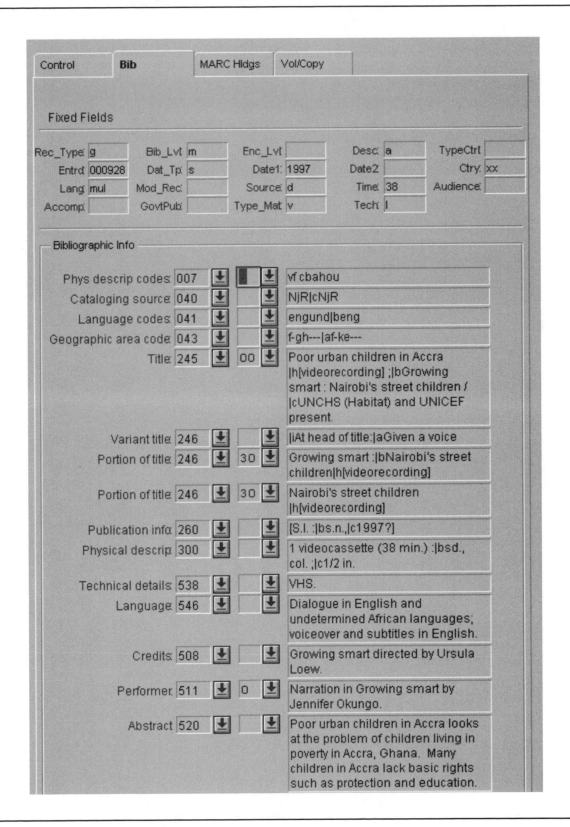

Figure 4-3 *Continued*

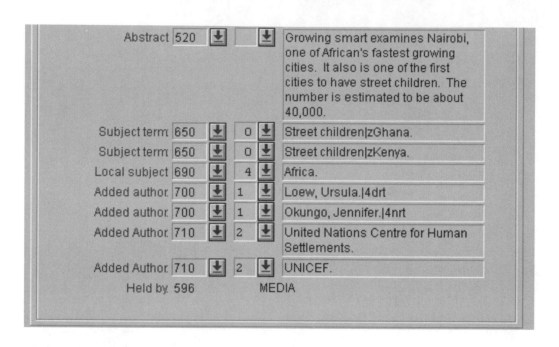

Figure 4-4 Digital Video Disc

Control	**Bib**	MARC Hldgs	Vol/Copy

Fixed Fields

Rec_Type: g	Bib_Lvt m	Enc_Lvt	Desc: a	TypeCtrl
Entrd: 970709	Dat_Tp: p	Date1: 1997	Date2 1996	Ctry. onc
Lang eng	Mod_Rec	Source: d	Time: 251	Audience:
Accomp:	GovtPub:	Type_Mat: v	Tech: l	

Bibliographic Info

Control number:	001			NJRG97-F230
Control # identifier.	003			CStRLIN
Phys descrip codes:	007			vd cgaizu
ISBN	020			0774701919
Cataloging source:	040			NjR|cNjR
Title:	245		00	Scanning television |h[videorecording] /|cFace to Face Media and Harcourt Brace & Company present ; conceived and directed by John Pungente ; produced by Gary Marcuse.
Publication info:	260			[Toronto] :|bFace to Face Media, |cc1997, 1996.
Physical descrip:	300			4 optical discs :|bsd., col. ;|c4 3/4 in.
General Note:	500			Jesuit Communication Project.
General Note:	500			Produced with the participation of CityTV, National Film Board of Canada, Ontario Ministry of Health, TVOntario, Warner Brothers Canada, YTV.
General Note:	500			"Videos for Media Literacy in class"--Container.
General Note:	500			For Media Television, producer/director, Reid Willis.
Credits:	508			Editor, Paul Lievesley ; music, Graeme Coleman ; online facilities, British Columbia Television.
Contents:	505		0	Disc 1. Seeing ourselves: Media and representation -- disc 2. Selling images and values -- disc 3. Our constructed worlds: Media environments -- disc 4. The global citizen; New and converging technologies.

Figure 4-4 *Continued*

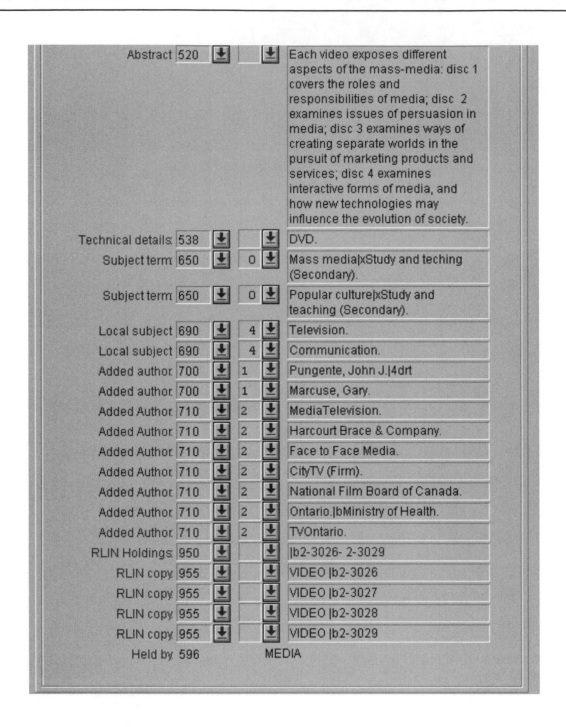

Figure 4-5 Motion Picture

| Control | **Bib** | MARC Hldgs | Vol/Copy |

Fixed Fields

Rec_Type:	s	Bib_Lvt	m	Enc_Lvt		Desc:	a	TypeCtrl	
Entrd:	870925	Dat_Tp:	s	Date1:	1985	Date2:		Ctry:	cau
Lang:	eng	Mod_Rec:		Source:	d	Time:	060	Audience:	g
Accomp:		GovtPub:		Type_Mat:	m	Tech:	l		

Bibliographic Info

Old Geac BCN: 980			00987396	
Date/time stamp:	005			19900925073155.0
Phys descrip codes:	007			mr caahdu
Local system #:	035			(CStRLIN)NJRG87-F200
Cataloging source:	040			NjR|cNjR
Local LC call number:	090			|i09/25/90 CT
Local call number:	099			6-156
Title:	245		00	Einstein on the beach|h[motion picture] :|bthe changing image of opera /|cdirected and photographed by Mark Obenhaus ; produced by Chrisann Verges.
Portion of title:	246		30	Changing image of opera|h[motion picture]
Publication info:	260			Los Angeles, CA :|bDirect Cinema [distributor],|cc1985.
Physical descrip:	300			1 film reel (60 min.) :|bsd., col. ;|c16 mm.
Credits:	508			Edited by Sarah Stein ; designer/director, Robert Wilson ; music/lyrics, Philip Glass.
Performer:	511		0	Narrator, Gerald Jonas.
Performer:	511		0	Music performed by the Philip Glass Ensemble.
Abstract:	520			Einstein on the beach is like no other opera. It has no story, no hero or heroine, and there are no obvious links between words, images, and music. Dancers are the featured performers. The premier in 1976 of Einstein on the beach changed the face of opera forever. Through performance and

Figure 4-5 *Continued*

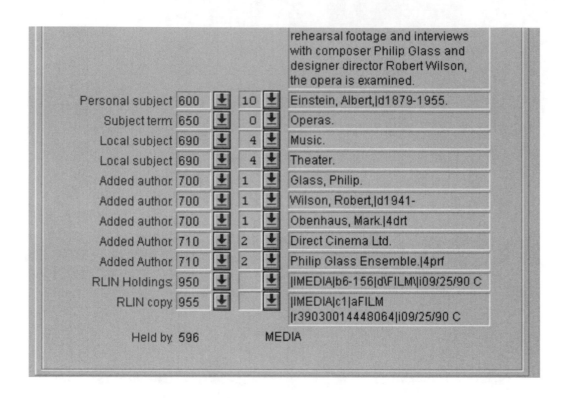

REFERENCES

Cataloging Policy and Support Office, Library of Congress. 1996. "Order of Subject Headings," from *Subject Cataloging Manual: Subject Headings*. Washington, D.C.: Library of Congress, Cataloging Distribution Service.

Joint Steering Committee for the Revision of AACR2. 1998. *Anglo-American Cataloguing Rules, Second Edition, 1998 Revision*. Chicago: American Library Association.

Network Development and MARC Standards Office, Library of Congress in cooperation with Standards and Support, National Library of Canada. 1999. *MARC 21 Format for Bibliographic Data Including Guidelines for Content Designation, 1999 Edition*. Washington, D.C.: Library of Congress Distribution Service.

5 ELECTRONIC RESOURCES

OVERVIEW

Electronic resources (formerly "computer files") have become an essential part of the collections of many libraries. In the early 1990s, electronic resources were the newest material type to be collected by libraries. At that time, there was debate as to whether these resources should be cataloged. Little was known about the format, and computers and operating systems were going through a period of rapid growth and change. Although computers and operating systems continue to rapidly evolve, standards for cataloging electronic resources have become much more established and regular.

Electronic resources typically receive full level cataloging. All examples included in this chapter use full level description. In addition, electronic resources are one format type to which a library may choose to assign Library of Congress Classification Numbers, rather than an accession number scheme, alphabetical arrangement by title, or arrangement by subject area, etc.

The glossary in *AACR2R* (1998:617) defines electronic resources as "A file (data and/or programs) encoded for manipulation by computer." Electronic resources (floppy disks and CD-ROMs) are covered in this chapter. Internet resources and databases are covered in Chapter Eight.

ELEMENTS OF BIBLIOGRAPHIC RECORDS FOR ELECTRONIC RESOURCES

The category of resources referred to as electronic resources includes floppy disks (3 1/2 inches and 5 1/4 inches) and compact discs, or CD-ROMs (4 3/4 in.).

The following information is necessary to create bibliographic records for electronic resources:

- Chief Source of Information
- Prescribed Sources of Information
- Choice of Main Entry
- International Standard Book Number (ISBN)
- Cataloging Source

- Language Code
- Geographic Information
- Library of Congress Call Number
- Title
- Title Variations
- General Material Designation (GMD)
- Statement of Responsibility
- Edition
- File Characteristics
- Place of Publication and/or Distribution, or Manufacture, etc.
- Name of Publisher(s) and/or Distributor(s)
- Date of Publication, Distribution, Copyright, Manufacture, etc.
- Physical Description
- Series
- Notes
- Subject Access
- Added Entries (Personal and/or Corporate Names, Title Added Entries)
- Classification

CHIEF SOURCE OF INFORMATION

The chief source of information for electronic resources is the title screen or other information available internally from the file itself, such as ReadMe screens and online documentation. If a cataloger is unable to access the electronic resource (such as lacking the appropriate equipment to view it), information may be taken from the disk/disc surface or external labels, accompanying documentation, the external container, or packaging (Joint Steering Committee for the Revision of *AACR2R, 1998)*.

PRESCRIBED SOURCES OF INFORMATION

Rule 9.0B2, *AACR2R (1998)* states that the following sources of information should be consulted when creating bibliographic records for electronic resources:

- Title/statement of responsibility- Chief source of information, disk/disc surface, accompanying documentation, external container or packaging
- Edition- Chief source of information, disk/disc surface, accompanying documentation, external container or packaging
- File Characteristics- Any source of information may be consulted
- Publication, distribution, manufacture, etc.- Chief source of information, disk/disc surface, accompanying documentation, external container or packaging
- Physical Description- Any source of information may be consulted
- Series- Chief source of information, disk/disc surface, accompanying documentation, external container or packaging
- Notes- Any source of information may be consulted

CHOICE OF MAIN ENTRY

Main entry may be under personal authorship or corporate authorship, or title main entry may be chosen. Rule 21.1A1, *AACR2R (1998)* defines a personal author as the individual chiefly responsible for a resource's intellectual or artistic content. Rule 21.1B1, *AACR2R (1998)* defines a corporate author as an organization or group of persons with a particular name that functions as an entity. Lastly, Rule 21.1C1, *AACR2R (1998)* states that a resource should be entered under title proper (or uniform title if appropriate) when: personal authorship is unknown or shared by a large number of individuals, and authorship can not be attributed to one particular individual or when a resource is not issued by a corporate body; or when a resource is a collection of works by different individuals or corporate bodies.

In some cases, title main entry is the most logical choice since the electronic resource is the result of the work of many individuals and/or corporate bodies, and it is not possible to attribute authorship to a particular individual or corporate body. Lack of a statement of responsibility is another reason why title main entry is chosen for some electronic resources.

Maxwell's states that electronic resources are typically entered under title main entry since more than one individual or corporate body is responsible for their creation. However, author or corporate body main entry may be chosen when responsibility for the creation of an electronic resource is very straightforward.

example

245	00	Temperature handbook and encyclopedia‡h[electronic resource].

100	1	Piermatti, Patricia A.
245	10	Rx for pharmaceutical science research‡h[electronic resource] /‡cPatricia A. Piermatti.

Physical Description

Physical description is provided both in fixed fields and the 300 field, **Physical Description**. The 007 field, **Physical Description Fixed Field—General Information** provides information on physical description in alphabetic coded form.

The 007 field for electronic resources has fourteen characters defined for use. The first six positions are those which are most frequently used; discussion in this text is limited to those six positions. Selected values are provided in the following text.

Position 00- Category of material; is always **c** for "electronic resource"

Position 01- SMD; **j** (magnetic disk); **o** (optical disc)

Position 02- Undefined; leave blank

Position 03- Color characteristics; **b** (black and white); **c** (multicolored); **m**(mixed)

Position 04- Dimensions; **a** (3 1/2 in.); **g** (4 3/4 in. or 12 in.)

Position 05- Sound; blank (no sound); **a** (sound); **u** (unknown)

example

```
007          co cga
c = electronic resource
o = optical disc
blank
c = multicolored
g = 4 3/4 in.
a = sound
```

A full list of values for the 007 field is available on the USMARC Web page at http://lcweb.loc.gov/marc/bibliographic/ecbd007s.html

International Standard Book Number (ISBN)

Monographic resources are often assigned ISBNs. Provide this information in the 020 field, **International Standard Book Number,** which is repeatable. This information can be helpful in identifying specific versions of an electronic resource.

The following subfields are used in the 020: ‡a ISBN; ‡c terms of availability (price).

There are no indicators defined for the 020 field.

example

```
020        1582560226
```

Cataloging Source

Information on the origin of a bibliographic record, plus any institutions that have modified a record, is provided in the 040 field, **Cataloging Source**, which is not repeatable.

The following subfields are available for use in the 040 field: ‡a original cataloging agency; ‡c transcribing agency (which is typically the institution in ‡a); and ‡d modifying agency. There are other subfields that may be used in the 040; this discussion is limited to those that are most predominantly used.

There are no indicators defined for the 040 field.

example

Original cataloging record created and transcribed by Rutgers University Libraries
```
040        NjR‡cNjR
```

Original cataloging record created and transcribed by Rutgers University Libraries, modified by Library X.
```
040        NjR‡NjR‡dXyZ
```

Original cataloging record created and transcribed by Rutgers University Libraries, modified at a later date by Rutgers University Libraries.
```
040        NjR‡NjR‡dNjR
```

Language Code

Provide information on language(s) present in an electronic resource in the 041 field, **Language Code**, which is not repeatable. Information in the 041 is provided in alphabetic coded form. The 041 works in conjunction with the 546 field, **Language Note**.

Codes are provided according to their predominance in the electronic resource (Network Development and MARC Standards Office, Library of Congress, 1999). The 041 field can provide codes for a maximum of six languages. If more than six languages are present in the electronic resource, the language for the title is coded as "mul" (multiple) to represent all the languages.

The following subfields are used in the 041: ‡a language code for text, sound track, or separate title; ‡b language code for summary or subtitle; ‡d language code for sung or spoken text; ‡g language code for accompanying materials other than librettos; ‡h language code for original and/or intermediate translations of text.

The initial indicator value indicates whether an electronic resource is or includes a translation. An initial indicator of 0 indicates that the electronic resource is not a translation and does not include a translation; a value of 1 indicates that the item is a translation or includes a translation.

example

041	1	freita‡gengfreita
546		In French and Italian; program notes in English, French, and Italian.
041	1	‡dgerita‡egeritaengfre‡hgerita‡genggerfreita spa‡henggerfre
546		Program notes by Alan Newcombe, Richard Osborne, Klaus Bennert, and Francis Drêsel, in English, German and French, with Italian and Spanish translations

Geographic Information

Provide information on the geographic area presented, described, covered, etc. by the electronic resource in the 043 field, **Geographic Area Code**, which is not repeatable. The 043 can accommodate 1-3 codes, which are represented in alphabetic coded form. Multiple geographic codes are separated by a ‡a.

Indicator values are not defined for the 043 field.

example

Resource contains information pertaining to New Jersey, in the United States
043   n-us-nj

Resource contains information pertaining to the Great Plains region in the United States
043   np- - - - -

Resource contains information pertaining to Japan
043   a-ja- - -

Resource contains information pertaining to Spain and Mexico
043   e-sp- - -‡an-mx- - -

A full list of geographic area codes is available on the USMARC Web page at http://lcweb.loc.gov/marc/geoareas/.

Library of Congress Call Number

Provide a Library of Congress Call Number (if applicable according to the cataloging agency's policies and procedures for electronic resources) in the 050 field, **Library of Congress Call Number**, which is repeatable. Some institutions have policies governing whether an LC Call Number is included in the bibliographic portion of a record when their records are submitted to a national online bibliographic utility such as RLIN or OCLC.

The following subfields are available for use in the 050 field: ‡a classification number; ‡b item number.

The initial indicator value indicates whether the item is in Library of Congress's collection. An initial value of blank indicates that no information is provided, and is used when libraries other than the Library of Congress provide classification numbers. The second indicator value indicates source of call number. Classification numbers provided by Library of Congress have a second indicator value of zero; classification numbers provided by other libraries have a second indicator value of 4.

example

| 050 | 0 | HB1335‡b.M84 |
| 050 | 4 | GB1399.4.N5‡bF566 1971 |

TITLE INFORMATION

Includes title, general material designation, remainder of title, and statement of responsibility.

Title

Consult the chief source of information first. If it is lacking or provides limited or no information, consult the prescribed sources of information. In the absence of chief or prescribed sources of information, a title may be supplied by the cataloger. The supplied title must be bracketed, and the source of title must be documented in a general note.

Title information is provided in the 245 field, **Title Statement**. The following subfields are available for use in the 245 field: ‡a title; ‡b remainder of title; ‡c statement of responsibility; ‡h GMD; ‡n number of part/section; ‡p name of part/section. One method of presenting subfields is to discuss them in the order in which they are used in bibliographic records, rather than alphabetically. However, the alphabetic approach is used in this text, and has been modeled after authoritative sources of information, such as *Concise MARC Format* and the RLIN and OCLC cataloging manuals. Placement of the subfields is illustrated in examples and illustrations. There are additional subfields that may be used in the 245; this text focuses discussion and examples on those that are most predominantly used.

Rule 1.1B1, *AACR2R (1998)*, instructs catalogers to transcribe the title proper exactly as to wording, order, and spelling, but not necessarily to capitalization and punctuation. Titles are provided in the 245 field, ‡a, which is not repeatable. Title information should be taken from the chief source of information whenever possible. For convenience and ease in cataloging, it is often preferable to print a copy of the title screen or any relevant internal information. As is the case for many nonprint resources, the title provided in the chief source of information may differ significantly from that on the external packaging provided by the manufacturer or distributor. Note title variations. Rule 9.1B2, *AACR2R (1998)* states that the source of title proper for electronic resources must always be cited.

Indicator values in the 245 field indicate if a title added entry will be generated. Many nonprint resources are cataloged using title main entry. A first indicator value of 0 is used when a title added entry will not be generated ; a first indicator value of 1 is used to generate a title added entry. The second indicator specifies number of nonfiling characters, with a range of 0-9 available.

example

> *Title from chief source of information:*
> 245   00   Kyushu-Okinawa Summit 2000 official guide

> *Title supplied by cataloger:*
> 245   00   [Documentary on Douglass College, Rutgers University]
> 500   Title supplied by cataloger.

Remainder of Title

The 245 field also provides the remainder of a title or other information, such as parallel titles. Provide this information in the ‡b, which is not repeatable.
example

> 245   00   Visions of research in music geology‡h[electronic resource] :‡bVRME

Title Variations

Provide title variations in the 246 field, **Varying Form of Title,** which is repeatable. The 246 provides other titles by which an electronic resource may be known; this includes abbreviations or acronyms, parallel titles in another language, or when one title appears on external packaging and another title is given in the chief source of information. Providing access to title variations permits users to search for an electronic resource in multiple ways.

The following subfields are available for use in the 246 field: ‡a title; ‡b remainder of title or parallel title; ‡h medium; ‡i display text; ‡n number of part/section of a work; ‡p name of a part/section of a work. There are additional subfields that may be used with the 246; this text focuses discussion and examples on those that are most predominantly used.

The initial indicator value indicates note or added entry. The second indicator value is used to provide information on type of title. A complete list of indicator values is available on the USMARC Web page at http://lcweb.loc.gov/marc/bibliographic/ecbdtils.html#mrcb246.

example

| 245 | 00 | Atlas of coal geology‡h[electronic resource]. |
| 246 | 30 | Coal geology‡h[electronic resource] |

| 245 | 00 | ITE digital library‡h[electronic resource]. |
| 246 | 3 | Institute of Transportation Engineers digital library‡h[electronic resource] |

Portions of the main title

245	10	Kyushu-Okinawa Summit 2000 official guide CD-ROM‡h[electronic resource].
246	30	Kyushu-Okinawa Summit 2000 official guide‡h[electronic resource]
246	30	Kyushu-Okinawa Summit 2000‡h[electronic resource]

Remainder of title

| 245 | 00 | To steal or not to steal‡h[videorecording] :‡bthat is the copyright question. |
| 246 | 30 | That is the copyright question‡h[videorecording] |

Title on chief source and container differ

| 245 | 04 | The Beatles live at the Star Club in Hamburg, Germany, 1962‡h[sound recording]. |
| 246 | 1 | ‡iTitle on container:‡aLingasong Records presents the Beatles live at the Star Club in Hamburg, Germany, 1962 |

Portion of the main title

| 245 | 00 | Excavating the Bible.‡nVolume two,‡pMarine archaeology ‡h[videorecording]. |
| 246 | 30 | Marine archaeology‡h[videorecording] |

GENERAL MATERIAL DESIGNATION (GMD)

Use of a GMD is deemed optional by Rule 1.1C, *AACR2R (1998)*. There are several reasons why a library may choose to use GMDs. It indicates to users the format of an electronic resource when a search is done in an online catalog since all resources with a specific GMD will cluster together. Additionally, the resource described in an online catalog may not readily be apparent to users even when the bibliographic record includes a physical description that includes type of resource and characteristics. Use of a GMD helps users to distinguish between different formats in which a title is available. For example, *Midnight Express* is the title of a book, as well as a motion picture, a motion picture sound track, and is also available on videorecording. However, there is a growing sentiment that GMDs are no longer useful, particularly in a Web-based environment in which some libraries use one bibliographic record to represent multiple manifestations of a title (a paper and an electronic version of a serial title, for example).

The GMD is included in the 245 field, ‡h and is enclosed in brackets. It immediately follows the information provided in ‡a and precedes the ‡b. It is not repeatable.

Use the GMD "electronic resource." This term was changed from "computer file" when the *Amendments 2001* were issued. The terms "compact disc" or "floppy disk" are not GMDs and should not be used. Provide the GMD in the 245 field, ‡h, which is not repeatable.

example

| 245 | 00 | Search and discovery challenge‡h[electronic resource]. |
| 245 | 00 | Racial profiling archives‡h[electronic resource]. |

STATEMENT OF RESPONSIBILITY

The statement of responsibility provides names of corporate bodies and/or individuals responsible for production, creation, manufacture, etc. of an electronic resource. This information is taken from the chief or prescribed sources of information.

The statement of responsibility is included in the 245 field, ‡c, is preceded by a forward slash, and is not repeatable. Each corporate body or individual presented in the statement of responsibility is separated by semicolons. Per Rule 1.1F1, *AACR2R (1998)*, statements of responsibility are to be transcribed as they appear. Information taken from sources other than the chief source of information will be bracketed.

The statement of responsibility for electronic resources includes the names of individuals (creators, programmers, researchers, etc.) and corporate bodies responsible for production of the resource.

Rule 9.1F2, *AACR2R (1998)* states that a word or short phrase may be added to the statement of responsibility when the relationship between the title and individuals or corporate bodies named in the statement of responsibility is unclear. Provide this information in the 245 field, ‡c.

example

245	00	Search and discovery challenge‡h[electronic resource] / ‡ccreated by Donna Wilson ; program written by Diane Urbanski.
245	00	Kyushu-Okinawa Summit 2000 official guide CD-ROM‡h[electronic resource] /‡cpresented by the Government of Japan ; produced by Nippon Koho Center and NHK Enterprises 21.

EDITION

Provide edition information in the 250 field, **Edition Statement,** which is not repeatable. The concept of "edition" is important for electronic resources since software, programs, databases, etc. often undergo many updates, and typically in a short time period. A particular edition of an electronic resource may require a different operating system, memory, peripherals, etc. than an earlier edition. Edition statements are not limited to numeric terms, such as "3rd edition." The terms "release," "version," "revision," or others deemed appropriate by a cataloging agency may be used. Rule 1.2B1, *AACR2R (1998)*, instructs catalogers to transcribe edition statements in the form found on the item.

The following subfields are available for use in the 250 field: ‡a edition statement; ‡b remainder of edition statement. There are additional subfields that may be used with the 250; this text focuses discussion and examples on those that are most predominantly used.

There are no indicators defined for the 250 field.

example

250	1st ICPSR ed.
250	Version 1.00.
250	Bertelsmann electronic edition.

Additionally, Rule 9.2B1, *AACR2R (1998)* states that the source of an edition statement must be provided in a note when it dif-

fers from the source of the title proper. This information is provided in a 500 general note.
example

| 500 | Edition statement from accompanying user guide. |
| 500 | Edition statement from publisher's World Wide Web page. |

FILE CHARACTERISTICS

Provide information on file characteristics for electronic resources in the 256 field, **Electronic Resource Characteristics,** which is not repeatable. File characteristics include: designation and number of records, statements, etc.

DESIGNATION

The *Amendments 2001* instruct catalogers to use the following designations to indicate type of file when readily available: *electronic data, electronic program(s)*, and *electronic data and program(s)*.

Maxwell's defines a program as "...an electronic file containing a set of instructions that tells a computer to perform certain tasks," and data as "...electronic text...that is manipulated by a program" (Maxwell, 1997: 233-234).
example

| 256 | Electronic data. |
| 256 | Electronic data and program. |

NUMBER OF RECORDS, STATEMENTS, ETC.

Rule 9.3B2, *Amendments 2001* states that when a file designation is provided, and if the information is available, the number of files contained in an electronic resource may be provided. This portion of the 256 may also include *data* (number of records), *programs* (number of statements), or *multipart files* (number of records and/or bytes, or number of statements and/or bytes).
example

256	Electronic data (1 file : 83565 bytes).
256	Electronic data (1 file : 165,490 records).
256	Electronic program (2 files : 2 megabytes).
256	Electronic data (1 file : 10,469 logical records) and programs (2 files : 2 megabytes).

PUBLICATION INFORMATION

Consult the chief and/or prescribed sources of information to obtain information on where and when an electronic resource was published, distributed, manufactured, etc. Publication, distribution, manufacture, etc. information is provided in the 260 field, **Publication, Distribution, etc. (Imprint)**, which is not repeatable.

PLACE OF PUBLICATION, DISTRIBUTION, MANUFACTURE, ETC.

The place of publication, distribution, manufacture, etc. is provided in the 260 field, ‡a. It is repeatable if there is more than one place of publication, or if an electronic resource is published in one location and distributed in another, for example.

Generally, the city and country or state of publication are given. If only a city name is given, and it is necessary to record the country, state, etc., for purposes of identification and clarification, record the supplied information in brackets, as per Rule 1.4C3, *AACR2R (1998)*.

example

260	Detroit, Mich.
260	Schmalkalden [Germany]

If a place of publication, distribution, manufacture, etc. is not provided, but may be ascertained, record in brackets with a question mark. Consult Rule 1.4C6, *AACR2R (1998)* for further discussion of this topic.

example

260	[Denver?]

If no place of publication, distribution, manufacture, etc. is provided, and may not be ascertained, the abbreviation for the term "Sine loco," [S.l.], is used per Rule 1.4C6, *AACR2R (1998)*. The abbreviation is always bracketed.

example

260	[S.l.] :‡bMedia Mix Productions

NAME OF PUBLISHER(S) AND/OR DISTRIBUTOR(S)

Consult the chief and/or prescribed sources of information first. Record the publisher's name following the place of publication as per Rule 1.4D1, *AACR2R (1998)*. If the distributor (or another body with a function related to the material being described) is included, transcribe the distributor, etc. name as it appears in the chief or prescribed sources of information. If the distributor's location differs from that of the publisher, record both locations.

Provide this information in the 260 field, ‡b, which is repeatable when there is more than one publisher, distributor, etc.
example

260   [S.l.] :‡bMedia Mix Productions ;‡aChicago :‡bDistributed by Light Pharmacy Films

The term "distributor" is added in brackets following distributor information only when this function (or other related functions) is not clear in the chief or prescribed sources of information, as per Rule 1.4E1, *AACR2R (1998)*. If distributor information is taken from a label affixed to the electronic resource, external packaging, etc., this must be noted.
example

260   New Brunswick, N.J. :‡bT. Meyer Publishers ;‡aRobinson Media Group [distributor]

260   San Francisco, CA :‡bNan Hai Co., Inc. [distributor], ‡cc1988.

500   Distributor information from label affixed to external container.

500   Distributor information from disk label.

If there is no information provided for publisher, distributor, etc., and it may not be ascertained, use the abbreviation for the term "sine nomine," [s.n.], as per Rule 1.4D7, *AACR2R (1998)*. The abbreviation is always bracketed.
example

260   Chicago :‡b[s.n.]

DATE OF PUBLICATION, DISTRIBUTION, COPYRIGHT, MANUFACTURE, ETC.

Provide this information in the 260 field, ‡c, which is repeatable. However, the practice of repeating the ‡c is not widely used.

Multiple dates, such as for date of production and copyright, may be included in the 260 field, ‡c.

Consult the chief and/or prescribed sources of information first. Record publication date, or distribution date if publication date is not available. In the absence of either dates, record copyright date, which is preceded by a lower case "c". Information on date of publication, distribution, etc. is further outlined in Rule 1.4F, *AACR2R (1998)*.

example

Publication date
260   Media, Pa. :‡bEducational Clearinghouse,‡c1990.

Copyright date
260   Oxford :‡bIRL Press Ltd.,‡cc1986.

If information on publication, distribution, etc. date is not provided in either the chief or prescribed sources of information, approximate the date of publication. Approximated dates are bracketed.

example

Approximated date
260   [S.l.] :‡bT. Meyer Publishers,‡c[ca. 1997]

Probable date
260   Cherry Hill, N.J. :‡bAriel Press,‡[1990?]

Decade certain
260   Clifton, N.J. :‡bPiermatti Educational Resources,‡c[198-]

Probable decade
260   Chicago :‡bScholars Press,‡c[199-?]

Note: More information on dates is available in *AACR2R (1998)*, Chapter 1, "General Rules for Description."

Multipart items: Include a beginning date if the electronic resource is not complete and/or is expected to continue indefinitely. An ending date may be included when an electronic resource is complete. Rule 1.4F8, *AACR2R (1998)* notes that this practice is optional.

example

260	Palo Alto, Calif. :‡bDIALOG Information Services,‡c1965-
260	New Brunswick, N.J. :‡bRutgers University Libraries, ‡c1995-2000.

Unpublished items: Do not attempt to provide a place of publication, etc. or publisher, distributor, manufacturer, etc. name for unpublished items, as per Rule 1.4D9, *AACR2R (1998).* Do not use the abbreviations "S.l." or "s.n." A date may be included for the item.
example

260	‡c1999.
260	‡c[2000?]

There are no indicators defined for the 260 field.

PHYSICAL DESCRIPTION

Includes extent (number and Specific Material Designation (SMD) of physical parts of an item), other physical details (color or sound characteristics, for example), dimensions, and information about accompanying materials.

The physical description is provided in the 300 field, **Physical Description**. The physical description field is repeatable, permitting a multilevel description, yet this option is not commonly applied.

EXTENT

Provide the number and SMD of the parts of an item, as per Rule 9.5B1, *AACR2R (1998).* The SMD is not identical to the GMD. It is used to specify material types, while the GMD describes the broad category of materials into which a resource may fall. Extent is provided in the ‡a, and is not repeatable.

The International Standard Bibliographic Description for Electronic Resources (ISBD-ER), as proposed by IFLA, provides other terms that may be used for this field. Suggested terms include: electronic disk(s), electronic optical disc(s). According to the ISBD-ER, "electronic disk" is to be used for magnetically encoded electronic disks; "electronic optical disc" is to be used for optically encoded electronic discs. This information is available on the Web

at: http://ifla.inist.fr/VRII/s13/pubs/isbd.htm. Additionally, the *Amendments 2001* provide an option for using conventional terminology to record the specific format of the physical carrier. Examples provided cite "CD-ROM," "Photo CD," and "DVD." However, there is no additional data available at this time to provide more guidance if catalogers choose to apply this option. It is expected that this information will be forthcoming.
example

260	1 computer disk
260	4 computer optical discs

Note: Rule 9.5B1, *AACR2R (1998)* states that the terms "computer" and "optical" can be omitted from the SMD if a GMD is used. This choice is at the discretion of the cataloging agency. Note that the spelling differs by physical carrier: 3 inch and 5 1/4 inch floppies are "disks," while 4 3/4 inch CD-ROMs are "discs."

Serially issued resources that are not yet complete include a SMD preceded by three blank spaces, as per Rule 1.5B5, *AACR2R (1998)*. Serially issued resources are not limited to periodicals, and may include any resource that is intended to be published indefinitely.
example

300	computer optical discs
300	computer disk

Other Physical Details
Provide a description of characteristics other than extent or dimensions, as per Rule 1.5C, *AACR2R (1998)*. This information is provided in the ‡b, which is not repeatable.
example

Electronic resource- sound, color

300	2 computer optical discs :‡bsd., col.

SOUND CHARACTERISTICS
Provide only when an electronic resource has sound capability.
example

300	2 computer optical discs :‡bsd.
300	2 computer disks :‡bsd.

COLOR CHARACTERISTICS

Provide only when a program is in color or has portions in color.
example

300	2 computer optical discs :‡bsd., col.
300	2 computer disks :‡bsd., col.

DIMENSIONS

Provide information on size, width, etc. as appropriate, as per Rule 1.5D1, *AACR2R (1998)*. Dimensions are included in the ‡c, which is not repeatable. Provide dimensions in inches (in.). The standard size for floppy disks is 3 1/2 inches and 5 1/4 inches. However, it has become increasingly uncommon for items to be issued on 5 1/4 inch disks. The standard size for CD-ROMs is 4 3/4 inches.
example

300	2 computer optical discs :‡bsd., col. ;‡4 3/4 in.
300	2 computer discs :‡bsd., col. ;‡c3 1/2 in.

ADDITIONAL PHYSICAL CHARACTERISTICS

This information is deemed optional by Rule 9.5C2, *AACR2R (1998)* yet is useful in describing electronic resources. Description of number of sides, density, etc. may be provided in the 300 field, **Physical Description**, rather than in a separate note.
example

300	2 computer discs :‡bsd., col., double sided, double density ;‡c3 1/2 in.

ACCOMPANYING MATERIALS

Provide information describing accompanying materials in one of three ways, per Rule 1.5E1, *AACR2R (1998)*: (1) at the end of the physical description; (2) in a note separate from the physical description; or (3) as part of a multilevel description.
example

As part of the physical description:

300	1 computer disc :‡bsd., col. ;‡c4 3/4 in. +‡e 1 user's guide (30 p. : ill. ; 12 cm.) + 1 videocassette (20 min., VHS)

Note: If more than one item is included in the ‡e, 300, each item is preceded by a space and a plus sign.

In a separate note:

| 300 | 1 computer disc :‡bsd., col. ;‡c4 3/4 in. |
| 500 | Accompanied by user's guide. |

Multilevel description:

300	1 computer disc :‡bsd., col. ;‡c4 3/4 in.
300	30 p. :‡bill. ;‡c12cm.
300	1 videocassette (20 min.) :‡bsd., col. ;‡c 1/2 in.

SERIES

Provide series treatment if available in the chief and/or prescribed sources of information. This text provides general series information; a detailed discussion of various types of series treatments is beyond the focus of this text. Series are represented in this text by the 440 field, **Series Statement/Added Entry—Title**, which is repeatable.

The following subfields are available for use in the 440 field: ‡a title; ‡n number of part/section; ‡p name of part/section; ‡v volume or numbering designation.

Provide series title in the 440, ‡a, which is not repeatable.

The first indicator value for the 440 field is undefined. The second indicator specifies number of nonfiling characters, with a range of 0-9 available.

Detailed information on series is available on the USMARC Web page at http://lcweb.loc.gov/marc/bibliographic/ecbdhome.html#mrcb440.

example

| 440 | 0 | Library of African cinema |
| 440 | 0 | BMG classics |

Provide information on numbered parts in the ‡n Number of Part/Section of a Work.

example

| 440 | 0 | Langues de l'Orient.‡nl,‡pManuals |
| 440 | 0 | Baseball.‡nVolume 7,‡pFourth inning |

Provide the specific name of the part(s)/section(s) of a series in the ‡p Name of Part/Section of a Work.

example

440	0	The Great explorers.‡pThe Columbus series
440	0	Janua linguarum.‡pSeries minor

Provide numbering designation, such as "volume" or "part" in the ‡v.
example

440	0	BMG classics ;‡vvol. 32
440	0	Medicine at the crossroads ;‡vMECR108

NOTES

Notes for electronic resources provide a variety of information, including contents, summary, file characteristics, and program language. They are also used to describe characteristics of the electronic resource or to note features unique to a library's copy of an item.

The notes in this section are provided in the order which they appear in MARC records. Notes are not arranged in numeric order by MARC tag number.

Notes of a very general nature are provided in the 500 field, **General Note**, which is repeatable. This type of note is more prevalent in nonprint cataloging than in cataloging for print resources.

NATURE AND SCOPE

Provide a note on nature and scope of the electronic resource in the 516 field, **Type of Electronic Resource or Data Note**, only when it is not apparent from the description. This field is repeatable.
example

516	Novel.
516	Statistical spreadsheet.

SYSTEM REQUIREMENTS

Provide information on system requirements in the 538 field, **Systems Detail Note**, which is repeatable. Information is provided in the 538 in the following order: make and model of the computer(s) on which the program will run; required memory; operating system; software requirements, including programming language; kind and characteristics of required and recommended peripherals (Joint Steering Committee for the Revision of *AACR2R (1998):* *235).*

This note is repeatable when software can run on more than one type of computer.
example

| 538 | System requirements: IBM PC, XT, AT or compatible; 256K memory; DOS 2.0 or higher; CGA or EGA graphics card with display; at least one floppy disk drive. |
| 538 | System requirements: IBM PC or compatible; Internet browser; Adobe Acrobat reader; CD-ROM drive. |

Systems Details Note repeated

538	System requirements for Macintosh: 68020 or greater processor ; 6MB RAM (11MB RAM for Power Macintosh) ; System 7.0 or greater ; hard disk with at least 20MB free space ; CD-ROM drive.
538	System requirements for Adobe Photoshop Deluxe CD-ROM: Color monitor with 8-bit or a 24-bit display card (color monitor with a 24-bit display card recommended).
538	System requirements for Type on call disc for Macintosh: Macintosh computer, including SE, Classic, LC, II family, Portable PowerBook, Performa, Centris, Quadra, and Power Macintosh; 4MB RAM for Apple System software 7.0 or later; hard disk; CD ROM drive; Adobe PostScript printer or other laser, dot matrix, or inkjet printer support by Macintosh.

LANGUAGE

Provide information on language(s) if more than one language is present in the electronic resource, or if it is in a language (or languages) other than the primary language of the cataloging agency. Information on programming language(s) is provided in the 538 field, **Systems Detail Note.** Use the 546 field, **Language Note,** which is repeatable. It is used in conjunction with the 041 field, **Language Code,** which is not repeatable.

The initial article value of 0 indicates that the electronic resource is not a translation or does not include a translation; an initial article value of 1 indicates that the electronic resource is a translation or includes a translation.
example

| 041 | 0 | spa |
| 546 | | In Spanish. |

041	1	fre‡beng
546		In French with English subtitles.

A full list of language codes is available on the USMARC Web page at http://lcweb.loc.gov/marc/languages/.

SOURCE OF TITLE PROPER

Rule 9.7B3, *AACR2R (1998)* stipulates that the source of title proper must always be cited for electronic resources.

Provide this information in the 500 field, **General Note**, which is repeatable.

example

500	Title supplied in correspondence by creator of file.
500	Title from disk label.
500	Title from user guide.
500	Title from introductory screen.

CREDITS

Provide the names of individuals or corporate bodies not named in the statement of responsibility who have contributed to the production of the electronic resource. This information is provided in the 508 field, **Creation/Production Credits Note**, which is not repeatable.

example

508	Data contributed by Ronald Jantz and Rudolph Bell.
508	Translations by Elizabeth Leister.
508	Accompanying printed user guide edited by Rhonda Marker.

EDITION AND HISTORY

Provide information on the resource being cataloged, or use to provide history of the electronic resource. This note is also used to provide information on changes to the file, to cite other works upon which the electronic resource is based, or to provide date information (dates covered, dates when data was collected) (Joint Steering Committee for the Revision of *AACR2R (1998)*: 237).

This information is provided in the 500 field, **General Note**, which is repeatable, and differs from what is provided in the 250 field.

example

500	Transcribed from: The vision of William concerning Piers the Plowman : in three parallel texts together with Richard the

Redeless / by William Langland ; edited from numerous manuscripts with preface, notes, and a glossary by Walter W. Skeat. Oxford : Clarendon Press, 1986.

500   Version statement from about screen.

FILE CHARACTERISTICS

Rule 9.7B8, *AACR2R (1998)* instructs catalogers to provide additional information on the type and extent of the resource not given in the 256 field, **Electronic Resource Characteristics** in a 500 field, **General Note**, which is repeatable.
example

500   File size undeterminable.
500   B text only.

PUBLICATION, DISTRIBUTION, ETC., AND DATE INFORMATION

"Make notes on publication, distribution, etc., details that are not included in the publication, distribution, etc., area and are considered to be important" (Joint Steering Committee for the Revision of *AACR2R (1998)*:196, 7.7B9).

Provide this information in the 500 field, **General Note**, which is repeatable.
example

500   Available from: Oxford Text Archive, Oxford University Computing Service, 13 Banbury Road, Oxford OX2 6NN, UK.
500   Distributor information taken from label affixed to jewel case.

PHYSICAL DESCRIPTION

Rule 9.7B10, *AACR2R (1998)* instructs catalogers to provide additional physical description not represented in the 007 field, **Physical Description Fixed Field—General Information,** or the 300 field, **Physical Description,** particularly when they have an impact on how an electronic resource may be used. This information is provided in the 500 field, **General Note,** or the 538 field, **Systems Details Note;** both are repeatable.
example

500   The program can be shown to a class on a single screen monitor or video projector, may be used by individuals on a PC, or may be transmitted over an IBM PC network to individual workstations.
500   Color monitor and monochrome monitor version supplied with package.

538	Software uses BRS/SEARCH.
538	Disc characteristics: CD-ROM.

ACCOMPANYING MATERIALS

Provide additional information on accompanying materials in the 500 field, **General Note**, which is repeatable. Rule 9.7B11, *AACR2R (1998)* states that details of accompanying materials may be provided in a note when they are not included in the physical description or in a separate description.
example

500	User's manual titled: Rx for pharmaceutical science research: a user's manual.

AUDIENCE

Provide information on the intended audience or intellectual level of an electronic resource in the 521 field, **Target Audience Note**, which is repeatable. Take this information from chief or prescribed sources of information.
example

521	Available for teaching and research purposes.
521	For individuals doing pharmaceutical science library research.

OTHER FORMATS

Provide information on other formats in which an electronic resource has been issued in the 530 field, **Additional Physical Form Available Note**, which is repeatable.
example

530	Also available in print.
530	Also available in an online ed.
530	Also available on the World Wide Web site.

SUMMARY

Provide a brief description of the contents of the electronic resource in the 520 field, **Summary, Etc.**, which is repeatable. While not required, this information is beneficial to users.

The first indicator value provides an introductory phrase for the 520 field. A blank first indicator value generates the display "Summary." The second indicator value is undefined. Additional information on indicator values for the 520 field is available on the USMARC Web page at http://lcweb.loc.gov/marc/bibliographic/ecbdnot1.html#mrcb520.

example

520	Each program provides an overview of an important abstracting/indexing reference service for individuals doing pharmaceutical science library research. Each tutorial runs approximately 40 to 50 minutes.

CONTENTS

Information detailing the contents of an electronic resource is provided in the 505 field, **Formatted Contents Note,** which is repeatable. It provides individual titles or parts contained in an electronic resource, and may include statements of responsibility. Additionally, Rule 9.7B18, *AACR2R (1998)* specifies that notes on additional or partial contents should be provided when appropriate.

Contents notes in which the various parts of the note are coded are referred to as "enhanced." Enhanced contents notes contain a ‡t (title) and ‡r (statement of responsibility).

The first indicator value for the 505 field indicates completeness of the contents. A first indicator value of 0 indicates complete contents, a value of 1 is used for incomplete contents, and a value of 2 is used for partial contents. The second indicator value provides information on content designation. A second indicator value of 0 is used for enhanced contents. A second value of blank is used for nonenhanced contents notes. The indicators for an enhanced contents note are 00 (a nonenhanced contents has a single first indicator with a value from 0-2, or 8).

example

505	0	AIDS knowledge base from San Francisco General Hospital - - AIDS subset from MEDLINE - - Full text of AIDS-related articles from leading journals - - The AIDS database from the Bureau of Hygiene and Tropical Diseases (London) - - AmFAR's AIDS/HIV experimental treatment directory.

505	0	Part 1. An introduction to Drug literature index - - pt. 2. An introduction to Index medicus - - pt. 3. An introduction to International pharmaceutical abstracts.

Enhanced contents note

505	00	‡tBalcony rock /‡rD. Brubeck, P. Desmond - - ‡tOut of nowhere /‡r Heyman, J.W. Green - - ‡tLe souk /‡rD. Brubeck, P. Desmond - - ‡t Take the "A" train /‡rStrayhorn - - ‡tThe song is you /‡rHammerstein II, Kern - - ‡tDon't

worry 'bout me /‡rKoehler, Bloom - - ‡tI want to be happy /‡rCaesar, Youmans.

NUMBERS

Provide numbers other than the ISBN that are important for identification of the electronic resource in the 500 field, **General Note,** which is repeatable.
example

500	"AC/323(AVT)TP/13."
500	"2000055753" - - Disc label.

DESCRIPTIVE OR LIBRARY SPECIFIC NOTES

Provide descriptive or copy specific information regarding an electronic resource in a 500 field, **General Note,** which is repeatable.
example

500	Access to this database is available at designated workstations in the following Rutgers University Libraries: Chang Library, Chemistry Library, Dana Library, Library of Science and Medicine, Physics Library, Robeson Library.
500	Access restricted to Rutgers University faculty, staff, and students.

"WITH" NOTES

Provide notes for titles that are not the first in a collective title. This information is provided in the 500 field, **General Note,** which is repeatable. Additionally, information provided in this type of note may also be used as the basis for a 740 field, **Added Entry—Uncontrolled Related/Analytical Title.**
example

500	With: Power Chinese.

SUBJECT ACCESS

Subject access to electronic resources helps users to identify and locate resources, particularly when resources are maintained in a closed collection or are not available in a physical format, as is the case for Internet resources. Subject headings are used to provide access to electronic resources through *personal names, corporate names, topical terms,* or *geographic names.* Subject headings may be further subdivided by form division (format of material), general subdivisions, chronological subdivisions, and geographic subdivisions. Meeting names and subject added entries for uniform titles are not included in this text.

PERSONAL NAME

Provide subject access to personal names in the 600 field, **Subject Added Entry—Personal Name,** which is repeatable. Personal names are included in a bibliographic record when an electronic resource is about an individual or individuals, or contains a significant portion of information about an individual or individuals.

The following subfields are available for use in the 600 field: ‡a personal name; ‡c titles associated with a name; ‡d dates associated with a name; ‡v form subdivision; ‡x general subdivision; ‡y chronological subdivision; ‡z geographic subdivision. There are additional subfields that may be used with the 600; this text focuses discussion and examples on those that are most predominantly used.

The initial indicator value indicates type of name. An initial article value of 0 indicates entry under forename; 1 indicates entry under single surname. The second indicator value provides source of name heading. A second indicator value of 0 indicates that a name is from the Library of Congress Name Authority file. Additional information is available on the USMARC Web page at http://lcweb.loc.gov/marc/bibliographic/ecbdsubj.html #mrcb600.

example

600	00	Cher,‡d1946-
600	10	Day-Lewis, Daniel.
600	10	Weinberg, Valerie Ann.
600	10	Irving, Henry,‡cSir,‡d1838-1905.
600	10	Ellington, Duke,‡d1899-1974.
600	10	King, Martin Luther,‡cJr.,‡d 1929-1968‡xAssassination.
600	10	Krupa, Gene,‡d1909-1973‡vBiography.
600	10	Shakespeare, William,‡d1564 1616‡xStage history‡y 1800-1950.
600	10	Gogh, Vincent van,‡d1853-1890‡xMuseums‡zNetherlands‡zAmsterdam.

CORPORATE NAME

Provide subject access to corporate names in the 610 field, **Sub-**

ject Added Entry—Corporate Name, which is repeatable. Corporate names are included in a bibliographic record when an electronic resource is about a corporation or corporations, or contains a significant portion of information about a corporation or corporations.

The following subfields are available for use in the 610 field: ‡a corporate or jurisdiction names; ‡b subordinate units; ‡v form subdivision; ‡x general subdivision; ‡y chronological subdivision; ‡z geographic subdivision. There are additional subfields that may be used with the 610; this text focuses discussion and examples on those that are most predominantly used.

The initial indicator value indicates form of entry for names. An initial indicator value of 1 is for jurisdiction name; 2 is for a name presented in direct order. A second indicator value of 0 indicates that a name is from the Library of Congress Name Authority file. Additional information is available on the USMARC Web page at http://lcweb.loc.gov/marc/bibliographic/ecbdsubj.-html#mrcb610.

example

610	20	Lyceum Theatre (London, England)
610	10	United States.‡bDept. of the Interior.
610	20	Harvard University‡xFunds and scholarships‡v Handbooks, manuals, etc.
610	20	Microsoft Corporation‡xHistory.
610	20	Grand Central Terminal (New York, N.Y.)‡xHistory‡y20th century.
610	20	Salvation Army‡zEngland.

TOPICAL TERMS

Provide subject access to topical terms in the 650 field, Subject Added Entry—Topical Term, which is repeatable. Terms used in the 650 may describe form of the electronic resource (Dictionaries) or content (Jazz, Bicycle touring).

The following subfields are available for use in the 650 field: ‡a topical term or geographic name as entry element; ‡v form division; ‡x general subdivision; ‡y chronological subdivision; ‡z geographic subdivision. There are additional subfields that may be used with the 650; this text focuses discussion and examples on those that are most predominantly used.

The initial article value indicates level of subject; blank indicates that no information has been provided. In most cases, subject headings supplied by catalogers or provided in records available through union databases will have an initial indicator value of blank. A second indicator value of 0 indicates that a

name is from the Library of Congress Name Authority file. Additional information is available on the USMARC Web page at http://lcweb.loc.gov/marc/bibliographic/ecbdsubj.html#mrcb650
example

650	0	Violence in art.
650	0	Grandparents as parents‡xServices for‡zNew Jersey ‡vDirectories.
650	0	Crime prevention‡xCitizen participation.
650	0	American prose literature‡y19th century.
650	0	Artists‡zUnited States.

GEOGRAPHIC TERMS

Provide subject access to geographic terms in the 651 field, **Subject Added Entry—Geographic Name**, which is repeatable. The following subfields are available for use in the 651 field: ‡a geographic name; †v form division; ‡x general subdivision; ‡y chronological subdivision; ‡z geographic subdivision. There are additional subfields that may be used with the 651; this text focuses discussion and examples on those that are most predominantly used.

The initial indicators are undefined for this field. A second indicator value of 0 indicates that a name is from the Library of Congress Name Authority file. Additional information is available on the USMARC Web page at http://lcweb.loc.gov/marc/bibliographic/ecbdsubj.html#mrcb651.
example

651	0	Brooklyn (New York, N.Y.)
651	0	Manhattan (New York, N.Y.)‡vTours‡vMaps.
651	0	United States‡xPopulation‡xStatistics.
651	0	United States‡xHistory‡yCivil War, 1861-1865.
651	0	United States‡xHistory‡xStudy and teaching (Higher) ‡zNew Jersey.

ADDED ENTRIES

Added entries provide access to personal and corporate names that are not main entries yet serve as important additional access points. This information is provided in the 7XX fields, which are discussed in detail in the following paragraphs as they relate to electronic resources. Title added entries provide additional access for titles related to the main work.

PERSONAL NAME

Provide access to personal names in the 700 field, **Added Entry— Personal**, which is repeatable. It is used to include additional access points in the form of names taken from the 245, **Title Statement**, or other fields deemed appropriate by the cataloging agency. Personal name added entries differ from personal names in the 600 in that they provide different types of information, and would be found in an online catalog using different types of searches (subject versus personal name).

The following subfields are available for use in the 700 field: ‡a personal name; ‡c titles or other words associated with a particular name; ‡d dates; ‡4 relator code. A list of relator codes is available on the USMARC Web page at http://lcweb.loc.gov/marc/relators/. There are additional subfields that may be used with the 700; this text focuses discussion and examples on those that are most predominantly used.

The initial indicator value indicates type of name. An initial article value of 0 indicates entry under forename; 1 indicates entry under single surname. The second indicator value indicates type of added entry. A blank second indicator value indicates that no information is provided; a second indicator value of 2 indicates an analytical entry, and means the item in the bibliographic record contains the work represented by the added entry. Additional information is available on the USMARC Web page at http://lcweb.loc.gov/marc/bibliographic/ecbdadde.html#mrcb700.
example

700	0	Liberace,‡d1919-
700	1	Glenn, Tyree.
700	1	Irving, Henry,‡cSir,‡d1838-1905.
700	1	Severinsen, Doc,‡d1927-
700	1	Fellini, Federico.‡4drt
700	1	Binoche, Juliette,‡d1964- ‡4prf

CORPORATE NAME

Provide access to corporate names in the 710 field, **Added Entry—Corporate Name**, which is repeatable. It is used to include additional access points in the form of names taken from the 245, **Title Statement**, or 260, **Publication, Distribution, etc. (Imprint)**, or other fields deemed appropriate by the cataloging agency.

The following subfields are available for use in the 710 field: ‡a corporate name or jurisdiction name; ‡b subordinate unit; and ‡4 relator code. There are additional subfields that may be used with the 710; this text focuses discussion and examples on those that are most predominantly used.

The initial indicator value indicates type of corporate name. An initial article value 1 indicates entry in jurisdiction order; a value of 2 indicates entry in direct order. The second indicator value indicates type of added entry. A blank second indicator value indicates that no information is provided; a second indicator value of 2 indicates an analytical entry, and means the item in the bibliographic record contains the work represented by the added entry. Additional information is available on the USMARC Web page at http://lcweb.loc.gov/marc/bibliographic/ecbdadde.html#mrcb710.
example

| 260 | | Clifton, N.J. :‡bPiermatti Educational Resources,‡c1999. |
| 710 | 2 | Piermatti Educational Resources. |

UNIFORM TITLE

Provide access to uniform titles in the 730 field, **Added Entry—Uniform Title**, which is repeatable. Uniform titles provide a title related to the electronic resource being cataloged.

The following subfields are available for use in the 730 field: ‡a uniform title; ‡f date of a work; ‡h medium; ‡k form subheading; ‡l language. There are additional subfields that may be used with the 730; this text focuses discussion and examples on those that are most predominantly used.

The initial indicator value indicates number of nonfiling characters (0-9). The second indicator value indicates type of added entry. A blank second indicator value indicates that no information is provided; a second indicator value of 2 indicates an analytical entry, and means the item in the bibliographic record contains the work represented by the added entry. Additional information is available on the USMARC Web page at http://lcweb.loc.gov/marc/bibliographic/ecbdadde.html#mrcb730.

example

| 245 | 00 | Curtis botanical‡h[electronic resource]. |
| 730 | 0 | Curtis's botanical magazine. |

RELATED TITLES

Provide access to titles related to the work described in the 245 field, **Title Statement** using the 740 field, **Added Entry—Uncontrolled Related/Analytical Title**, which is repeatable. The 740 field is created using information taken from 500, **General Note**, or 505, **Formatted Contents Note** fields, or other fields deemed appropriate by the cataloging agency.

The following subfields are available for use in the 740 field: ‡a uncontrolled related/analytical title; ‡h medium; ‡n number of part/section of a work; ‡p name of part/section of a work. There are additional subfields that may be used with the 740; this text focuses discussion and examples on those that are most predominantly used.

The initial indicator value indicates number of nonfiling characters (0-9). The second indicator value indicates type of added entry. A blank second indicator value indicates that no information is provided; a second indicator value of 2 indicates an analytical entry, and means the item in the bibliographic record contains the work represented by the added entry. Additional information is available on the USMARC Web page at http://lcweb.loc.gov/marc/bibliographic/ecbdadde.html#mrcb740.

example

245	00	Atlas of coal geology‡h[electronic resource].
505	0	v.1. Coal geology - - v. 2. Coal petrology.
740	02	Coal geology‡h[electronic resource].
740	02	Coal petrology‡h[electronic resource].

CLASSIFICATION

Libraries may choose to classify their electronic resources using a scheme such as LCC or DDC. If LCC is used, the Q schedule for Science or T for Technology are often used. Classifying electronic resources provides access to their subject content. "Classification policy should allow software to be mainstreamed according to the subject instead of developing accession number schemes or grouping together all software in the computer science area."

(Frost, 1989: 191). The main subject heading indicates topic or genre of the resource. A form division may be added to indicate that it is an electronic resource.

EXAMPLES OF BIBLIOGRAPHIC RECORDS

Examples follow on the next page.

Figure 5-1 Computer Optical Disc

| Control | **Bib** | MARC Hldgs | Vol/Copy |

Fixed Fields

Rec_Type: a	Bib_Lvt: m	Enc_Lvt:	Desc: a	TypeCtrl:
Entrd: 000000	Dat_Tp: s	Date1: 1999	Date2:	Ctry: nmu
Lang: eng	Mod_Rec:	Source: d	Frequn: u	Regulr: u
Audience:	FileType: m	GovtPub: f		

TypeCode: m	Frequn: u	Regulr: u	Audience:	FileType: m
GovtPub: f				

Bibliographic Info

Phys descrip codes:	007	↓	↓	co cgu
ISBN:	020	↓	↓	1582560226
Cataloging source:	040	↓	↓	NjR|cNjR|dNjR
LC Call Number:	050	↓	4 ↓	QE5|b.I48 1999
Title:	245	↓	00 ↓	Illustrated dictionary of earth science|h[computer file].
Variant title:	246	↓	3 ↓	Dictionary of earth science |h[computer file]
Publication info:	260	↓	↓	Albuquerque, NM :|bTASA Graphic Arts ;|a[S.I.] :|bAmerican Geological Institute,|cc1999.
Physical descrip:	300	↓	↓	1 computer optical disc :|bcol. ;|c4 3/4 in. +e1 col. map (90 x 46 cm., folded to 20 x 16 cm.)
General Note:	500	↓	↓	Accompanied by map: Topography, bathymetry, and the lithospheric plates of the world.
Technical details:	538	↓	↓	System requirements: Windows 95/98/NT with16MB free RAM or Macintosh System 7 or later with 7MB free RAM; 13 in. or larger display (16 Bit or better video recommendation).
Technical details:	538	↓	↓	Disc characteristics: CD-ROM.
Abstract:	520	↓	↓	Title from disc label.
Abstract:	520	↓	↓	"Based on the authoritative American Geological Institute's Glossary of geology, 4th edition, the Illustrated dictionary of earth science offers quick access to up-

Figure 5-1 *Continued*

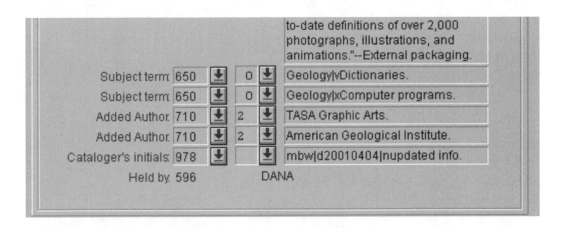

Figure 5-2 Computer Optical Disc

| Control | **Bib** | MARC Hldgs | All Volumes |

Fixed Fields

Rec_Type: m	Bib_Lvt m	Enc_Lvt	Desc: a	TypeCtrl
Entrd: 000816	Dat_Tp: s	Date1: 2000	Date2	Ctry: ja
Lang: eng	Mod_Rec:	Source: d	Frequn:	Regulr:
Audience:	FileType: m	GovtPub: f		

Bibliographic Info

Phys descrip codes:	007	⬇	⬇	co cga
Cataloging source:	040	⬇	⬇	NjR|cNjR
Language codes:	041	⬇	0 ⬇	engjpn|bengjpn
Geographic area code:	043	⬇	⬇	a-ja
Corporate Author:	110	⬇	2 ⬇	Summit Conference (26th : 2000 : Kyushu Region, Japan and Okinawa-shi, Japan)
Title:	245	⬇	10 ⬇	Kyushu-Okinawa Summit 2000 official guide CD-ROM|h[computer file] /|cpresented by the Government of Japan ; produced by Nippon Koho Center and NHK Enterprises 21.
Portion of title:	246	⬇	30 ⬇	Kyushu-Okinawa Summit 2000 |h[computer file]
Edition:	250	⬇	⬇	Japanese/English version.
Publication info:	260	⬇	⬇	[Japan] :|bNippon Koho Center, |cc2000.
Physical descrip:	300	⬇	⬇	1 computer optical disc :|bsd., col. ; |c4 3/4 in. +|e2 informational pamphlets ([3] p. : ill. ; 18 cm.) in English and Japanese + 4 sheets of col. images which correspond to interactive photographs appearing in the guide (15 x 21 cm.)
General Note:	500	⬇	⬇	Contents in 16 x 21 x 22 cm. container.
Language:	546	⬇	⬇	Online guide is available in English or Japanese; accompanying documentation is in English and Japanese.
General Note:	500	⬇	⬇	Title from readme file.
Abstract:	520	⬇	⬇	"...contains information about the Kyushu-Okinawa Summit

Figure 5-2 *Continued*

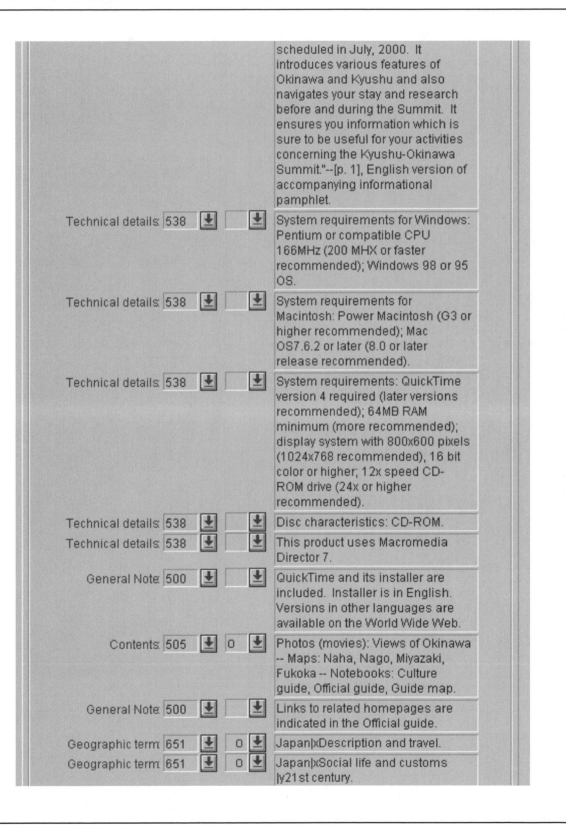

Figure 5-2 *Continued*

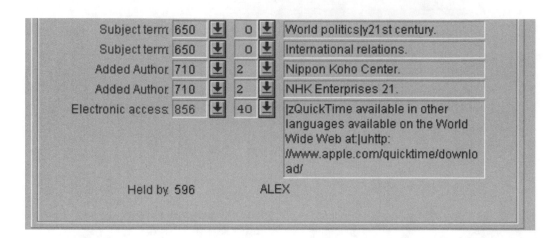

Figure 5-3 Computer Optical Disc

| Control | **Bib** | MARC Hldgs | All Volumes |

Fixed Fields

Rec_Type: m	Bib_Lvl: m	Enc_Lvl:	Desc: a
TypeCtrl	Entrd: 010110	Dat_Tp: s	Date1: 2000
Date2	Ctry: nju	Lang: eng	Mod_Rec:
Source: d	Frequn:	Regulr:	Audience:
FileType: c	GovtPub: s		

Bibliographic Info

001			a1507269
007			co ng
040			NjR|cNjR
043			n-us-nj
050		4	HV8141|b.R33
110		1	New Jersey.|bDept. of Law and Public Safety.
245		10	Racial profiling archives|h[electronic resource].
260			[Trenton] :|bThe Dept.,|c[2000?]
300			20 computer optical discs ;|c4 3/4 in.
500			Title from disc label.
505		0	[Disc 1]. CO-D-SO: (CO) = Commercial documents (0001-000903): newsletters, journal articles, operational plans, citizen complaints -- (D) = Troop D audit (00001-001184): stop data, Staff Inspection Unit-Trooper Transaction Reports from Troop D Turnpike Audit -- (SO) = Standard operating procedures (00001-002810): New Jersey State Police's standard operating procedures, related charge notices -- [disc 2]. IA-T: (IA) = Internal Affairs (00001-00548): citizen complaints, Advisory Board Findings -- (T) = Training (00001-005088): New Jersey State Police lesson plans, Academy orders, gang training materials, Drug Interdiction Training Unit (DITU) checklists -- [disc 3]. GC-ST: (GC) = Government correspondence (00001-002842): correspondence, memoranda, reports to and from the New Jersey State Policy and other government agencies -- (ST) = Statistics (00001-002234): investigation statistics, DWI arrests, consent to search statistics, race code stop reports -- [disc 4]. OR: (OR) = Other relevant documents (00001-000697): newspaper articles, operational plans, citizen complaints -- [disc 5]. OAG: (OAG) = Office of the Attorney General (00001-006339): correspondence and interoffice memoranda

Figure 5-3 Continued

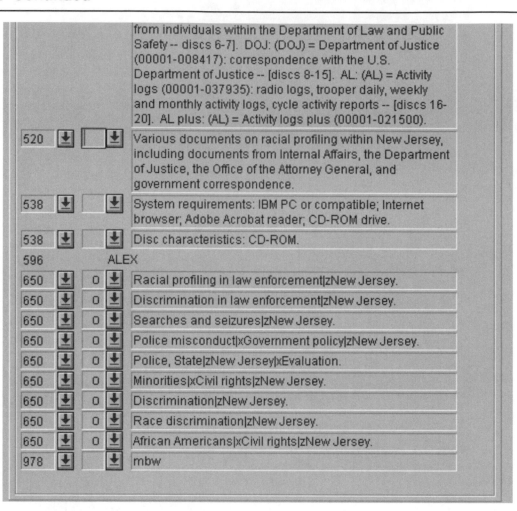

from individuals within the Department of Law and Public Safety -- discs 6-7]. DOJ: (DOJ) = Department of Justice (00001-008417): correspondence with the U.S. Department of Justice -- [discs 8-15]. AL: (AL) = Activity logs (00001-037935): radio logs, trooper daily, weekly and monthly activity logs, cycle activity reports -- [discs 16-20]. AL plus: (AL) = Activity logs plus (00001-021500).

520 | | | Various documents on racial profiling within New Jersey, including documents from Internal Affairs, the Department of Justice, the Office of the Attorney General, and government correspondence.

538 | | | System requirements: IBM PC or compatible; Internet browser; Adobe Acrobat reader; CD-ROM drive.

538 | | | Disc characteristics: CD-ROM.

596 | ALEX

650 | 0 | Racial profiling in law enforcement|zNew Jersey.

650 | 0 | Discrimination in law enforcement|zNew Jersey.

650 | 0 | Searches and seizures|zNew Jersey.

650 | 0 | Police misconduct|xGovernment policy|zNew Jersey.

650 | 0 | Police, State|zNew Jersey|xEvaluation.

650 | 0 | Minorities|xCivil rights|zNew Jersey.

650 | 0 | Discrimination|zNew Jersey.

650 | 0 | Race discrimination|zNew Jersey.

650 | 0 | African Americans|xCivil rights|zNew Jersey.

978 | | | mbw

Figure 5-4 Computer Optical Disc

| Control | **Bib** | MARC Hldgs | All Volumes |

Fixed Fields

Rec_Type: m   Bib_Lvt: m   Enc_Lvt: Desc: a   TypeCtrl:
Entrd: 000425   Dat_Tp: s   Date1: 2000   Date2:   Ctry: ctu
Lang: eng   Mod_Rec: Source: d   Frequn: Regulr:
Audience: FileType: i   GovtPub:

Bibliographic Info

Phys descrip codes: 007 [ ] co aga
Cataloging source: 040 NjR|cNjR|dNjR
LC Call Number: 050 4 TA413.5|b.P74 2000
Title: 245 1 Pressure strain and force handbook|h[computer file].
Edition: 250 Library ref. ed.
Publication info: 260 Stamford, CT :|bOmega Engineering,|cc2000.
Physical descrip: 300 1 computer optical disc :|bsd, col. ; |c4 3/4 in.
General Note: 500 Title from disc label.
Abstract: 520 Features over 700 color illustrations, covering pressure switches, load cells, strain gauges, controllers, recorders, dataloggers, transducers, and much more. Includes technical articles, prices (in U.S. Dollars) and selection guides.
Technical details: 538 System requirements for PC: Pentium processor-based system; 8MB RAM; Windows 95/98 or Windows NT; 256 color; 4X speed CD-ROM drive.
Technical details: 538 System requirements for Macintosh: 8MB RAM; 256 color monitor; 4X CD-ROM drive.
Technical details: 538 Disc characteristics: CD-ROM.
Corporate subject: 610 20 Omega Engineering, Inc.|vCatalogs |vInteractive multimedia.
Subject term: 650 0 Pressure|xMeasurement |xInstruments|vCatalogs |vInteractive multimedia.

Figure 5-4 *Continued*

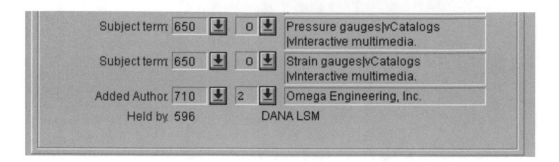

Figure 5-5 Computer Optical Disc

| Control | **Bib** | MARC Hldgs | Vol/Copy |

Fixed Fields

Rec_Type: a	Bib_Lvt: m	Enc_Lvt:	Desc: a	TypeCtrl:
Entrd: 000000	Dat_Tp: s	Date1: 1999	Date2:	Ctry: nmu
Lang: eng	Mod_Rec:	Source: d	Frequn: u	Regulr: u
Audience:	FileType: m	GovtPub: f		

| TypeCode: m | Frequn: u | Regulr: u | Audience: | FileType: m |
| GovtPub: f | | | | |

Bibliographic Info

Phys descrip codes	007		▮	co cgu
ISBN	020			1582560226
Cataloging source	040			NjR|cNjR|dNjR
LC Call Number	050		4	QE5|b.I48 1999
Title	245		00	Illustrated dictionary of earth science|h[computer file].
Variant title	246		3	Dictionary of earth science |h[computer file]
Publication info	260			Albuquerque, NM :|bTASA Graphic Arts ;|a[S.l.] :|bAmerican Geological Institute,|cc1999.
Physical descrip	300			1 computer optical disc :|bcol. ;|c4 3/4 in. +e1 col. map (90 x 46 cm., folded to 20 x 16 cm.)
General Note	500			Accompanied by map: Topography, bathymetry, and the lithospheric plates of the world.
Technical details	538			System requirements: Windows 95/98/NT with16MB free RAM or Macintosh System 7 or later with 7MB free RAM; 13 in. or larger display (16 Bit or better video recommendation).
Technical details	538			Disc characteristics: CD-ROM.
Abstract	520			Title from disc label.
Abstract	520			"Based on the authoritative American Geological Institute's Glossary of geology, 4th edition, the Illustrated dictionary of earth science offers quick access to up-

Figure 5-5 *Continued*

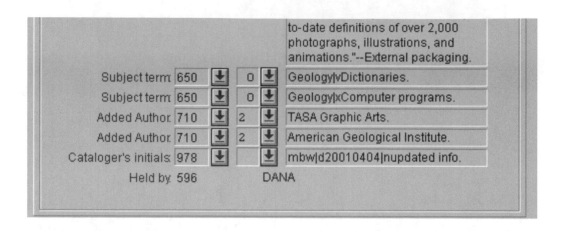

Figure 5-6 Computer Disks

| Control | **Bib** | MARC Hldgs | Vol/Copy |

Fixed Fields

Rec_Type: m	Bib_Lvt m	Enc_Lvt	Desc: a	TypeCtrl
Entrd: 010727	Dat_Tp: s	Date1: 1995	Date2	Ctry: nyu
Lang: eng	Mod_Rec:	Source: d	Frequn:	Regulr:
Audience:	FileType: e	GovtPub:		

Bibliographic Info

Phys descrip codes:	007		■		cj aa
Cataloging source:	040				NjR|cNjR
LC Call Number:	050		4		BX5943.A1|bA55 1995
Title:	245		04		The Anglican electronic library |h[computer file].
Variant title:	246		1		|iTitle on disk label:|aElectronic BCP
Variant title:	246		3		Electronic book of common Prayer |h[computer file]
Edition:	250				Windows version, second ed. 2.02.
Publication info:	260				Bronx, N.Y. :|bTSH Electronic Publishing,|cc1995.
Physical descrip:	300				2 computer disks :|bcol. ;|c3 1/2 in.
General Note:	500				Title from introductory screen.
Technical details:	538				System requirements: IBM PC or compatible (386 or higher processor); Windows 3.1 or Windows 95; mouse or other Windows-compatible pointing device.
Incomplete contents:	505		1		Electronic Book of Common Prayer, with lesser feasts -- Electronic book of occasional services
Abstract:	520				The Electronic Book of Common Prayer includes lesser feasts, administration of the sacraments and other rites and ceremonies of the church, together with the Psalter or Psalms of David, according to use of the Episcopal Church.

Figure 5-6 *Continued*

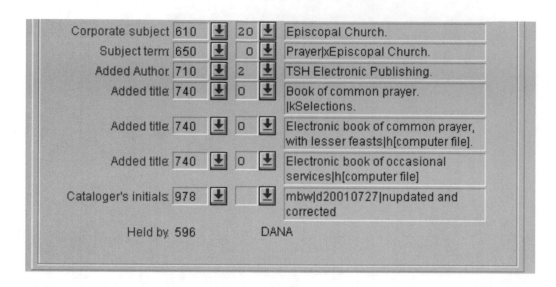

Figure 5-7 Computer Disks

| Control | **Bib** | MARC Hldgs | Vol/Copy |

Fixed Fields

Rec_Type: m	Bib_Lvl: m	Enc_Lvl:	Desc: a
TypeCtrl	Entrd: 970411	Dat_Tp: s	Date1: 1994
Date2	Ctry: xxu	Lang: eng	Mod_Rec:
Source: d	Frequn:	Regulr:	Audience:
FileType: c	GovtPub:		

Bibliographic Info

001			a1101578
005			19970414082311.0
035			(CStRLIN)NJRG97-D42
040			NjR|cNjR
050		4	QM465.N48|bC66 1994
090			QM465.N48|bC66 1994|i04/14/97 T
100		1	Coor, Sam.
245		10	Neuroanatomy review|h[electronic resource] :|bthe spinal cord /|can interactive multimedia production by Sam Coor.
250			V[ersion] 1.1.
260			[S.l.] :|bHamCoor, Inc. ;|aSeattle, WA :|bdistributed by the University of Washington,|cc1994.
300			5 computer disks :|bcol. ;|c3 1/2 in. +|e1 pamphlet (19 x 19 cm., folded to 9 x 9 cm.)
520			Reference work about the spinal cord.
538			System requirements: IBM 386 25MHz PC; Windows 3.1 or 3.0 with multimedia extensions; 4MB RAM (8MB recommended); 640 x 480 resolution with 256 colors, at least 17MB free hard disk space.
596		DANA	
650		0	Spinal cord.
650		0	Spine.
710		2	HamCoor, Inc.
710		2	University of Washington.
950			|IDANA|i04/14/97 N
978			mbw|d20010727|nupdated and corrected

REFERENCES

Frost, Carolyn O. 1989. *Media Access and Organization: A Cataloging and Reference Sources Guide for Nonbook Materials.* Englewood, Colo.: Libraries Unlimited.

Joint Steering Committee for the Revision of AACR2. 1998. *Anglo-American Cataloguing Rules, Second Edition, 1998 Revision.* Chicago: American Library Association.

Maxwell, Robert L., and Margaret F. Maxwell. 1997. *Maxwell's Handbook for AACR2R: Explaining and Illustrating the Anglo-American Cataloging Rules and the 1993 Amendments.* Chicago: American Library Association.

Network Development and MARC Standards Office, Library of Congress in cooperation with Standards and Support, National Library of Canada. 1999. *MARC 21 Format for Bibliographic Data Including Guidelines for Content Designation, 1999 Edition.* Washington, D.C.: Library of Congress Distribution Service.

KITS

OVERVIEW

Kits may be defined as a set or collection of various material types intended for use as a unit. *AACR2R (1998:619)* defines this category of resources as "kits," or "multimedia materials." The glossary of *AACR2R (1998)* defines kits as "An item containing two or more categories of material, no one of which is identifiable as the predominant constituent of the item; also designated 'kit'." It should also be noted that *AACR2R (1998)* uses this term only in reference to the GMD (Frost, 1989). There is not a separate chapter on kits as there is for other formats. Instead, guidelines for cataloging kits are provided in Chapter One, which provides general guidelines for description that may be applied to all material types.

When choosing an appropriate format for cataloging a kit, it is necessary to determine which format best represents the resource. For example, a resource titled "Introduction to Jazz" consists of a videorecording, a sound cassette, and a teacher's guide. Choice of format is not always clear cut, and may depend on factors such as the focus of the cataloging agency (sound recording or visual material), running time for each nonbook resource (that with the longest running time may be deemed as the predominant resource). Choice of format may also be decided based on material or packaging provided by the publisher, distributor, etc.

Level of description provided for kits depends on a library's collection, available staff, and the importance of kits to their holdings. All examples included in this text use full level description.

The type of classification provided for kits varies with type and size of library as well as by kind of collection in which the resources are housed (circulating or noncirculating). Libraries may provide Library of Congress Classification numbers or Dewey Decimal numbers, accession numbers, may arrange kits alphabetically by title or subject. Arrangement and classification varies by library and how they provide access.

ELEMENTS OF BIBLIOGRAPHIC RECORDS FOR KITS

The following information is necessary to create bibliographic records for kits:

- Chief Source of Information
- Prescribed Sources of Information
- Choice of Main Entry
- International Standard Book Number (ISBN)
- Publisher Number
- Cataloging Source
- Language Code
- Geographic Information
- Library of Congress Call Number
- Edition
- Title
- Title Variations
- General Material Designation (GMD)
- Statement of Responsibility
- Place of Publication and/or Distribution, or Manufacture, etc.
- Name of Publisher(s) and/or Distributor(s)
- Date of Publication, Distribution, Copyright, Manufacture, etc.
- Physical Description
- Series
- Notes
- Subject Access
- Added Entries (Personal and/or Corporate Names, Title Added Entries)
- Classification

CHIEF SOURCE OF INFORMATION

Consult the primary item in the kit. The chief source of information typically includes title information and credits, and publication/distribution information. Follow instructions for chief source of information as provided in the previous format-specific chapters.

PRESCRIBED SOURCES OF INFORMATION

Prescribed sources of information for kits is determined by the format chosen to describe the item. Follow instructions for prescribed sources of information as provided in the previous format-specific chapters.

CHOICE OF MAIN ENTRY

Main entry may be under personal authorship or corporate authorship, or title main entry may be chosen. Some library professionals feel that the issue of main entry is not as pressing in an online environment where a variety of types of searches may be performed to locate an item. However, Rule 21.1A1, *AACR2R (1998)* defines a personal author as the individual chiefly responsible for a resource's intellectual or artistic content. Rule 21.1B1, *AACR2R (1998)* defines a corporate author as an organization or group of persons with a particular name that functions as an entity. Lastly, Rule 21.1C1, *AACR2R (1998)* states that a resource should be entered under title proper (or uniform title if appropriate) when: personal authorship is unknown or shared by a large number of individuals, and authorship can not be attributed to one particular individual or when a resource is not issued by a corporate body; or when a resource is a collection of works by different individuals or corporate bodies.

For some resources, title main entry is the most logical choice since the nonprint resource is the result of the work of many individuals and/or corporate bodies, and it is not possible to attribute authorship to a particular individual or corporate body. Lack of a statement of responsibility is another reason why title main entry is chosen for some nonprint resources.
example

| 110 | 2 | Centre for Educational Research and Innovation. |
| 245 | 10 | Piagetian inventories‡h[kit] :‡bthe experiments of Jean Piaget. |

| 245 | 00 | Intervention and referral services for general educations pupils‡h[kit] :‡ba four-part series and companion guide. |

Physical Description

Physical description is provided both in fixed fields and the 300 field, **Physical Description**. The 007 field, **Physical Description Fixed Field—General Information** provides information on physical description in alphabetic coded form. Some bibliographic utilities and cataloging modules display the 007 field at the top of the bibliographic record with other fixed fields; other utilities and modules provide this information in the bibliographic record with the variable fields. In this text, the 007 field is displayed with the variable fields in examples of bibliographic records.

Coding for the 007 field indicates that the item is a kit, which the USMARC Web page (2001) describes as "...a mixture of various components issued as a unit and intended primarily for instructional purposes. No one component is identifiable as the predominant component of the kit." Coding the 007 field for kits is new; previously, kits were coded using the predominant format (and GMD) of the components. There are only two ways in which a kit may be coded; both are shown below.

There are no subfields or indicators defined for the 007 field.

The 007 field for kits begins with the letter "o."
example

```
007            ou
o = kit
u = unspecified
007            o
o = kit
blank = No attempt to code
```

International Standard Book Number (ISBN)

Monographic resources are often assigned ISBNs. Provide this information in the 020 field, **International Standard Book Number**, which is repeatable. This information can be helpful in identifying specific versions of a resource.

The following subfields are used in the 020: ‡a ISBN; ‡c terms of availability (price).

There are no indicators defined for the 020 field.
example

```
020            0780619900 (set) :‡c$300.00
020            0333776151 (Macmillan ISBN)
```

Publisher Number

Provide information on a formatted publisher number in the 028 field, **Publisher Number**, which is repeatable. Publisher numbers may also be provided in the 500 field, **General Note**, in an unformatted form. Publisher numbers are used for kits cataloged using the visual materials or sound recordings format.

The following subfields are available for use in the 028 field:

‡a publisher number; ‡b source.
example

028	02	8034-2‡bNew World Records
500		LRC: EJ-1005.
028	4	LSP 2061‡bLOB
500		"IMMW101-IMMW106"- -Container.

Cataloging Source

Information on the origin of a bibliographic record, plus any institutions that have modified a record, is provided in the 040 field, **Cataloging Source**, which is not repeatable.

The following subfields are available for use in the 040 field: ‡a original cataloging agency; ‡c transcribing agency (which is typically the institution in ‡a); and ‡d modifying agency. There are other subfields that may be used in the 040; this discussion is limited to those that are most predominantly used.

There are no indicators defined for the 040 field.
example

Original cataloging record created and transcribed by Rutgers University Libraries
040   NjR‡cNjR

Original cataloging record created and transcribed by Rutgers University Libraries, modified by Library X.
040   NjR‡NjR‡dXyZ

Original cataloging record created and transcribed by Rutgers University Libraries, modified at a later date by Rutgers University Libraries.
040   NjR‡NjR‡dNjR

Language Code

Provide information on language(s) present in a resource in the 041 field, **Language Code**, which is not repeatable. Information in the 041 is provided in alphabetic coded form. The 041 works in conjunction with the 546 field, **Language Note**.

Codes are provided according to their predominance in the resource (Network Development and MARC Standards Office, Library of Congress, 1999). The 041 field can provide codes for a maximum of six languages. If more than six languages are present in the resource, the language for the title is coded as "mul"(multiple) to represent all the languages.

The following subfields are used in the 041: ‡a language code for text, sound track, or separate title; ‡b language code for summary or subtitle; ‡d language code for sung or spoken text; ‡e language code for librettos; ‡g language code for accompanying materials other than librettos; ‡h language code for original and/ or intermediate translations of text.

The initial indicator value indicates whether a resource is or includes a translation. An initial indicator of 0 indicates that the resource is not a translation and does not include a translation; a value of 1 indicates that the item is a translation or includes a translation.

example

| 041 | 0 | ‡beng |
| 546 | | Silent with captions in English. |

041	1	freita‡gengfreita
546		In French and Italian; program notes in English, French, and Italian.
041	1	‡dgerita‡egeritaengfre‡hgerita‡genggerfreitaspa‡henggerfre
546		Program notes by Alan Newcombe, Richard Osborne, Klaus Bennert, and Francis Drêsel, in English, German and French, with Italian and Spanish translations, and texts of the vocal works, in German and Italian, with English and French translations (16 p. : ill.) included.

Geographic Information

Provide information on the geographic area presented, described, covered, etc. by the resource in the 043 field, **Geographic Area Code**, which is not repeatable. The 043 can accommodate 1-3 codes, which are represented in alphabetic coded form. Multiple geographic codes are separated by a ‡a.

Indicator values are not defined for the 043 field.

example

Resource contains information pertaining to New Jersey, in the United States
043   n-us-nj

Resource contains information pertaining to the Great Plains region in the United States
043   np- - - - -

Resource contains information pertaining to Japan
043   a-ja- - -

Resource contains information pertaining to Spain and Mexico

043   e-sp- - -‡an-mx- - -

A full list of geographic area codes is available on the USMARC Web page at http://lcweb.loc.gov/marc/geoareas/.

Library Of Congress Call Number

Provide a Library of Congress Call Number (if applicable according to the cataloging agency's policies and procedures for nonprint resources) in the 050 field, **Library of Congress Call Number**, which is repeatable. Some institutions have policies governing whether an LC Call Number is included in the bibliographic portion of a record when their records are submitted to a national online bibliographic utility such as RLIN or OCLC.

The following subfields are available for use in the 050 field: ‡a classification number; ‡b item number.

The initial indicator value indicates whether the item is in Library of Congress's collection. An initial value of blank indicates that no information is provided, and is used when libraries other than the Library of Congress provide classification numbers. The second indicator value indicates source of call number. Classification numbers provided by Library of Congress have a second indicator value of zero; classification numbers provided by other libraries have a second indicator value of 4.

example

| 050 | 0 | HB1335‡b.M84 |
| 050 | 4 | GB1399.4.N5‡bF566 1971 |

TITLE INFORMATION

Includes title, general material designation, remainder of title, and statement of responsibility.

Title

Consult the chief source of information first. If it is lacking or provides limited or no information, consult the prescribed sources of information. In the absence of chief or prescribed sources of information, a title may be supplied by the cataloger. The supplied title must be bracketed, and the source of title must be documented in a general note.

Title information is provided in the 245 field, **Title Statement**. The following subfields are available for use in the 245 field: ‡a title; ‡b remainder of title; ‡c statement of responsibility; ‡h GMD; ‡n number of part/section; ‡p name of part/section. One method of presenting subfields is to discuss them in the order in which they are used in bibliographic records, rather than alphabetically. However, the alphabetic approach is used in this text, and has been modeled after authoritative sources of information, such as *Concise MARC Format* and the RLIN and OCLC cataloging manuals. Placement of the subfields is illustrated in examples and illustrations. There are additional subfields that may be used in the 245; this text focuses discussion and examples on those that are most predominantly used.

Rule 1.1B1, *AACR2R (1998)*, instructs catalogers to transcribe the title proper exactly as to wording, order, and spelling, but not necessarily to capitalization and punctuation. Titles are provided in the 245 field, ‡a, which is not repeatable.

Indicator values in the 245 field indicates if a title added entry will be generated. Most nonprint items are cataloged using title main entry. Nonprint resources are rarely entered under an author (corporate or personal) main entry. (A discussion of choice of main entry for nonbook resources is provided in the following paragraph). For this reason, the majority of nonprint resources will have a first indicator value of 0. A first indicator value of 1 is used when a title added entry will be generated. The second indicator specifies number of nonfiling characters, with a range of 0-9 available.

example

Title from chief source of information:

245	00	Kyushu-Okinawa Summit 2000 official guide

Title supplied by cataloger:

245	00	[Documentary on Douglass College, Rutgers University]
500		Title supplied by cataloger.

Remainder of Title

The 245 field also provides the remainder of a title or other information, such as parallel titles. Provide this information in the ‡b, which is not repeatable.
example

245	00	Powwow songs :‡bmusic of the Plains Indians
245	03	L'Homme sur les quais‡h[videorecording] =‡bThe man by the shore

Title Variations

Provide title variations in the 246 field, **Varying Form of Title**, which is repeatable. The 246 provides other titles by which a resource may be known; this includes abbreviations or acronyms, parallel titles in another language, or when one title appears on external packaging and another title is given in the chief source of information. Providing access to title variations permits users to search for a resource in multiple ways.

The following subfields are available for use in the 246 field: ‡a title; ‡b remainder of title or parallel title; ‡h medium; ‡i display text; ‡n number of part/section of a work; ‡p name of a part/section of a work. There are additional subfields that may be used with the 246; this text focuses discussion and examples on those that are most predominantly used.

The initial indicator value indicates note or added entry. The second indicator value is used to provide information on type of title. A complete list of indicator values is available on the USMARC Web page at http://lcweb.loc.gov/marc/bibliographic/ ecbdtils.html#mrcb246.

example

Portions of the main title

245	10	Kyushu-Okinawa Summit 2000 official guide CD-ROM‡h[electronic resource].
246	30	Kyushu-Okinawa Summit 2000 official guide‡h[electronic resource]
246	30	Kyushu-Okinawa Summit 2000‡h[electronic resource]

Remainder of title

| 245 | 00 | To steal or not to steal‡h[videorecording] :‡bthat is the copyright question. |
| 246 | 30 | That is the copyright question‡h[videorecording] |

Title on chief source and container differ

| 245 | 04 | The Beatles live at the Star Club in Hamburg, Germany, 1962‡h[sound recording]. |
| 246 | 1 | ‡iTitle on container:‡aLingasong Records presents the Beatles live at the Star Club in Hamburg, Germany, 1962 |

Portion of the main title

| 245 | 00 | Excavating the Bible.‡nVolume two,‡pMarine archaeology ‡h[videorecording]. |
| 246 | 30 | Marine archaeology‡h[videorecording] |

| 245 | 00 | Elements of protein synthesis‡h[kit]. |
| 246 | 30 | Protein synthesis‡h[kit]. |

GENERAL MATERIAL DESIGNATION (GMD)

Use of a GMD is deemed optional by Rule 1.1C, *AACR2R (1998)*.

There are several reasons why a library may choose to use GMDs. It indicates to users the format of a resource when a search is done in an online catalog since all resources with a specific GMD will cluster together. Additionally, the resource described in an online catalog may not readily be apparent to users even when the bibliographic record includes a physical description that includes type of resource and characteristics. Use of a GMD helps users to distinguish between different formats in which a title is available. For example, *Midnight Express* is the title of a book, as well as a motion picture, a motion picture sound track, and is also available on videorecording. However, there is a growing sentiment that GMDs are no longer useful, particularly in a Web-based environment in which some libraries use one bibliographic record to represent multiple manifestations of a title (a paper and an electronic version of a serial title, for example).

The GMD is included in the 245 field, ‡h and is enclosed in brackets. It immediately follows the information provided in ‡a and precedes the ‡b. It is not repeatable.

Two lists of GMDs are provided in *AACR2R (1998)*. The first list is for British cataloging agencies; Australian, Canadian, and American cataloging agencies use terms from the second list. Use the GMD "kit" as instructed in Rule 1.1C1, *AACR2R (1998)*. A cataloging agency may also use the GMD of the predominant format in the kit. Provide the GMD in the 245 field, ‡h, which is not repeatable.

example

245   00   McGruff's drug prevention and child protection program‡h[kit].

STATEMENT OF RESPONSIBILITY

The statement of responsibility provides names of corporate bodies and/or individuals responsible for production, creation, manufacture, etc. of a nonprint resource. This information is taken from the chief or prescribed sources of information.

The statement of responsibility is included in the 245 field, ‡c, is preceded by a forward slash, and is not repeatable. Each corporate body or individual presented in the statement of responsibility is separated by semicolons. Per Rule 1.1F1, *AACR2R (1998)*, statements of responsibility are to be transcribed as they appear. Information taken from sources other than the chief source of information will be bracketed.

The information provided in the statement of responsibility for kits is determined by the format chosen to describe the resource.

Follow instructions for statement of responsibility as provided in the previous format specific chapters.

Provide the statement of responsibility in the 245 field, ‡c.
example

245	00	McGruff's drug prevention and child protection program‡h[kit] /‡cconceived and produced by Bill Hawes ; material adapted by Robin L. Nelson.

Edition

Provide edition information in the 250 field, **Edition Statement,** which is not repeatable. Edition information for nonprint resources is not limited to the term "edition," and includes "version," "release," "revision," or other terms deemed appropriate by the cataloging agency. Rule 1.2B1, *AACR2R (1998)*, instructs catalogers to transcribe edition statements in the form found on the item.

The following subfields are available for use in the 250 field: ‡a edition statement; ‡b remainder of edition statement. There are additional subfields that may be used with the 250; this text focuses discussion and examples on those that are most predominantly used.

There are no indicators defined for the 250 field.
example

250	Japanese/English version.
250	Version 1.00.
250	Teacher's edition.
250	Limited anniversary edition.

PUBLICATION INFORMATION

Consult the chief and/or prescribed sources of information to obtain information on where and when a resource was published, distributed, manufactured, etc. Publication, distribution, manufacture, etc. information is provided in the 260 field, **Publication, Distribution, etc. (Imprint),** which is not repeatable.

PLACE OF PUBLICATION, DISTRIBUTION, MANUFACTURE, ETC.

The place of publication, distribution, manufacture, etc. is provided in the 260 field, ‡a. It is repeatable if there is more than one place of publication, or if a resource is published in one location and distributed in another, for example.

Generally, the city and country or state of publication are given. If only a city name is given, and it is necessary to record the country, state, etc., for purposes of identification and clarification, record the supplied information in brackets, as per Rule 1.4C3, *AACR2R (1998)*.
example

| 260 | Detroit, Mich. |
| 260 | Schmalkalden [Germany] |

If a place of publication, distribution, manufacture, etc. is not provided, but may be ascertained, record in brackets with a question mark. Consult Rule 1.4C6, *AACR2R (1998)*, for further discussion of this topic.
example

| 260 | [Denver?] |

If no place of publication, distribution, manufacture, etc. is provided, and may not be ascertained, the abbreviation for the term "Sine loco" [S.l.], is used per Rule 1.4C6, *AACR2R (1998)*. The abbreviation is always bracketed.
example

| 260 | [S.l.] :‡bMedia Mix Productions |

NAME OF PUBLISHER(S) AND/OR DISTRIBUTOR(S)

Consult the chief and/or prescribed sources of information first. Record the publisher's name following the place of publication as per Rule 1.4D1, *AACR2R (1998)*. If the distributor (or another body with a function related to the material being described) is included, transcribe the distributor, etc. name as it appears in the chief or prescribed sources of information. If the distributor's location differs from that of the publisher, record both locations.

Provide this information in the 260 field, ‡b, which is repeatable when there is more than one publisher, distributor, etc.
example

| 260 | [S.l.] :‡bMedia Mix Productions ;‡aChicago :‡bDistributed by Light Pharmacy Films |

The term "distributor" is added in brackets following distribu-

tor information only when this function (or other related functions) is not clear in the chief or prescribed sources of information, as per Rule 1.4E1, *AACR2R (1998)*. If distributor information is taken from a label affixed to the resource, external packaging, etc., this must be noted.
example

260	New Brunswick, N.J. :‡bT. Meyer Publishers ;‡aRobinson Media Group [distributor]
260	San Francisco, CA :‡bNan Hai Co., Inc. [distributor], ‡cc1988.
500	Distributor information from label affixed to external container.
500	Distributor information from cassette label.

If there is no information provided for publisher, distributor, etc., and it may not be ascertained, use the abbreviation for the term "sine nomine," [s.n.], as per Rule 1.4D7, *AACR2R (1998)*. The abbreviation is always bracketed.
example

260	Chicago :‡b[s.n.]

DATE OF PUBLICATION, DISTRIBUTION, COPYRIGHT, MANUFACTURE, ETC.

Provide this information in the 260 field, ‡c, which is repeatable. However, the practice of repeating the ‡c is not widely used. Multiple dates, such as for date of production and copyright, may be included in the 260 field, ‡c.

Consult the chief and/or prescribed sources of information first. Record publication date, or distribution date if publication date is not available. In the absence of either date, record copyright date, which is preceded by a lower case "c." Information on date of publication, distribution, etc. is further outlined in Rule 1.4F, *AACR2R (1998)*.
example

Publication date
260	Media, Pa. :‡bEducational Clearinghouse,‡c1990.

Copyright date
260	Oxford :‡bIRL Press Ltd.,‡cc1986.

If information on publication, distribution, etc. date is not pro-

vided in either the chief or prescribed sources of information, approximate the date of publication. Approximated dates are bracketed.
example

Approximated date
260   [S.l.] :‡bT. Meyer Publishers,‡c[ca. 1997]

Probable date
260   Cherry Hill, N.J. :‡bAriel Press,‡[1990?]

Decade certain
260   Clifton, N.J. :‡bPiermatti Educational Resources,‡c[198-]

Probable decade
260   Chicago :‡bScholars Press,‡c[199-?]

Note: More information on dates is available in *AACR2R (1998)*, Chapter 1, "General Rules for Description."
Multipart items: Include a beginning date if the resource is not complete and/or is expected to continue indefinitely. An ending date may be included when a resource is complete. Rule 1.4F8, *AACR2R (1998)* notes that this practice is optional.
example

260   Palo Alto, Calif. :‡bDIALOG Information Services,‡c1965-
260   New Brunswick, N.J. :‡bRutgers University Libraries,‡c1995-2000.

Unpublished items: Do not attempt to provide a place of publication, etc. or publisher, distributor, manufacturer, etc. name for unpublished items, as per Rule 1.4D9, *AACR2R (1998)*. Do not use the abbreviations "S.l." or "s.n." A date may be included for the item.
example

260   ‡c1999.
260   ‡c[2000?]

There are no indicators defined for the 260 field.

PHYSICAL DESCRIPTION

Includes extent (number and Specific Material Designation (SMD) of physical parts of an item), other physical details (color or sound characteristics, for example), dimensions, and information about accompanying materials.

The physical description is provided in the 300 field, **Physical Description**. The physical description field is repeatable, permitting a multilevel description, yet this option is not commonly applied.

Kits may be described in a variety of ways. The physical description may be general or specific, or a multilevel description may be provided to describe each component part in full detail. Rule 1.10B, *AACR2R (1998)* states that when a kit contains a predominant format, the kit should be described in terms of that particular format. The remaining components should be described as accompanying materials. If the contents of the resource are in a container, it is helpful to provide the dimensions in centimeters (length x width x height).

EXTENT

Provide the number and SMD of the parts of an item, as per Rule 1.5B1, *AACR2R (1998)*. Format-specific information is provided in Subrule .5B in Chapters 3, 6-7, 9, and 11, *AACR2R (1998)*. The SMD is not identical to the GMD. It is used to specify material types, while the GMD describes the broad category of materials into which a resource may fall. Extent is provided in the ‡a, and is not repeatable.

Use the physical description to provide the number and SMD of the physical parts when a specific physical description is provided. Do not confuse the GMD with the SMD. Provide the GMD in the 245 field, ‡h, which is not repeatable.

Component parts may be described as "various pieces" for resources with a large number of different parts.
example

General description

300	4 film reels, 4 sound discs
300	30 various pieces
300	various pieces*

*A very general physical description is best suited for a kit with a large number of different parts.

Specific description

300		2 sound cassettes (ca. 49 min. ea.) :‡banalog, 1 7/8 ips +‡e1 teacher's guide (78 p. : ill. ; 28 cm.) + 1 student workbook (100 p. : ill. ; 28 cm.) + flash cards + 2 puppets in container 40 x 45 x 40 cm.

Multilevel description

300	2 sound cassettes (ca. 49 min. ea.) :‡banalog, 1 7/8 ips
300	1 videocassette (30 min.) :‡bsd., col. ;‡c1/2 in.
300	xi, 200 p. :‡bill. ;‡c28 cm. +‡e 1 teacher's guide (78 p. : ill. ; 28 cm.) + 1 student workbook (100 p. : ill. ; 28 cm.)

OTHER PHYSICAL DETAILS

Provide a description of characteristics other than extent or dimensions, as per Rule 1.5C, *AACR2R (1998)*. This information is provided in the ‡b, which is not repeatable. The format specific chapters provide greater detail on physical details as related to various resources.
example

Motion picture- silent, black and white

300	1 film reel (30 min.) :‡bsi., b&w

Videorecording- sound, color

300	2 videocassettes (180 min.) :‡bsd., col.

Sound recording- digital recording, stereophonic sound

300	1 sound disc (50 min.) :‡bdigital, stereo.

Electronic resource- sound, color

300	2 computer optical discs :‡bsd., col.

DIMENSIONS

Provide information on size, width, etc. as appropriate, as per Rule 1.5D1, *AACR2R (1998)*. The format specific chapters provide more detail on dimensions. Dimensions are included in the ‡c, which is not repeatable.
example

300	2 film reels (180 min.) :‡bsd., col. with b&w sequences ;‡c16 mm.
300	2 computer optical discs :‡bsd., col. ;‡c4 3/4 in.
300	38 microfilm reels :‡bcol., ill. ;‡c35 mm.
300	2 fiche :‡bmaps ;‡c11 x 15 cm.

SERIES

Provide series treatment if available in the chief and/or prescribed sources of information. This text provides general series information; a detailed discussion of various types of series treatments is beyond the focus of this text. Series are represented in this text by the 440 field, **Series Statement/Added Entry—Title**, which is repeatable.

The following subfields are available for use in the 440 field: ‡a title; ‡n number of part/section; ‡p name of part/section; ‡v volume or numbering designation.

Provide series title in the 440, ‡a, which is not repeatable.

The first indicator value for the 440 field is undefined. The second indicator specifies number of nonfiling characters, with a range of 0-9 available.

Detailed information on series is available on the USMARC Web page at http://lcweb.loc.gov/marc/bibliographic/ecbdhome.html#mrcb440.

example

```
440      0      Library of African cinema
440      0      BMG classics
```

Provide information on numbered parts in the ‡n number of Part/Section of a Work.

example

```
440      0      Langues de l'Orient.‡nl,‡pManuals
440      0      Baseball.‡nVolume 7,‡pFourth inning
```

Provide the specific name of the part(s)/section(s) of a series in the ‡p name of Part/Section of a Work.

example

```
440      0      The Great explorers.‡pThe Columbus series
440      0      Janua linguarum.‡pSeries minor
```

Provide numbering designation, such as "volume" or "part" in the ‡v.

example

```
440      0      BMG classics ;‡vvol. 32
440      0      Medicine at the crossroads ;‡vMECR108
```

NOTES

Notes for kits provide a variety of information, including contents, summary, and additional information about the resource. Notes may also describe characteristics of the resource unique to the library's copy of the item.

The notes in this section are provided in the order which they appear in MARC records. Notes are not arranged in numeric order by MARC tag number.

Notes of a very general nature are provided in the 500 field, **General Note**, which is repeatable. This type of note is more prevalent in nonprint cataloging than in cataloging for print resources.

NATURE AND FORM

Provide a note on nature and form of kits in the 500 field, **General Note** only when it is not apparent from the description. The 500 field is repeatable.
example

500	Reading tutorial.
500	Statistical package for accountants.

LANGUAGE

Provide information on language(s) if more than one language is present in the nonprint resource, or if the resource is in a language (or languages) other than the primary language of the cataloging agency. Use the 546 field, **Language Note**, which is repeatable. It is used in conjunction with the 041 field, **Language Code**, which is not repeatable.

The initial article value of 0 indicates that the resource is not a translation or does not include a translation; an initial article value of 1 indicates that the resource is a translation or includes a translation.
example

041	0	spa
546		In Spanish.

041	1	fre‡beng
546		In French with English subtitles.

A full list of language codes is available on the USMARC Web page at http://lcweb.loc.gov/marc/languages/.

SOURCE OF TITLE PROPER

Indicate source of title if not taken from chief or prescribed sources of information, or has been supplied by the cataloger, as per Rule 1.7B3, *AACR2R (1998)*.

Provide this information in the 500 field, **General Note**, which is repeatable

example

500	Title supplied by cataloger.
500	Title from accompanying teacher's guide.

CREDITS

Provide the names of individuals or corporate bodies not named in the statement of responsibility who have contributed to the production of the kit, when applicable. This information is provided in the 508 field, **Creation/Production Credits Note**, which is not repeatable.

example

245	00	Insight‡h[kit].‡pGraphics I.
508		Writer/visual editor, Janice Mallin.

EDITION AND HISTORY

Provide information on the resource, or use to provide history of the kit. This information is provided in the 500 field, **General Note**, which is repeatable, and differs from what is provided in the 250 field.

example

500	An expansion of McGruff's Elementary School Puppet Program.

PUBLICATION, DISTRIBUTION, ETC., AND DATE INFORMATION

"Make notes on publication, distribution, etc., details that are not included in the publication, distribution, etc., area and are considered to be important" (Joint Steering Committee for the Revision of *AAC2R2, [1998]*:196, 7.7B9).

Provide this information in the 500 field, **General Note**, which is repeatable.
example

500	Additional copies of this publication may be ordered from ALA Publishing.

500   Distributor information taken from accompanying printed matter.

PHYSICAL DESCRIPTION

Provide additional physical description not represented in the 007 field, **Physical Description Fixed Field—General Information,** or the 300 field, **Physical Description.** This information is provided in the 500 field, **General Note,** or 538 field, **System Details Note** (depending on criteria described); both are repeatable.

Additional physical description includes sound characteristics, color, videorecording system, and other information deemed important by the cataloging agency. Information provided for kits depends on format chosen to represent the item. Consult the preceding format-specific chapters for detailed information on additional physical description.

example

500   Video closed captioned for the hearing impaired.
500   Java compatible.
500   The accompanying sound cassette contains 4 public service announcements. The accompanying electronic resource is in WordPerfect format, and allows users to modify and adapt written materials to their specific needs. The Toolkit also includes camera-ready handouts for easy duplication and distribution of select materials.

AUDIENCE

Provide information on the intended audience or intellectual level of a kit. Take this information from chief or prescribed sources of information. This information is provided in the 521 field, **Target Audience Note,** which is repeatable.

The first indicator value provides an introductory phrase for the 521 field that describes audience or intellectual level of materials. A first indicator value of blank provides the display constant "Audience." The second indicator value is undefined. Additional information on indicator values for the 521 field is available on the USMARC Web page at http://lcweb.loc.gov/marc/bibliographic/ecbdnot1.html#mrcb521.

example

521   Audience: Rated PG-13.
521   2   Interest grade level: Grades 4-6.

SUMMARY

Provide a brief description of the contents of the kit. Since users may not browse for nonprint resources in the manner used for print resources, the summary should provide specific information to accurately describe the resource. Information taken from the container, external sources of information, or other sources should be noted. Generally, summaries should be limited to two-three sentences unless more information is warranted; this is determined by individual cataloging agencies.

The first indicator value provides an introductory phrase for the 520 field. A blank first indicator value generates the display "Summary." The second indicator value is undefined. Additional information on indicator values for the 520 field is available on the USMARC Web page at http://lcweb.loc.gov/marc/bibliographic/ecbdnot1.html#mrcb520.
example

520	Summary: Discusses the field of advertising and career opportunities.
520	Summary: Designed for teachers to help students from being victims of crime and accidents.

CONTENTS

Information detailing the contents of a resource is provided in the 505 field, **Formatted Contents Note**, which is repeatable. It provides individual titles or parts contained in a resource, and may include statements of responsibility and durations (for sound recordings and visual materials, for example).

Contents notes in which the various parts of the note are coded are referred to as "enhanced." Enhanced contents notes contain a ‡t (title) and ‡r (statement of responsibility).

The first indicator value for the 505 field indicates completeness of the contents. A first indicator value of 0 indicates complete contents, a value of 1 is used for incomplete contents, and a value of 2 is used for partial contents. The second indicator value provides information on content designation. A second indicator value of 0 is used for enhanced contents. A second value of blank is used for nonenhanced contents notes. The indicators for an enhanced contents note are 00 (a nonenhanced contents has a single first indicator with a value from 0-2, or 8).

While not required, a contents note is useful to providing a description since the contents of a nonprint resource may not be browsed in the manner used for print resources.

example

505	0	Crime prevention - - Drugs - - Strangers - - Just say no - - At home alone.
505	0	Introduction to Drug literature index - - Introduction to Index medicus - - Introduction to International pharmaceutical abstracts.
505	0	Currency exchanges (Metz) - - Currency exchanges (Mueller) - - Currency exchanges (Spufford) - - Prices (Metz) - - Prices (Posthumus).

Enhanced contents note

| 505 | 00 | ‡tBalcony rock /‡rD. Brubeck, P. Desmond - - ‡tOut of nowhere /‡r Heyman, J.W. Green - - ‡tLe souk /‡rD. Brubeck, P. Desmond - - ‡t Take the "A" train /‡rStrayhorn - - ‡tThe song is you/‡rHammerstein II, Kern - - ‡tDon't worry 'bout me /‡rKoehler, Bloom - - ‡tI want to be happy /‡rCaesar, Youmans. |

DESCRIPTIVE OR LIBRARY SPECIFIC NOTES

Provide descriptive or copy specific information regarding a kit in a 500 field, **General Note**, which is repeatable.
example

| 500 | | Use restricted to Media Services Reading Room. |
| 500 | | Access restricted to faculty and full-time registered students. |

Additional Physical Form

Provide information on additional formats in which a resource is available in the 530 field, **Additional Physical Form Available Note**, which is repeatable.

Indicator values are not defined for the 530 field.
example

| 530 | | Also available on the World Wide Web. |

System Requirements

Provide information on physical characteristics, coding, recording system, etc. in the 538 field, **System Details Note**, which is repeatable. The description of system details may be preceded by a note specifying the type of information which follows.

Indicator values are not defined for the 538 field.
example

| 538 | | System requirements: Graphical Web browser (Netscape |

	Navigator 3.0 or higher, or Microsoft Internet Explorer)
538	Mode of access: World Wide Web.
538	VHS.
538	Disc characteristics: CD-ROM.
538	Requires a DVD player.

SUBJECT ACCESS

Subject access to nonprint resources helps users to identify and locate resources, particularly when resources are maintained in a closed collection or are not available in a physical format, as is the case for Internet resources. Subject headings are used to provide access to resources through *personal names*, *corporate names*, *topical terms*, or *geographic names*. Subject headings may be further subdivided by form division (format of material), general subdivisions, chronological subdivisions, and geographic subdivisions. Meeting names and subject added entries for uniform titles are not included in this text.

PERSONAL NAME

Provide subject access to personal names in the 600 field, **Subject Added Entry—Personal Name**, which is repeatable. Personal names are included in a bibliographic record when a resource is about an individual or individuals, or contains a significant portion of information about an individual or individuals.

The following subfields are available for use in the 600 field: ‡a personal name; ‡c titles associated with a name; ‡d dates associated with a name; ‡v form subdivision; ‡x general subdivision; ‡y chronological subdivision; ‡z geographic subdivision. There are additional subfields that may be used with the 600; this text focuses discussion and examples on those that are most predominantly used.

The initial indicator value indicates type of name. An initial article value of 0 indicates entry under forename; 1 indicates entry under single surname. The second indicator value provides source of name heading. A second indicator value of 0 indicates that a name is from the Library of Congress Name Authority file. Additional information is available on the USMARC Web page at http://lcweb.loc.gov/marc/bibliographic/ecbdsubj.html #mrcb600.

example

600	00	Cher,‡d1946-
600	10	Day-Lewis, Daniel.
600	10	Weinberg, Valerie Ann.
600	10	Irving, Henry,‡cSir,‡d1838-1905.
600	10	Ellington, Duke,‡d1899-1974.
600	10	King, Martin Luther,‡cJr.,‡d 1929-1968‡xAssassination.
600	10	Krupa, Gene,‡d1909-1973‡vBiography.
600	10	Shakespeare, William,‡d1564 1616‡xStage history ‡y1800-1950.
600	10	Gogh, Vincent van,‡d1853-1890‡xMuseums‡zNetherlands‡zAmsterdam.

CORPORATE NAME

Provide subject access to corporate names in the 610 field, **Subject Added Entry—Corporate Name,** which is repeatable. Corporate names are included in a bibliographic record when a resource is about a corporation or corporations, or contains a significant portion of information about a corporation or corporations.

The following subfields are available for use in the 610 field: ‡a corporate or jurisdiction names; ‡b subordinate units; ‡v form subdivision; ‡x general subdivision; ‡y chronological subdivision; ‡z geographic subdivision. There are additional subfields that may be used with the 610; this text focuses discussion and examples on those that are most predominantly used.

The initial indicator value indicates form of entry for names. An initial indicator value of 1 is for jurisdiction name; 2 is for a name presented in direct order. A second indicator value of 0 indicates that a name is from the Library of Congress Name Authority file. Additional information is available on the USMARC Web page at http://lcweb.loc.gov/marc/bibliographic/ ecbdsubj.html#mrcb610.

example

610	20	Lyceum Theatre (London, England)
610	10	United States.‡bDept. of the Interior.
610	20	Harvard University‡xFunds and scholarships‡vHandbooks, manuals, etc.
610	20	Microsoft Corporation‡xHistory.
610	20	Grand Central Terminal (New York, N.Y.)‡xHistory‡y20th century.
610	20	Salvation Army‡zEngland.

TOPICAL TERMS

Provide subject access to topical terms in the 650 field, **Subject Added Entry—Topical Term**, which is repeatable. Terms used in the 650 may describe form of the resource (Motion pictures, Spanish) or content (Jazz, Bicycle touring).

The following subfields are available for use in the 650 field: ‡a topical term or geographic name as entry element; ‡v form division; ‡x general subdivision; ‡y chronological subdivision; ‡z geographic subdivision. There are additional subfields that may be used with the 650; this text focuses discussion and examples on those that are most predominantly used.

The initial article value indicates level of subject; blank indicates that no information has been provided. In most cases, subject headings supplied by catalogers or provided in records available through union databases will have an initial indicator value of blank. A second indicator value of 0 indicates that a name is from the Library of Congress Name Authority file. Additional information is available on the USMARC Web page at http://lcweb.loc.gov/marc/bibliographic/ecbdsubj.html#mrcb650.
example

650	0	Violence in art.
650	0	Grandparents as parents‡xServices for‡zNew Jersey ‡vDirectories.
650	0	Crime prevention‡xCitizen participation.
650	0	American prose literature‡y19th century.
650	0	Artists‡zUnited States.

GEOGRAPHIC TERMS

Provide subject access to geographic terms in the 651 field, **Subject Added Entry—Geographic Name**, which is repeatable.

The following subfields are available for use in the 651 field: ‡a geographic name; ‡v form division; ‡x general subdivision; ‡y chronological subdivision; ‡z geographic subdivision. There are additional subfields that may be used with the 651; this text focuses discussion and examples on those that are most predominantly used.

The initial indicators are undefined for this field. A second indicator value of 0 indicates that a name is from the Library of Congress Name Authority file. Additional information is available on the USMARC Web page at http://lcweb.loc.gov/marc/bibliographic/ecbdsubj.html#mrcb651.

example

651	0	Brooklyn (New York, N.Y.)
651	0	Manhattan (New York, N.Y.)‡vTours‡vMaps.
651	0	United States‡xPopulation‡xStatistics.
651	0	United States‡xHistory‡yCivil War, 1861-1865.
651	0	United States‡xHistory‡xStudy and teaching (Higher) ‡zNew Jersey.

ADDED ENTRIES

Added entries provide access to personal and corporate names that are not main entries yet serve as important additional access points. Name added entries include directors, cast, editors, publishers, or production companies. Title added entries provide additional access for titles related to the main work.

PERSONAL NAME

Provide access to personal names in the 700 field, **Added Entry—Personal,** which is repeatable. Personal name added entries differ from personal names in the 600 in that they provide different types of information, and would be found in an online catalog using different types of searches (subject versus personal name).

The following subfields are available for use in the 700 field: ‡a personal name; ‡c titles or other words associated with a particular name; ‡d dates; ‡4 relator code. A list of relator codes is available on the USMARC Web page at http://lcweb.loc.gov/marc/relators/. There are additional subfields that may be used with the 700; this text focuses discussion and examples on those that are most predominantly used.

The initial indicator value indicates type of name. An initial article value of 0 indicates entry under forename; 1 indicates entry under single surname. A blank second indicator value indicates that no information is provided; a second indicator value of 2 indicates an analytical entry, and means the item in the bibliographic record contains the work represented by the added entry. Additional information is available on the USMARC Web page at http://lcweb.loc.gov/marc/bibliographic/ecbdadde.html #mrcb700.

example

700	0	Liberace,‡d1919-
700	1	Glenn, Tyree.
700	1	Irving, Henry,‡cSir,‡d1838-1905.
700	1	Severinsen, Doc,‡d1927-
700	1	Fellini, Federico.‡4drt
700	1	Binoche, Juliette,‡d1964- ‡4prf

CORPORATE NAME

Provide access to corporate names in the 710 field, **Added Entry—Corporate Name**, which is repeatable. Corporate name added entries differ from corporate names in the 610 in that they provide different types of information, and would be found in an online catalog using different types of searches (subject versus corporate name). It is used to include additional access points in the form of names taken from the 245, **Title Statement**, 260, **Publication, Distribution, etc. (Imprint)**, or 511, **Participant or Performer Note** fields, or other fields deemed appropriate by the cataloging agency.

The following subfields are available for use in the 710 field: ‡a corporate name or jurisdiction name; ‡b subordinate unit; and ‡4 relator code. There are additional subfields that may be used with the 710; this text focuses discussion and examples on those that are most predominantly used.

The initial indicator value indicates type of corporate name. An initial article value 1 indicates entry in jurisdiction order; a value of 2 indicates entry in direct order. A blank second indicator value indicates that no information is provided; a second indicator value of 2 indicates an analytical entry, and means the item in the bibliographic record contains the work represented by the added entry. Additional information is available on the USMARC Web page at http://lcweb.loc.gov/marc/bibliographic/ecbdadde.html#mrcb710.

example

710	1	United States.‡bArmy.
710	2	Warner Home Video.
710	2	United States.‡bBureau of the Census.
710	2	Beatles.‡4prf
260		San Diego, CA :‡bPuppet Productions,‡cc1986.
710	2	Puppet Productions, Inc.

UNIFORM TITLE

Provide access to uniform titles in the 730 field, **Added Entry—Uniform Title**, which is repeatable. Uniform titles provide a title related to the resource. Examples include radio or television programs, or motion pictures.

The following subfields are available for use in the 730 field: ‡a uniform title; ‡f date of a work; ‡h medium; ‡k form subheading; ‡l language. There are additional subfields that may be used with the 730; this text focuses discussion and examples on those that are most predominantly used.

The initial indicator value indicates number of nonfiling characters (0-9). A second blank second indicator value indicates that no information is provided; a second indicator value of 2 indicates an analytical entry, and means the item in the bibliographic record contains the work represented by the added entry. Additional information is available on the USMARC Web page at http://lcweb.loc.gov/marc/bibliographic/ecbdadde.html#mrcb730. example

245	00	Radio nostalgia‡h[kit].
505	0	Amos 'n Andy - - Charlie McCarthy show - - Fibber McGee & Molly - - You bet your life.
730	0	Amos 'n Andy (Radio program)
730	0	You bet your life (Radio program)

RELATED TITLES

Provide access to titles related to the work described in the 245 field, **Title Statement** using the 740 field, **Added Entry—Uncontrolled Related/Analytical Title**, which is repeatable. The 740 field is created using information taken from 500, **General Note**, or 505, **Formatted Contents Note** fields, or other fields deemed appropriate by the cataloging agency.

The following subfields are available for use in the 740 field: ‡a uncontrolled related/analytical title; ‡h medium; ‡n number of part/section of a work; ‡p name of part/section of a work. There are additional subfields that may be used with the 740; this text focuses discussion and examples on those that are most predominantly used.

The initial indicator value indicates number of nonfiling characters (0-9). A blank second indicator value indicates that no information is provided; a second indicator value of 2 indicates an analytical entry, and means the item in the bibliographic record contains the work represented by the added entry. Additional information is available on the USMARC Web page at http://lcweb.loc.gov/marc/bibliographic/ecbdadde.html#mrcb740. example

245	00	Insight‡h[kit].‡pGraphics I.
505	0	Part 1. Advertising : art at work - - pt. 2. Advertising : layout design.
740	0	Advertising : art at work.
740	0	Advertising : layout design.
740	0	Art at work.
740	0	Layout design.

EXAMPLES OF BIBLIOGRAPHIC RECORDS

Examples follow on the next page.

Figure 6-1 Kit With Various Component Parts

Control   **Bib**   MARC Hldgs   All Volumes

Fixed Fields

Rec_Type: a	Bib_Lvt: m	Enc_Lvt:	Desc: a	TypeCtrl:
Entrd: 941216	Dat_Tp: q	Date1: 1990	Date2: 1994	Ctry: dcu
Lang: eng	Mod_Rec:	Source: d	Illus: a	Audience:
Repr:	Cont:	GovtPub:	ConfPub: 0	Festschr: 0
Indx: 0	Fiction: 0	Biog:		

Bibliographic Info

Old Geac BCN: 980			01239576	
Date/time stamp: 005	⬇	⬇	19941219064414.0
Phys descrip codes: 007	⬇	⬇	ou
Local system #: 035	⬇	⬇	(CStRLIN)NJRG94-B33866
Cataloging source: 040	⬇	⬇	NjR|cNjR|dNjR
Local LC call number: 090	⬇	⬇	|i12/19/94 TZ
Corporate author: 110	⬇	1 ⬇	United States.|bNational Education Goals Panel.
Title: 245	⬇	10 ⬇	Community action toolkit|h[kit] :|ba do-it-yourself kit for education renewal /|cNational Education Goals Panel.
Portion of title: 246	⬇	30 ⬇	Do-it-yourself kit for education renewal|h[kit]
Publication info: 260	⬇	⬇	Washington, D.C. :|bThe Panel, |c[199-?]
Physical descrip: 300	⬇	⬇	1 v. (various pagings) :|bill. (some col.) ;|c28 cm. +|e1 guide to goals and standards (36 p. : col. ill. ; 22 cm.) + 1 community organizing guide (56 p. ; 22 cm.) + 1 local goals reporting handbook (80 p. : col. ill. ; 22 cm.) + 1 guide to getting out your message (80 p. ; 22 cm.) + 1 sound cassette + 1 computer disk (3 1/2 in.) in container 29 x 29 x 8 cm.
General Note: 500	⬇	⬇	The accompanying sound cassette contains 4 public service announcements. The accompanying computer file is in WordPerfect format, and allows

Figure 6-1 *Continued*

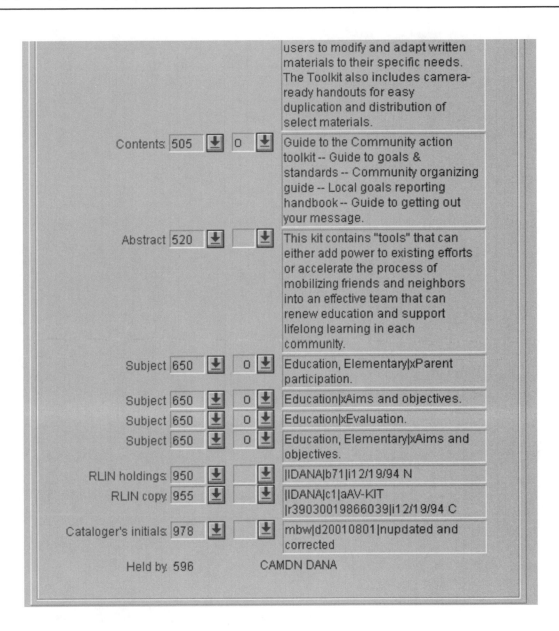

Figure 6-2 Kit With Various Component Parts

| Control | **Bib** | MARC Hldgs | Vol/Copy |

Fixed Fields

Rec_Type: a	Bib_Lvl: m	Enc_Lvl:	Desc: a	TypeCtrl:
Entrd: 010726	Dat_Tp: s	Date1: 2000	Date2:	Ctry: nju
Lang: eng	Mod_Rec:	Source: d	Illus:	Audience:
Repr:	Cont: b	GovtPub: s	ConfPub: 0	Festschr: 0
Indx: 0	Fiction: 0	Biog:		

Bibliographic Info

Field	Tag	Ind	Data
Phys descrip codes:	007		ou
Cataloging source:	040		NjR|cNjR
Geographic area code:	043		n-us-nj
LC Call Number:	050	4	QE445.N5|bN4 2000
Corporate author:	110	2	New Jersey Geological Survey.
Title:	245	10	New Jersey rocks and sediments |h[kit] /|cSterling Hills Mining Museum.
Variant title:	246	3	NJ rocks and sediments|h[kit]
Variant title:	246	3	New Jersey rocks & sediments |h[kit]
Variant title:	246	3	NJ rocks & sediments|h[kit]
Publication info:	260		Trenton, N.J. :|bThe Survey : |bDistributed by New Jersey Department of Environmental Protection, Division of Science and Research,|c2000.
Physical descrip:	300		various pieces +|e1 rock and sediment container + 1 guide (36 p. : ill. ; 28 cm.) + 1 booklet (20 p. ; 22 cm.) + 1 looseleaf (26 x 30 cm.) in kit (32 x 27 x 13 cm.)
General Note:	500		Container has set of 12 rocks, 5 sediments, and a geologic map of New Jersey
General Note:	500		Map includes text and small physiographic map on verso.
General Note:	500		Guide titled New Jersey rocks and sediments kit.

Figure 6-2 *Continued*

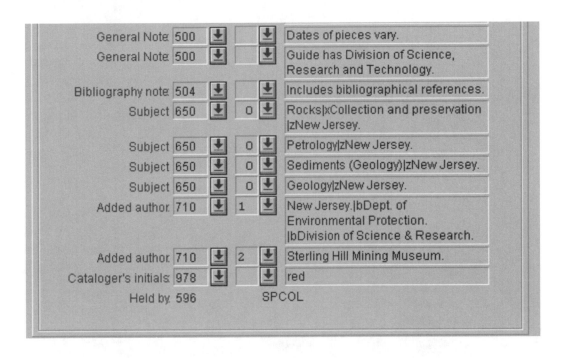

Figure 6-3 Kit With Various Pieces

| Control | **Bib** | MARC Hldgs | Vol/Copy |

Fixed Fields

Rec_Type:	Bib_Lvt: m	Enc_Lvt:	Desc:		TypeCtrl:
Entrd: 80425	Dat_Tp: s	Date1: 1968	Date2:	Ctry: cau
Lang: eng	Mod_Rec:	Source: d	Time:	Audience: g
Accomp:	GovtPub:	Type_Mat: g	Tech: n	

Bibliographic Info

Old Geac BCN: 980	00352117
Phys descrip codes: 007	ou
Local system #: 035	(CStRLIN)NJRGMG10137702F
Cataloging source: 040	|dNjR
Local call number: 099	80
Title: 245	00	Election U.S.A.|h[kit].
Publication info: 260	Lakewood, Calif. :|bCivic Educational Aids,|cc1968.
Physical descrip: 300	various pieces in container (29 x 52 x 4 cm.)
Subject term: 650	0	Presidents|zUnited States |xElection.
Subject term: 650	0	Educational games.
Added Author: 710	21	Civic Educational Aids (Firm)
RLIN Holdings: 950	|IDGLSS|a80|d\A-V KIT|i01/01/01 N |p4|x560
RLIN copy: 955	A-V KIT|c1|r39030004836518
Cataloger's initials: 978	mbw|d20010801|nupdated and corrected
Held by: 596	DGLSS

REFERENCES

Frost, Carolyn O. 1989. *Media Access and Organization: A Cataloging and Reference Sources Guide for Nonbook Materials.* Englewood, Colo.: Libraries Unlimited.

Joint Steering Committee for the Revision of AACR2. 1998. *Anglo-American Cataloguing Rules, Second Edition, 1998 Revision.* Chicago: American Library Association.

Library of Congress. Network Development and MARC Standards Office. "MARC 21 Concise Format for Bibliographic Data, 1999 English Edition, Update No. 2 (October 2001)" Washington, D.C.: Library of Congress (October 2001) Available at: *http://lcweb.loc.gov/marc/bibliographic/ecbd007s.html#mrcb0070.*

Network Development and MARC Standards Office, Library of Congress in cooperation with Standards and Support, National Library of Canada. 1999. *MARC 21 Format for Bibliographic Data Including Guidelines for Content Designation, 1999 Edition.* Washington, D.C.: Library of Congress Distribution Service.

7 MICROFORMS

OVERVIEW

Microforms have long been a fundamental part of the collections of libraries. This format enables libraries to provide access to large collections that may no longer be available in print, or when print counterparts are fragile and handling is not advised. Microforms also provide additional access when print counterparts are unavailable. They allow libraries to provide access to older runs of serials or other large collections that could not be housed as easily if available in print. Microforms continue to be a challenging format to catalog. Collection development and management of microforms, as well as cataloging of microforms, is often a speciality since this format has unique issues.

Level of description provided for microforms depends on a library's collection, available staff, and the importance of microforms to their holdings. A library may choose brief (or at least less full treatment) cataloging for very large microform sets. All examples included in this chapter use full level description.

The type of classification provided for microforms varies with type and size of library. Libraries may provide Library of Congress Classification numbers or Dewey Decimal numbers, accession numbers, may arrange microforms alphabetically by title, or arrangement may be according to type of material represented (serials, government documents, monographs). Arrangement and classification varies by library and how they provided access.

The glossary in *AACR2R (1998:619)* defines microfiche as "A sheet of film bearing a number of microimages in a two-dimensional array." The glossary defines microfilm as "A length of film bearing a number of microimages in linear array." Last, the glossary defines microforms as "A generic term for any medium, transparent or opaque, bearing microimages." The following categories of microforms are covered in this chapter: microforms and microfiche. Microopaques and aperture cards are not included in this text.

ELEMENTS OF BIBLIOGRAPHIC RECORDS FOR MICROFORMS

The category of resources referred to as microforms includes microform reels (16 and 35 mm.) and microfiche.

The following information is necessary to create bibliographic records for microforms:

- Chief Source of Information
- Prescribed Sources of Information
- Choice of Main Entry
- International Standard Book Number (ISBN)
- Cataloging Source
- Language Code
- Geographic Information
- Library of Congress Call Number
- Title
- Title Variations
- General Material Designation (GMD)
- Statement of Responsibility
- Edition
- Place of Publication and/or Distribution, or Manufacture, etc.
- Name of Publisher(s) and/or Distributor(s)
- Date of Publication, Distribution, Copyright, Manufacture, etc.
- Physical Description
- Series
- Notes
- Subject Access
- Added Entries (Personal and/or Corporate Names, Title Added Entries)
- Classification

CHIEF SOURCE OF INFORMATION

The chief source of information for microforms is the title frame or title card. In microfiche sets, the title card or first card often serves as the chief source of information. Rule 11.0B1, *AACR2R (1998)* states that when a title card is lacking, eye-readable information on the top of the cards may be used. If a title appears in abbreviated form on the microform while the full title appears on the container or is available in accompanying materials, the container or accompanying materials may be used as the chief source of information. In such cases, the source of title must be provided in a note.

PRESCRIBED SOURCES OF INFORMATION

Rule 11.0B2, *AACR2R (1998)* states that the following sources of information should be consulted when creating bibliographic records for microforms:

- Title/statement of responsibility- Chief source of information
- Edition- Chief source of information, remainder of resource, or container
- Publication, distribution, manufacture, etc.- Chief source of information, remainder of resource, or container
- Physical Description- Any source of information may be consulted
- Series- Chief source of information, remainder of resource, or container
- Notes- Any source of information may be consulted

CHOICE OF MAIN ENTRY

Main entry may be under personal authorship or corporate authorship, or title main entry may be chosen. Some library professionals feel that the issue of main entry is not as pressing in an online environment where a variety of types of searches may be performed to locate an item. However, Rule 21.1A1, *AACR2R (1998)* defines a personal author as the individual chiefly responsible for a resource's intellectual or artistic content. Rule 21.1B1, *AACR2R (1998)* defines a corporate author as an organization or group of persons with a particular name that functions as an entity. Lastly, Rule 21.1C1, *AACR2R (1998)* states that a resource should be entered under title proper (or uniform title if appropriate) when: personal authorship is unknown or shared by a large number of individuals, and authorship can not be attributed to one particular individual or when a resource is not issued by a corporate body; or when a resource is a collection of works by different individuals or corporate bodies.

For some resources, title main entry is the most logical choice since the nonprint resource is the result of the work of many individuals and/or corporate bodies, and it is not possible to attribute authorship to a particular individual or corporate body. Lack of a statement of responsibility is another reason why title main entry is chosen for some nonprint resources.

example

| 110 | 2 | Unesco.‡bExecutive Board. |
| 245 | 10 | List of Executive Board documents‡h[microform] :‡b1946-1982. |

| 100 | 1 | Hakluyt, Richard,‡d1552?-1616. |
| 245 | 14 | The principal navigations, voyages, traffiques and discoveries of the English nation‡h[microform]. |

| 245 | 00 | North American Phalanx‡h[microform]. |

Physical Description

Physical description is provided both in fixed fields and the 300 field, **Physical Description**. The 007 field, **Physical Description Fixed Field—General Information** provides information on physical description in alphabetic coded form.

The 007 field for microforms has 13 characters defined for use. Selected values are provided in the following text.

Position 00- Category of material; is always **h** for "microform"

Position 01- SMD;"**d** for "microfilm reel"; **e** for "microfiche"

Position 02- Undefined; leave blank

Position 03- Positive/Negative characteristics; **a** positive; **b** negative; **m** mixed polarity

Position 04- Dimensions; **a** 8 mm; **d** 16 mm

Position 05- Reduction ratio range; **a** low reduction; **b** normal reduction; **c** high reduction; **u** unknown

Position 06-08- Reduction ratio

Position 09- Color; **b** black and white; **c** multicolored; **m** mixed

Position 10- Emulsion on film; **a** silver halide; **b** diazo; **m** mixed emulsion; **u** unknown

Position 11- Generation; **a** first generation; **b** printing master; **c** service copy

Position 12- Base of film; **a** safety base, undetermined; **i** nitrate base; **m** mixed base; **u** unknown

example

```
007              hd afabaca
h = microform
d = microfilm reel
blank
a = a positive
f = 35 mm.
a = low reduction ratio
b = monochrome
a = silver halide emulsion
c = service copy
a = safety base, undetermined

007              he mlbcubu
h = microform
e = microfiche
blank
m = mixed polarity
l = 3 x 5 in.
b = normal reduction ratio
c = color
u = emulsion unknown
b = printing master
u = safety base unknown
```

A full list of values for the 007 field is available on the USMARC Web page at http://lcweb.loc.gov/marc/bibliographic/ecbd007s.html.

International Standard Book Number (ISBN)

Monographic resources are often assigned ISBNs. Provide this information in the 020 field, **International Standard Book Number,** which is repeatable. This information can be helpful in identifying specific versions of a resource.

The following subfields are used in the 020: ‡a ISBN; ‡c terms of availability (price).

There are no indicators defined for the 020 field.
example

```
020        0780619900 (set) :‡c$300.00
020        0333776151 (Macmillan ISBN)
```

Cataloging Source

Information on the origin of a bibliographic record, plus any institutions that have modified a record, is provided in the 040 field, **Cataloging Source**, which is not repeatable.

The following subfields are available for use in the 040 field: ‡a original cataloging agency; ‡c transcribing agency (which is typically the institution in ‡a); and ‡d modifying agency. There are other subfields that may be used in the 040; this discussion is limited to those that are most predominantly used.

There are no indicators defined for the 040 field.
example

Original cataloging record created and transcribed by Rutgers University Libraries
040   NjR‡cNjR

Original cataloging record created and transcribed by Rutgers University Libraries, modified by Library X.
040   NjR‡NjR‡dXyZ

Original cataloging record created and transcribed by Rutgers University Libraries, modified at a later date by Rutgers University Libraries.
040   NjR‡NjR‡dNjR

Language Code

Provide information on language(s) present in a resource in the 041 field, **Language Code**, which is not repeatable. Information in the 041 is provided in alphabetic coded form. The 041 works in conjunction with the 546 field, **Language Note**.

Codes are provided according to their predominance in the resource (Network Development and MARC Standards Office, Library of Congress, 1999). The 041 field can provide codes for a maximum of six languages. If more than six languages are present in the resource, the language for the title is coded as "mul"(multiple) to represent all the languages.

The following subfields are used in the 041: ‡a language code for text, sound track, or separate title; ‡b language code for summary or subtitle; ‡d language code for sung or spoken text; ‡e language code for librettos; ‡g language code for accompanying materials other than librettos; ‡h language code for original and/or intermediate translations of text.

The initial indicator value indicates whether a resource is or includes a translation. An initial indicator of 0 indicates that the resource is not a translation and does not include a translation; a value of 1 indicates that the item is a translation or includes a translation.

example

| 041 | 1 | freita‡gengfreita |
| 546 | | In French and Italian; program notes in English, French, and Italian. |

| 041 | 1 | ‡dgerita‡egeritaengfre‡hgerita‡genggerfreitaspa‡ henggerfre |
| 546 | | Program notes by Alan Newcombe, Richard Osborne, Klaus Bennert, and Francis Drêsel, in English, German and French, with Italian and Spanish translations, and texts of the vocal works, in German and Italian, with English and French translations (81, 16 p. : ill.) included. |

Geographic Information

Provide information on the geographic area presented, described, covered, etc. by the resource in the 043 field, **Geographic Area Code,** which is not repeatable. The 043 can accommodate 1-3 codes, which are represented in alphabetic coded form. Multiple geographic codes are separated by a ‡a.

Indicator values are not defined for the 043 field.

example

Resource contains information pertaining to New Jersey, in the United States
043   n-us-nj

Resource contains information pertaining to the Great Plains region in the United States
043   np- - - - -

Resource contains information pertaining to Japan
043   a-ja- - -

Resource contains information pertaining to Spain and Mexico
043   e-sp- - -‡an-mx- - -

A full list of geographic area codes is available on the USMARC Web page at http://lcweb.loc.gov/marc/geoareas/.

Library of Congress Call Number

Provide a Library of Congress Call Number (if applicable according to the cataloging agency's policies and procedures for nonprint resources) in the 050 field, **Library of Congress Call Number,** which is repeatable. Some institutions have policies governing whether an LC Call Number is included in the bibliographic portion of a record when their records are submitted to a national online bibliographic utility such as RLIN or OCLC.

The following subfields are available for use in the 050 field: ‡a classification number; ‡b item number.

The initial indicator value indicates whether the item is in Library of Congress's collection. An initial value of blank indicates that no information is provided, and is used when libraries other than the Library of Congress provide classification numbers. The second indicator value indicates source of call number. Classification numbers provided by Library of Congress have a second indicator value of zero; classification numbers provided by other libraries have a second indicator value of 4.

example

| 050 | 0 | HB1335‡b.M84 |
| 050 | 4 | GB1399.4.N5‡bF566 1971 |

TITLE INFORMATION

Includes title, general material designation, remainder of title, and statement of responsibility.

Title

Consult the chief source of information first. If it is lacking or provides limited or no information, consult the prescribed sources of information. In the absence of chief or prescribed sources of information, a title may be supplied by the cataloger. The supplied title must be bracketed, and the source of title must be documented in a general note.

Title information is provided in the 245 field, **Title Statement**. The following subfields are available for use in the 245 field: ‡a title; ‡b remainder of title; ‡c statement of responsibility; ‡h GMD; ‡n number of part/section; ‡p name of part/section. One method of presenting subfields is to discuss them in the order in which they are used in bibliographic records, rather than alphabetically. However, the alphabetic approach is used in this text, and has been modeled after authoritative sources of information, such as *Concise MARC Format* and the RLIN and OCLC cataloging manuals. Placement of the subfields is illustrated in examples and illustrations. There are additional subfields that may be used in the 245; this text focuses discussion and examples on those that are most predominantly used.

Rule 1.1B1, *AACR2R (1998)*, instructs catalogers to transcribe the title proper exactly as to wording, order, and spelling, but not necessarily to capitalization and punctuation. Titles are provided in the 245 field, ‡a, which is not repeatable.

Indicator values in the 245 field indicate if a title added entry will be generated. Most nonprint items are cataloged using title main entry. Nonprint resources are rarely entered under an author (corporate or personal) main entry. (A discussion of choice of main entry for nonbook resources is provided in the following paragraph.) For this reason, the majority of nonprint resources will have a first indicator value of 0. A first indicator value of 1 is used when a title added entry will be generated. The second indicator specifies number of nonfiling characters, with a range of 0-9 available.

example

Title from chief source of information:

| 245 | 00 | Kyushu-Okinawa Summit 2000 official guide |

Title supplied by cataloger:

| 245 | 00 | [Documentary on Douglass College, Rutgers University] |
| 500 | | Title supplied by cataloger. |

| 245 | 04 | The Microfiche collection of information on gerontology & geriatric medicine |
| 245 | 00 | Socialist Party of America papers, 1919-1976, addendum |

Remainder of Title

The 245 field also provides the remainder of a title or other information, such as parallel titles. Provide this information in the ‡b, which is not repeatable.

example

| 245 | 00 | Relapse and conditioning‡h[microform] :‡bcognitive and physiological changes in alcoholics after exposure to alcohol. |
| 245 | 00 | Canterbury Cathedral library‡h[microform] :‡bcatalogue of pre-1801 printed books. |

Title Variations

Provide title variations in the 246 field, **Varying Form of Title,** which is repeatable. The 246 provides other titles by which a resource may be known; this includes abbreviations or acronyms, parallel titles in another language, or when one title appears on external packaging and another title is given in the chief source of information. Providing access to title variations permits users to search for a resource in multiple ways. The 246 field also generates a title display in online catalogs.

The following subfields are available for use in the 246 field: ‡a title; ‡b remainder of title or parallel title; ‡h medium; ‡i display text; ‡n number of part/section of a work; ‡p name of a part/section of a work. There are additional subfields that may be used with the 246; this text focuses discussion and examples on those that are most predominantly used.

The initial indicator value indicates note or added entry. The second indicator value is used to provide information on type of title. A complete list of indicator values is available on the USMARC Web page at http://lcweb.loc.gov/marc/bibliographic/ecbdtils.html#mrcb246.

example

Portion of the main title

| 245 | 00 | History and genealogy of Fenwick's Colony‡h[microform]. |
| 246 | 30 | Fenwick's Colony‡h[microform] |

Remainder of title

| 245 | 00 | Relapse and conditioning‡h[microform] :‡bcognitive and physiological changes in alcoholics after exposure to alcohol |
| 246 | 30 | Cognitive and physiological changes in alcoholics after exposure to alcohol‡h[microform] |

Title variations

| 245 | 00 | North American Phalanx‡h[microform] |
| 246 | 1 | ‡iTitle on microfilm also appears as:‡aCollection 5, North American Phalanx records, 1841-1972 |

GENERAL MATERIAL DESIGNATION (GMD)

Use of a GMD is deemed optional by Rule 1.1C, *AACR2R (1998)*. There are several reasons why a library may choose to use GMDs. It indicates to users the format of a resource when a search is done in an online catalog since all resources with a specific GMD will cluster together. Additionally, the resource described in an online catalog may not readily be apparent to users even when the bibliographic record includes a physical description that includes type of resource and characteristics. Use of a GMD helps users to distinguish between different formats in which a title is available. For example, *Midnight Express* is the title of a book, as well as a motion picture, a motion picture sound track, and is also available on videorecording. However, there is a growing sentiment that GMDs are no longer useful, particularly in a Web-based environment in which some libraries use one bibliographic record to represent multiple manifestations of a title (a paper and an electronic version of a serial title, for example).

The GMD is included in the 245 field, ‡h and is enclosed in brackets. It immediately follows the information provided in ‡a and precedes the ‡b. It is not repeatable.

Two lists of GMDs are provided in *AACR2R (1998)*. The first list is for British cataloging agencies; Australian, Canadian, and American cataloging agencies use terms from the second list. Use the GMD "microform." Do not confuse the GMD with the SMD, which specifies type of material. Provide the GMD in the 245 field, ‡h, which is not repeatable.

example

245	04	The Microfiche collection of information on gerontology & geriatric medicine‡h[microform].
245	00	Socialist Party of America papers, 1919-1976, addendum‡h[microform].

STATEMENT OF RESPONSIBILITY

The statement of responsibility provides names of corporate bodies and/or individuals responsible for production, creation, manufacture, etc. of a microform. This information is taken from the chief or prescribed sources of information. Provide this information in the 245 field, ‡c. Names provided in the 245 field, ‡c are typically used to create name added entries in 7XX personal and corporate name added entry fields.

The statement of responsibility is included in the 245 field, ‡c, is preceded by a forward slash, and is not repeatable. Each corporate body or individual presented in the statement of responsibility is separated by semicolons. Per Rule 1.1F1, *AACR2R (1998)*, statements of responsibility are to be transcribed as they appear. Information taken from sources other than the chief source of information will be bracketed.

example

245	00	Calendar of business‡h[microform] /‡cSenate of the United States.
245	00	Gazetteer of Lithuania‡h[microform] :‡bnames / ‡capproved by the United States Board on Geographic Names.

EDITION

Provide edition information in the 250 field, **Edition Statement,** which is not repeatable. Edition information for nonprint resources is not limited to the term "edition," and includes "version," "release," "revision," or other terms deemed appropriate by the cataloging agency. Rule 11.2B1, *AACR2R (1998)* states that an edition statement should be provided when the item in hand contains differences from other editions of the microform or from a reissue of the microform.

The following subfields are available for use in the 250 field: ‡a edition statement; ‡b remainder of edition statement. There are additional subfields that may be used with the 250; this text focuses discussion and examples on those that are most predominantly used.

There are no indicators defined for the 250 field.
example

250	1st ed.
250	Librarians' ed.
250	2nd ed., Feb. 1990.
250	10th rev. ed.

PUBLICATION INFORMATION

Consult the chief and/or prescribed sources of information to obtain information on where and when a resource was published, distributed, manufactured, etc. Publication, distribution, manufacture, etc. information is provided in the 260 field, **Publication, Distribution, etc. (Imprint),** which is not repeatable.

PLACE OF PUBLICATION, DISTRIBUTION, MANUFACTURE, ETC.

The place of publication, distribution, manufacture, etc. is provided in the 260 field, ‡a. It is repeatable if there is more than one place of publication, or if a resource is published in one location and distributed in another, for example.

Generally, the city and country or state of publication are given. If only a city name is given, and it is necessary to record the country, state, etc., for purposes of identification and clarification,

record the supplied information in brackets, as per Rule 1.4C3, *AACR2R (1998)*.
example

```
260        Detroit, Mich.
260        Schmalkalden [Germany]
```

If a place of publication, distribution, manufacture, etc. is not provided, but may be ascertained, record in brackets with a question mark. Consult Rule 1.4C6, *AACR2R (1998)*, for further discussion of this topic.
example

```
260        [Denver?]
```

If no place of publication, distribution, manufacture, etc. is provided, and may not be ascertained, the abbreviation for the term "Sine loco," [S.l.], is used per Rule 1.4C6, *AACR2R (1998)*. The abbreviation is always bracketed.
example

```
260        [S.l.] :‡bMedia Mix Productions
```

DATE OF PUBLICATION, DISTRIBUTION, COPYRIGHT, MANUFACTURE, ETC.

Provide this information in the 260 field, ‡c, which is repeatable. However, the practice of repeating the ‡c is not widely used. Multiple dates, such as for date of production and copyright, may be included in the 260 field, ‡c.

Consult the chief and/or prescribed sources of information first. Record publication date, or distribution date if publication date is not available. In the absence of either date, record copyright date, which is preceded by a lower case "c." Information on date of publication, distribution, etc. is further outlined in Rule 1.4F, *AACR2R (1998)*.
example

Publication date
```
260        Media, Pa. :‡bEducational Clearinghouse,‡c1990.
```

Copyright date
```
260        Oxford :‡bIRL Press Ltd.,‡cc1986.
```

If information on publication, distribution, etc. date is not pro-

vided in either the chief or prescribed sources of information, approximate the date of publication. Approximated dates are bracketed.
example

Approximated date
260   [S.l.] :‡bT. Meyer Publishers,‡c[ca. 1997]

Probable date
260   Cherry Hill, N.J. :‡bAriel Press,‡[1990?]

Decade certain
260   Clifton, N.J. :‡bPiermatti Educational Resources,‡c[198-]

Probable decade
260   Chicago :‡bScholars Press,‡c[199-?]

Note: More information on dates is available in *AACR2R (1998)*, Chapter 1, "General Rules for Description."

Multipart items: Include a beginning date if the resource is not complete and/or is expected to continue indefinitely. An ending date may be included when a resource is complete. Rule 1.4F8, *AACR2R (1998)* notes that this practice is optional.
example

260   Palo Alto, Calif. :‡bDIALOG Information Services,‡c1965-
260   New Brunswick, N.J. :‡bRutgers University Libraries,‡c 1995-2000.

Unpublished items: Do not attempt to provide a place of publication, etc. or publisher, distributor, manufacturer, etc. name for unpublished items, as per Rule 1.4D9, *AACR2R (1998)*. Do not use the abbreviations "S.l." or "s.n." A date may be included for the item.
example

260   ‡c1999.
260   ‡c[2000?]

There are no indicators defined for the 260 field.

PHYSICAL DESCRIPTION

Includes extent (number and Specific Material Designation (SMD) of physical parts of an item), other physical details (color or sound characteristics, for example), dimensions, and information about accompanying materials.

The physical description is provided in the 300 field, **Physical Description**. The physical description field is repeatable, permitting a multilevel description, yet this option is not commonly applied.

EXTENT

Provide information on extent (number and SMD of parts), negative characteristics, color and illustrative characteristics, dimensions, and accompanying materials as per Rule 11.5B1, *AACR2R (1998)*. The extent (number and SMD of parts) of a resource is provided in the 300 field, **Physical Description**, ‡a and is not repeatable. The SMD is not identical to the GMD. It is used to specify material types, while the GMD describes the broad category of materials into which a resource may fall.
example

300	3 film reels
300	29 fiches

Note: Rule 11.5B1, *AACR2R (1998)* states that the term "micro" can be omitted from the SMD if a GMD is used. This choice is at the discretion of the cataloging agency.

Number of Frames

Rule 11.5B2, *AACR2R (1998)* instructs catalogers to provide number of frames for microfiche when possible. Number of frames is provided in the 300 field, **Physical Description**, ‡a.
example

300	29 fiches (29 fr. each)

NEGATIVE CHARACTERISTICS

Indicate when a microform is negative. Provide this information in the 300 field, **Physical Description**, ‡b.
example

300	3 film reels :‡bnegative
300	29 fiches (29 fr. each) :‡bnegative

ILLUSTRATIVE AND COLOR CHARACTERISTICS

Indicate when a microform contains illustrations; provide detail on type of illustrations (music, maps). If a microform is in color, or contains colored illustrations, indicate this as well. Provide this information in the 300 field, **Physical Description**, ‡b.
example

Contains illustrations
300   3 film reels :‡bill.

Contains maps
300   2 fiche :‡bmaps

Microform is in color and also has illustrations
300   3 film reels :‡bcol. & ill.

Microform is in color; contains no illustrations
300   2 fiche :‡bcol.

DIMENSIONS

The standard size for fiche is 10.5 (height) x 14.8 (width) centimeters (cm.). Do not provide dimensions for fiche unless larger than the standard size. Provide width of film for reels in millimeters (mm.); width is 16 or 35 mm. This information is provided in the 300 field, **Physical Description**, ‡c, which is not repeatable.
example

300   2 fiche :‡bmaps ;‡c11 x 15 cm.
300   3 film reels :‡bcol. ill., music ;‡c35 mm.
300   1 film reel :‡bill. ;‡c16 mm.

ACCOMPANYING MATERIALS

Provide information describing accompanying materials in one of three ways, per Rule 1.5E1, *AACR2R (1998)*: (1) at the end of the physical description; (2) in a note separate from the physical description; or (3) as part of a multilevel description.
example

As part of the physical description:
300   2 film reels (180 min.) :‡bsd., col. ;‡c16 mm. +‡e1 teacher's guide (25 p. : ill. ; 28 cm.)

Note: If more than one item is included in the ‡e, 300, each item is preceded by a space and a plus sign.

300	2 film reels (180 min.) :‡bsd., col. ;‡c16 mm. +‡e1 teacher's guide (25 p. : ill. ; 28 cm.) +3 student guides (24 p. ; 21 cm.) in folder.

In a separate note:

300	2 film reels (180 min.) :‡bsd., col. ;‡c16 mm.
500	Accompanied by teacher's guide titled: Safety and your child.

Multilevel description:

300	2 film reels (180 min.) :‡bsd., col. ;‡c16 mm.
300	1 sound cassette (40 min.) :‡banalog
300	50 p. :‡bill. ;‡c28 cm.

SERIES

Provide series treatment if available in the chief and/or prescribed sources of information. This text provides general series information; a detailed discussion of various types of series treatments is beyond the focus of this text. Series are represented in this text by the 440 field, **Series Statement/Added Entry—Title**, which is repeatable.

The following subfields are available for use in the 440 field: ‡a title; ‡n number of part/section; ‡p name of part/section; ‡v volume or numbering designation.

Provide series title in the 440, ‡a, which is not repeatable.

The first indicator value for the 440 field is undefined. The second indicator specifies number of nonfiling characters, with a range of 0-9 available.

Detailed information on series is available on the USMARC Web page at http://lcweb.loc.gov/marc/bibliographic/ecbdhome.html#mrcb440.
example

440	0	Library of African cinema
440	0	BMG classics

Provide information on numbered parts in the ‡n number of Part/Section of a Work.

example

| 440 | 0 | Langues de l'Orient.‡nI,‡pManuals |
| 440 | 0 | Baseball.‡nVolume 7,‡pFourth inning |

Provide the specific name of the part(s)/section(s) of a series in the ‡p name of Part/Section of a Work.
example

| 440 | 0 | The Great explorers.‡pThe Columbus series |
| 440 | 0 | Janua linguarum.‡pSeries minor |

Provide numbering designation, such as "volume" or "part" in the ‡v.
example

| 440 | 0 | BMG classics ;‡vvol. 32 |
| 440 | 0 | Medicine at the crossroads ;‡vMECR108 |

NOTES

Notes used for microforms provide a variety of information, including edition, contents, language, source of title, and summary. They are also used to describe characteristics of the microform or to note features unique to a library's copy of an item.

The notes in this section are provided in the order which they appear in MARC records. Notes are not arranged in numeric order by MARC tag number.

Notes of a very general nature are provided in the 500 field, **General Note,** which is repeatable. This type of note is more prevalent in nonprint cataloging than in cataloging for print resources. Examples of various types of general notes are given below.

NATURE, SCOPE, OR ARTISTIC OR OTHER FORM OF ITEM

Rule 11.7B1, *AACR2R (1998)* instructs catalogers to provide a note on these characteristics in the 500 field, **General Note** only when it is not apparent from the description. The 500 field is repeatable.
example

| 500 | | Microfilm of the originals in the Manuscript Dept. of the William R. Perkins Library, Duke University, Durham, N.C. |

LANGUAGE

Provide information on language(s) if more than one language is present in the microform, or if the microform is in a language (or languages) other than the primary language of the cataloging agency. Use the 546 field, **Language Note**, which is repeatable. It is used in conjunction with the 041 field, **Language Code**, which is not repeatable.

The initial article value of 0 indicates that the resource is not a translation or does not include a translation; an initial article value of 1 indicates that the resource is a translation or includes a translation.

example

041	0	spa
546		In Spanish.

041	1	fre‡bfreeng
546		In French with accompanying documentation in French and English.

A full list of language codes is available on the USMARC Web page at http://lcweb.loc.gov/marc/languages/.

SOURCE OF TITLE PROPER

Indicate source of title if not taken from chief or prescribed sources of information, or has been supplied by the cataloger as per Rule 11.7B3, *AACR2R (1998)*.

Provide this information in the 500 field, **General Note**, which is repeatable.
example

500	Title from microfiche header.
500	Description based on: 1976-77; title from cover.
500	Title from caption.

CREDITS

Provide the names of individuals or corporate bodies not named in the statement of responsibility who have contributed to the content of the microform. This information is provided in the 508 field, **Creation/Production Credits Note**, which is not repeatable.
example

508	Editorial advisor to guide: Joseph Criscenti.

| 508 | Pamphlet listing and guide to the microfiche collection by David Shaw and Sheila Hingley, assisted by Margaret Brown and Lawrence Dethan. |

EDITION AND HISTORY

Provide information on the resource, or use to provide history of the microform. This information is provided in the 500 field, **General Note,** which is repeatable, and differs from what is provided in the 250 field.
example

500	Distributed to depository libraries in microfiche, 1994-
500	Microfilmed for the New York Public Library by 3M IM Press.
500	Microfilm of ms. originals from the collection of the American Antiquarian Society.

PUBLICATION, DISTRIBUTION, ETC., AND DATE INFORMATION

"Make notes on publication, distribution, etc., details that are not included in the publication, distribution, etc., area and are considered to be important" (Joint Steering Committee for the Revision of *AACR2 (1998)*: 270, Rule 11.7B9).

Provide this information in the 500 field, **General Note,** which is repeatable.
example

| 500 | Guide published by: CIS Academic Editions. |
| 500 | Abstracted in Dissertation abstracts, v.25 (1964) no.4, p. 2551. |

PHYSICAL DESCRIPTION

Provide additional physical description not represented in the 007 field, **Physical Description Fixed Field—General Information,** or the 300 field, **Physical Description.** This information is provided in the 500 field, **General Note,** or 538 field, **System Details Note** (depending on criteria described); both are repeatable. Additional physical description includes reduction ratio, type of reader required to use the microform, nature of film, and other information deemed important by the cataloging agency.

REDUCTION RATIO

Per Rule 11.7B10, *AACR2R (1998)* provide reduction ratio when it differs from the standard range, which is 16X –30X).

500	Reduction ratio varies.
500	Reduction ratio unknown.
500	Very high reduction ratio (61-90 x).

TYPE OF READER

If a specific type of reader is required to use the microform, or significantly enhances usage, indicate this is a note.

500	Requires an Indus reader.
500	Intended for use with a rotary filmer/scanner.

NATURE OF FILM

Provide information on the nature of the film if important to users.

500	Diazo.
500	Silver halide.
500	Vesicular.

ACCOMPANYING MATERIALS

Provide additional information on accompanying materials in the 500 field, **General Note,** which is repeatable. Rule 11.7B11, *AACR2R (1998)* states that details of accompanying materials may be provided in a note when they are not included in the physical description or in a separate description.
example

500	Accompanied by: Southern women's diaries, a guide / Jane DuPree Begos.
500	Accompanying guide titled: Guide and index to women's diaries : segment 1, New England women.

SERIES

Provide series information for series in which the print original (for microforms that are not the original manifestation of a work) was a part. This information is provided in the 500 field, **General Note,** which is repeatable.
example

500	Originally issued in the series: Gerritsen collection of women's history.

DISSERTATIONS

Libraries frequently collect microform copies of dissertations and theses. Provide this information and "...a brief statement of the degree for which the author was a candidate...." (Joint Steering Committee for the Revision of *AACR2R (1998)*: 52). This information is provided in the 502 field, **Dissertation Note**, which is repeatable.
example

502	Dissertation (Ph.D.)—Colorado State University, 1990.
502	Thesis (Ed. D.)—Fordham University, 1992.

Information is recorded in a 500, **General Note** when information is taken from the original thesis or dissertation, yet the item in hand is not the original.
example

500	Based on the author's Ph. D. dissertation, LSU, 1979.

AUDIENCE

Provide information on target audience in the 521 field, **Target Audience Note**, which is repeatable.
example

521	For grades 2-6.
521	Adult.
521	College and university.

OTHER FORMATS

Provide information on other formats in which a microform has been issued in the 530 field, **Additional Physical Form Available Note**, which is repeatable.
example

530	Also available in print.
530	Also issued on CD-ROM.
530	Cumulations available on the Web.

SUMMARY

Provide a brief description of the contents of the microform. Since users may not browse for nonprint resources in the manner used for print resources, the summary should provide specific information to accurately describe the resource. Information taken from external or other sources of information should be noted. Generally, summaries should be limited to two-three sentences unless more information is warranted; this is determined by individual cataloging agencies.

This information is provided in the 520 field, **Summary, Etc.,** which is repeatable as needed. While not required, this information is beneficial to users.

The first indicator value provides an introductory phrase for the 520 field. A blank first indicator value generates the display "Summary." The second indicator value is undefined.

Additional information on indicator values for the 520 field is available on the USMARC Web page at http://lcweb.loc.gov/marc/bibliographic/ecbdnot1.html#mrcb520.
example

520   Summary: Contains correspondence, minutes of committee meetings and proceedings of conventions, financial records, court records, copies of speeches, press releases, organizers' reports, lists, photographs, broadsides, leaflets, pamphlets, books, and serials.

520   Summary: Contains detailed descriptions of all printed items held in the Cathedral Library dating from the beginning of printing in the 15th century through to 1800.

CONTENTS

Information detailing the contents of a resource is provided in the 505 field, **Formatted Contents Note,** which is repeatable. It provides individual titles or parts contained in a resource.

Contents notes in which the various parts of the note are coded are referred to as "enhanced." Enhanced contents notes contain a ‡t (title) and ‡r (statement of responsibility).

The first indicator value for the 505 field indicates completeness of the contents. A first indicator value of 0 indicates complete contents, a value of 1 is used for incomplete contents, and a value of 2 is used for partial contents. The second indicator value provides information on content designation. A second indicator value of 0 is used for enhanced contents. A second value of blank is used for nonenhanced contents notes. The indicators for an enhanced contents note are 00 (a nonenhanced contents has a single first indicator with a value from 0-2, or 8).

While not required, a contents note is useful to providing a description since the contents of a nonprint resource may not be browsed in the manner used for print resources.
example

505   0   Introduction to Drug literature index - - Introduction to Index medicus - - Introduction to International pharma-

		ceutical abstracts.
505	0	Ser. A., Reels 1-16; National file, general papers, 1919-1976 - - Ser. B., Reels 17-25; Youth and Young People's Socialist League, 1954-1975 - - Ser. C., Reels 25-35; State and local party files, 1951-1975 - - Ser. D., Reels 34-38; Printed material, 1957-1975.

Enhanced contents note

505	00	‡tBalcony rock /‡rD. Brubeck, P. Desmond - - ‡tOut of nowhere /‡r Heyman, J.W. Green - - ‡tLe souk /‡rD. Brubeck, P. Desmond - - ‡t Take the "A" train /‡rStrayhorn - - ‡tThe song is you/‡rHammerstein II, Kern - - ‡tDon't worry 'bout me /‡rKoehler, Bloom - - ‡tI want to be happy /‡rCaesar, Youmans.

NUMBERS

Provide numbers other than the ISBN which are important for identification of the microform in the 500 field, **General Note**, which is repeatable.
example

500	"Readex #522"- - Container.
500	"4765"- - Container.

DESCRIPTIVE OR LIBRARY SPECIFIC NOTES

Provide descriptive or copy specific information regarding a microform in a 500 field, **General Note**, which is repeatable.
example

500	Accompanying guides housed in Reference.
500	Use restricted to Special Collections and only by appointment.

"WITH" NOTES

Provide notes for titles that are not the first in a collective title. This information is provided in the 500 field, **General Note**, which is repeatable. Additionally, information provided in this type of note may also be used as the basis for a 740 field, **Added Entry—Uncontrolled Related/Analytical Title**.
example

500	With: The letters of Elizabeth Cady Stanton.
500	With: Not by ourselves alone.

NOTE RELATING TO ORIGINAL

Since microforms are often reproductions of resources that originally appeared in print, information about the original resource should be provided when possible and as necessary. Provide this information in the 500 field, **General Note**, which is repeatable.

There are cases when a cataloging agency provides description for the original resource in the 300 field, **Physical Description**, and all details (including physical description) of the reproduction are provided in the 533 field, **Reproduction Note**, which is repeatable. This treatment is used since it is presumed that users are seeking information on the original resource.

The LCRI pertaining to Chapter One, *AACR2R (1998)* outlines Library of Congress cataloging practice for microform reproductions of previously published materials and for dissertations. The LCRI stipulates that bibliographic data appropriate to the original resource must be provided in: title and statement of responsibility; edition; material specific details; publication, distribution, etc. information; physical description; and series. The LCRI also instructs catalogers to use the GMD "microform" in the title. Lastly, the LCRI states that information relating to the reproduction should be provided in a single 533 field, **Reproduction Note**, and should include the following information in this order: SMD of the microform; place and name of agency responsible for the microform; date of reproduction; series statement of reproduction if applicable; and notes relating to the reproduction if applicable.

The following subfields are available for use in the 533 field: ‡a type of reproduction; ‡b place of reproduction; ‡c agency responsible for reproduction; ‡d date of reproduction; ‡e physical description of reproduction; ‡f series statement of reproduction; ‡m dates and/or sequential designation of issues reproduced; ‡n note about reproduction; ‡7 fixed length data elements regarding reproduction (/0 = type of date/publication status; /1-4 = date 1; /5-8 = date 2; /9-11 = place of publication, production, execution; /12 = frequency; /13 = regularity; /14 = form of item) (Network Development and MARC Standards Office, Library of Congress, 1999).

Indicator values are not defined for the 533 field.

example

533	Microfiche.‡bAnn Arbor, MI :‡cUniversity Microfilms International‡d1985.‡e2 microfiches.‡7s1985 miu b
533	Microfiche.‡bMillwood, N.Y. ;‡cKTO Microform,‡d[1991]. ‡e1 microfiche : negative ; 11 x 15 cm.

SUBJECT ACCESS

Subject access to microforms helps users to identify and locate resources, particularly when resources are maintained in a closed collection or are not available in a physical format, as is the case for Internet resources. Subject headings are used to provide access to resources through *personal names, corporate names, topical terms,* or *geographic names.* Subject headings may be further subdivided by form division (format of material), general subdivisions, chronological subdivisions, and geographic subdivisions. Meeting names and subject added entries for uniform titles are not included in this text.

PERSONAL NAME

Provide subject access to personal names in the 600 field, **Subject Added Entry–Personal Name,** which is repeatable. Personal names are included in a bibliographic record when a resource is about an individual or individuals, or contains a significant portion of information about an individual or individuals.

The following subfields are available for use in the 600 field: ‡a personal name; ‡c titles associated with a name; ‡d dates associated with a name; ‡v form subdivision; ‡x general subdivision; ‡y chronological subdivision; ‡z geographic subdivision. There are additional subfields that may be used with the 600; this text focuses discussion and examples on those that are most predominantly used.

The initial indicator value indicates type of name. An initial article value of 0 indicates entry under forename; 1 indicates entry under single surname. The second indicator value provides source of name heading. A second indicator value of 0 indicates that a name is from the Library of Congress Name Authority file. Additional information is available on the USMARC Web page at http://lcweb.loc.gov/marc/bibliographic/ecbdsubj.html #mrcb600.
example

600	00	Cher,‡d1946
600	10	Day-Lewis, Daniel.
600	10	Irving, Henry,‡cSir,‡d1838-1905.
600	10	Ellington, Duke,‡d1899-1974.
600	10	King, Martin Luther,‡cJr.,‡d 1929-1968‡xAssassination.
600	10	Krupa, Gene,‡d1909-1973‡vBiography.

| 600 | 10 | Shakespeare, William,‡d1564-1616‡xStage history‡y1800-1950. |
| 600 | 10 | Gogh, Vincent van,‡d1853-1890‡xMuseums‡zNetherlands‡zAmsterdam. |

CORPORATE NAME

Provide subject access to corporate names in the 610 field, **Subject Added Entry—Corporate Name**, which is repeatable. Corporate names are included in a bibliographic record when a resource is about a corporation or corporations, or contains a significant portion of information about a corporation or corporations.

The following subfields are available for use in the 610 field: ‡a corporate or jurisdiction names; ‡b subordinate units; ‡v form subdivision; ‡x general subdivision; ‡y chronological subdivision; ‡z geographic subdivision. There are additional subfields that may be used with the 610; this text focuses discussion and examples on those that are most predominantly used.

The initial indicator value indicates form of entry for names. An initial indicator value of 1 is for jurisdiction name; 2 is for a name presented in direct order. A second indicator value of 0 indicates that a name is from the Library of Congress Name Authority file. Additional information is available on the USMARC Web page at http://lcweb.loc.gov/marc/bibliographic/ecbdsubj.html#mrcb610.
example

610	20	Lyceum Theatre (London, England)
610	10	United States.‡bDept. of the Interior.
610	20	Harvard University‡xFunds and scholarships‡vHandbooks, manuals, etc.
610	20	Microsoft Corporation‡xHistory.
610	20	Grand Central Terminal (New York, N.Y.)‡xHistory‡y20th century.
610	20	Salvation Army‡zEngland.

TOPICAL TERMS

Provide subject access to topical terms in the 650 field, **Subject Added Entry—Topical Term**, which is repeatable. Terms used in the 650 may describe form of the resource (Motion pictures, Spanish) or content (Jazz, Bicycle touring).

The following subfields are available for use in the 650 field: ‡a topical term or geographic name as entry element; ‡v form division; ‡x general subdivision; ‡y chronological subdivision; ‡z geographic subdivision. There are additional subfields that may be used with the 650; this text focuses discussion and examples on those that are most predominantly used.

The initial article value indicates level of subject; blank indicates that no information has been provided. In most cases, subject headings supplied by catalogers or provided in records available through union databases will have an initial indicator value of blank. A second indicator value of 0 indicates that a name is from the Library of Congress Name Authority file. Additional information is available on the USMARC Web page at http://lcweb.loc.gov/marc/bibliographic/ecbdsubj.html#mrcb650.
example

650	0	Violence in art.
650	0	Grandparents as parents‡xServices for‡zNew Jersey ‡vDirectories.
650	0	Crime prevention‡xCitizen participation.
650	0	American prose literature‡y19th century.
650	0	Artists‡zUnited States.

GEOGRAPHIC TERMS

Provide subject access to geographic terms in the 651 field, **Subject Added Entry—Geographic Name**, which is repeatable.

The following subfields are available for use in the 651 field: ‡a geographic name; ‡v form division; ‡x general subdivision; ‡y chronological subdivision; ‡z geographic subdivision. There are additional subfields that may be used with the 651; this text focuses discussion and examples on those that are most predominantly used.

The initial indicators are undefined for this field. A second indicator value of 0 indicates that a name is from the Library of Congress Name Authority file. Additional information is available on the USMARC Web page at http://lcweb.loc.gov/marc/bibliographic/ecbdsubj.html#mrcb651.
example

651	0	Brooklyn (New York, N.Y.)
651	0	Manhattan (New York, N.Y.)‡vTours‡vMaps.
651	0	United States‡xPopulation‡xStatistics.
651	0	United States‡xHistory‡yCivil War, 1861-1865.
651	0	United States‡xHistory‡xStudy and teaching (Higher) ‡zNew Jersey.

ADDED ENTRIES

Added entries provide access to personal and corporate names that are not main entries yet serve as important additional access points. Title added entries provide additional access for titles related to the main work. This information is provided in the 7XX fields, which are discussed in detail in the following paragraphs as they relate to microforms.

PERSONAL NAME

Provide access to personal names in the 700 field, **Added Entry— Personal**, which is repeatable. It is used to include additional access points in the form of names taken from the 245, **Title Statement** or other fields deemed appropriate by the cataloging agency. Personal name added entries differ from personal names in the 600 in that they provide different types of information, and would be found in an online catalog using different types of searches (subject versus personal name).

The following subfields are available for use in the 700 field: ‡a personal name; ‡c titles or other words associated with a particular name; ‡d dates; ‡4 relator code. A list of relator codes is available on the USMARC Web page at http://lcweb.loc.gov/marc/relators/. There are additional subfields that may be used with the 700; this text focuses discussion and examples on those that are most predominantly used.

The initial indicator value indicates type of name. An initial article value of 0 indicates entry under forename; 1 indicates entry under single surname. A blank second indicator value indicates that no information is provided; a second indicator value of 2 indicates an analytical entry, and means the item in the bibliographic record contains the work represented by the added entry. Additional information is available on the USMARC Web page at http://lcweb.loc.gov/marc/bibliographic/ecbdadde.html#mrcb700.

example

700	0	Liberace,‡d1919-
700	1	Glenn, Tyree.
700	1	Irving, Henry,‡cSir,‡d1838-1905.
700	1	Severinsen, Doc,‡d1927-
700	1	Fellini, Federico.‡4drt
700	1	Binoche, Juliette,‡d1964- ‡4prf

CORPORATE NAME

Provide access to corporate names in the 710 field, **Added Entry—Corporate Name**, which is repeatable. It is used to include additional access points in the form of names taken from the 245, **Title Statement**, 260, **Publication, Distribution, etc. (Imprint)** or other fields deemed appropriate by the cataloging agency. Corporate name added entries differ from corporate names in the 610 in that they provide different types of information, and would be found in an online catalog using different types of searches (subject versus corporate name).

The following subfields are available for use in the 710 field: ‡a corporate name or jurisdiction name; ‡b subordinate unit; and ‡4 relator code. There are additional subfields that may be used with the 710; this text focuses discussion and examples on those that are most predominantly used.

The initial indicator value indicates type of corporate name. An initial article value 1 indicates entry in jurisdiction order; a value of 2 indicates entry in direct order. A blank second indicator value indicates that no information is provided; a second indicator value of 2 indicates an analytical entry, and means the item in the bibliographic record contains the work represented by the added entry. Additional information is available on the USMARC Web page at http://lcweb.loc.gov/marc/bibliographic/ecbdadde.html#mrcb710.
example

710	1	United States.‡bArmy.
710	2	Warner Home Video.
710	2	United States.‡bBureau of the Census.
710	2	Beatles.‡4prf

UNIFORM TITLE

Provide access to uniform titles in the 730 field, **Added Entry—Uniform Title**, which is repeatable. Uniform titles provide a title related to the resource. Examples include radio or television programs, or motion pictures.

The following subfields are available for use in the 730 field: ‡a uniform title; ‡f date of a work; ‡h medium; ‡k form subheading; ‡l language. There are additional subfields that may be used with the 730; this text focuses discussion and examples on those that are most predominantly used.

The initial indicator value indicates number of nonfiling characters (0-9). A blank second indicator value indicates that no information is provided; a second indicator value of 2 indicates an

analytical entry, and means the item in the bibliographic record contains the work represented by the added entry. Additional information is available on the USMARC Web page at http://lcweb.loc.gov/marc/bibliographic/ecbdadde.html#mrcb730.
example

245	00	Organized crime
730	0	Caucus New Jersey (Television program)
245	04	The collected works of Thomas Hobbes.
730	0	Thucydides.‡tHistory of the Peloponnesian War. ‡lEnglish.‡f1992.
245	00	Blade runner
730	0	Blade runner.‡hMotion picture.
245	00	James Joyce's "Anna Livia Plurabelle"
730	0	Finnegan's wake.‡kSelections.
245	00	65 songs, for voice and piano.
730	0	Songs.‡lEnglish & German.‡kSelections.
245	00	Salem a century ago‡h[microform] /‡ccompiled by Frank H. Stewart.
500		"Reprinted from the Salem standard and Jerseyman".
730	0	Salem standard and Jerseyman.

RELATED TITLES

Provide access to titles related to the work described in the 245 field, **Title Statement** using the 740 field, **Added Entry—Uncontrolled Related/Analytical Title,** which is repeatable. The 740 field is created using information taken from 500, **General Note,** or 505, **Formatted Contents Note** fields, or other fields deemed appropriate by the cataloging agency.

The following subfields are available for use in the 740 field: ‡a uncontrolled related/analytical title; ‡h medium; ‡n number of part/section of a work; ‡p name of part/section of a work. There are additional subfields that may be used with the 740; this text focuses discussion and examples on those that are most predominantly used.

The initial indicator value indicates number of nonfiling characters (0-9). A second blank second indicator value indicates that no information is provided; a second indicator value of 2 indicates an analytical entry, and means the item in the bibliographic record contains the work represented by the added entry. Additional information is available on the USMARC Web page at http://lcweb.loc.gov/marc/bibliographic/ecbdadde.html#mrcb740.
example

| 245 | 00 | 12th census of population, 1900, New Jersey ‡h[microform]. |
| 500 | | Microfilm of the population schedules of the United States |

Census Bureau from film deposited in the National Archives.

740   01   Population schedules, New Jersey‡h[microform].

CLASSIFICATION

Microforms present libraries with many challenges when deciding how best to classify. Libraries may use classification schemes such as LCC or DDC, or may provide local access schemes such as accession number arrangement based on when an item was added to the collection, based on format (microfiche, microform), broad topic area (women's studies, census). "For microforms, classification has its limitations since the items cannot be browsed, and any information gleaned by the user is limited to what the labeling on the container can provide. Moreover, subject classification is of relatively little value for items that have been grouped under broad subject categories, as is the case with general serials and large collections of titles in sets." (Frost, 1989: 240).

APPROACHES TO CATALOGING LARGE MICROFORM SETS

The time and effort frequently required to catalog large microform sets has unfortunately led to a lack of useable copy available through the RLIN and OCLC national online bibliographic utilities.

Libraries may devise their own local solutions to handling microform sets, including Web-accessible finding aids, accession numbering systems based on format, topic, or collection, or other in-house guides. In some cases, publishers provide card sets with microform collections, yet the cataloging is often not full level and subject access is poor or nonexistent. Another approach is to use analytics. "The most complete (and costly) method is to provide full cataloging for each bibliographic unit in the set, applying all author, title, and subject tracings appropriate to each individual item...Alternately, libraries may provide author/title analytics for items in sets, adding authors and/or titles of the individual works to unit cards representing the set as a whole." (Frost, 1989: 241)

EXAMPLES OF BIBLIOGRAPHIC RECORDS

Figure 7-1 Microfiche Set

| Control | **Bib** | MARC Hldgs | Vol/Copy |

Fixed Fields

Rec_Type: a	Bib_Lvl: m	Enc_Lvl:	Desc: a	TypeCtrl:
Entrd: 010718	Dat_Tp: s	Date1: 1998	Date2:	Ctry: fr
Lang: eng	Mod_Rec:	Source: d	Illus:	Audience:
Repr:	Cont:	GovtPub:	ConfPub: 0	Festschr: 0
Indx: 0	Fiction: 0	Biog:		

Bibliographic Info

Phys descrip codes: 007 ▼ █ ▼ he bmu---buuu

Cataloging source: 040 ▼ ▼ NjR|cNjR

Corporate author: 110 ▼ 2 ▼ Unesco.|bExecutive Board.

Title: 245 ▼ 10 ▼ List of Executive Board Documents |h[microform] :|b1946-1982.

Publication info: 260 ▼ ▼ [Paris :|bUnesco,|c1998?]

Physical descrip: 300 ▼ ▼ 9 microfiches ;|c11 x 15 cm.

General Note: 500 ▼ ▼ "List typed in the Unesco Archives for the series of bound volumes (1-115 EX) with indications of session, code, title, date and paging for every document."

General Note: 500 ▼ ▼ "This list exists in paper form in the Unesco Archives only and is obtainable for outside institutions and researchers on microfiche #84 S 0497 (9 fiches)."

General Note: 500 ▼ ▼ "84 S 0497"--Microfiche header.

Subject: 610 ▼ 20 ▼ Unesco.|vCongresses.

Subject: 610 ▼ 20 ▼ Unesco.|bExecutive Board. |vArchives.

Cataloger's initials: 978 ▼ ▼ red

Held by: 596   ALEX

Figure 7-2 Incomplete Microfiche Set

| Control | **Bib** | MARC Hldgs | All Volumes |

Fixed Fields

Rec_Type:	a	Bib_Lvt	m	Enc_Lvl		Desc:	a	TypeCtrl	
Entrd:	000412	Dat_Tp:	s	Date1:	1849	Date2		Ctry:	enk
Lang:	eng	Mod_Rec:		Source:	d	Illus:		Audience:	
Repr:		Cont		GovtPub:		ConfPub:	0	Festschr:	0
Indx:	0	Fiction:	0	Biog:					

Bibliographic Info

Phys descrip codes: 007 ▼ ■ ▼ he amb---buuu

Cataloging source: 040 ▼ ▼ NjR|cNjR

Personal author: 100 ▼ 1 ▼ Hakluyt, Richard,|d1552?-1616.

Title: 245 ▼ 14 ▼ The principal navigations, voyages, traffiques and discoveries of the English nation|h[microform] / |cRichard Hakluyt.

Publication info: 260 ▼ ▼ London :|bPrinted for the Hakluyt Society,|c1849.

Physical descrip: 300 ▼ ▼ v.

Series: 440 ▼ ▼ Works issued by the Hakluyt society ;|vextra ser., no. 1-12

Partial contents: 505 ▼ 2 ▼ V. 4. Sir Francis Drake, his voyage 1595 / by Thomas Maynarde; together with the Spanish account of Drake's attack on Puerto Rico / edited from the original manuscript by W.D. Cooley.

Reproduction note: 533 ▼ ▼ Microfiche.|bWakefield, Eng. : |cMicro Methods Ltd.|emicrofiches.

Subject: 650 ▼ 0 ▼ Voyages and travels.

Cataloger's initials: 978 ▼ ▼ mbw|d20010727|nupdated 300

Held by: 596   ALEX

Figure 7-3 Microform Thesis

| Control | **Bib** | MARC Hldgs | Vol/Copy |

Fixed Fields

Rec_Type: a	Bib_Lvt: m	Enc_Lvt:	Desc:	TypeCtrl:
Entrd: 971219	Dat_Tp: s	Date1: 1985	Date2:	Ctry: xxu
Lang: eng	Mod_Rec:	Source: d	Illus: a	Audience: f
Repr: b	Cont:	GovtPub:	ConfPub: 0	Festschr: 0
Indx: 0	Fiction: 0	Biog:		

Bibliographic Info

Phys descrip codes	007	⬇	█	⬇	he amu---bucu
Cataloging source	040	⬇		⬇	NjR|cNjR
Personal author	100	⬇	1	⬇	Gillespie, R. A.
Title	245	⬇	10	⬇	Relapse and conditioning |h[microform] :|bcognitive and physiological changes in alcoholics after exposure to alcohol /|cRobert A. Gillespie.
Portion of title	246	⬇	30	⬇	Cognitive and physiological changes in alcoholics after exposure to alcohol|h[microform]
Variant title	246	⬇	3	⬇	Relapse & conditioning |h[microform]
Variant title	246	⬇	3	⬇	Cognitive & physiological changes in alcoholics after exposure to alcohol|h[microform]
Publication info	260	⬇		⬇	|c1985.
Physical descrip	300	⬇		⬇	xv, 265 leaves :|bill.
Dissertation note	502	⬇		⬇	Thesis (Ph. D.)--Richard L. Connolly College, Long Island University, 1985.
Bibliography note	504	⬇		⬇	Includes bibliographical references (leaves 162-172).
Reproduction note	533	⬇		⬇	Microfiche.|bAnn Arbor, MI : |bUniversity Microfilms International, |d1985.|e3 microfiches.|7s1985 miu b
Subject	650	⬇	0	⬇	Alcoholism|xTreatment.
Subject	650	⬇	0	⬇	Alcoholics|xRehabilitation.
Subject	650	⬇	0	⬇	Alcohol|xPhysiological effect.
Held by	596				ALCHL

Figure 7-4 Incomplete Microfilm Set

| Control | **Bib** | MARC Hldgs | Vol/Copy |

Fixed Fields

Rec_Type: a	Bib_Lvl: m	Enc_Lvl:	Desc: a	TypeCtrl:
Entrd: 000410	Dat_Tp: c	Date1: 2000	Date2: 9999	Ctry: nju
Lang: eng	Mod_Rec:	Source: d	Illus:	Audience:
Repr:	Cont: b	GovtPub:	ConfPub: 0	Festschr: 0
Indx: 0	Fiction: 0	Biog:		

Bibliographic Info

Phys descrip codes	007	↓	■ ↓	hd afu---bucu
Local system #	035	↓	↓	(CStRLIN)NJRGa1460060
Cataloging source	040	↓	↓	NjR|cNjR|dNjR
Title	245	↓	10 ↓	North American Phalanx |h[microform] /|cprocessed by Lois R. Densky ; edited by Gregory J. Plunges ; updated and revised by Carla Tobias.
Variant title	246	↓	1 ↓	|iTitle on film also appears as: |aCollection 5, North American Phalanx records 1841-1972
Publication info	260	↓	↓	Freehold, N.J. :|bMonmouth County Historical Association,|c2000-
Physical descrip	300	↓	↓	v.
General Note	500	↓	↓	A non-sectarian experimental cooperative community.
General Note	500	↓	↓	Collection acquired through various donors.
Bibliography note	504	↓	↓	Includes bibliographical references.
Incomplete contents	505	↓	1 ↓	Reel 1. [1] Stock Book, 1843-1855 November -- [2] Record of the Proceedings of the North American Phalanx, 1843 March 18-1844 February 20 and 1847 January 5-February 1 -- [3] Record of the Proceedings of the North American Phalanx, 1847 October 29-1849 December 31 --[4] Record of the Proceedings of the North American Phalanx, 1854 January 1-1857 January 1 -- [5] Stock Ledger, 1843 September 12-1863 May 5 -- [6]

Figure 7-4 *Continued*

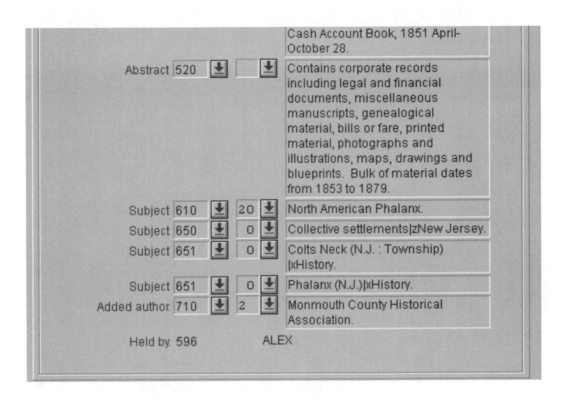

Figure 7-5 Microfiche Set

Control   **Bib**   MARC Hldgs   Vol/Copy

Fixed Fields

Rec_Type: a	Bib_Lvl: m	Enc_Lvl:	Desc: a	TypeCtrl:
Entrd: 981215	Dat_Tp: s	Date1: 1997	Date2:	Ctry: enk
Lang: eng	Mod_Rec:	Source: d	Illus:	Audience:
Repr:	Cont:	GovtPub:	ConfPub: 0	Festschr: 0
Indx: 0	Fiction: 0	Biog:		

Bibliographic Info

ISBN:	020	⤓	⤓	1857110862
Local system #:	035	⤓	⤓	(CStRLIN)NJRGa1366371
Cataloging source:	040	⤓	⤓	NjR|cNjR|dNjR
NAL call number:	070	⤓	⤓	he amu---bucu
Corporate author:	110	⤓	2 ⤓	Canterbury Cathedral Library.
Title:	245	⤓	10 ⤓	Canterbury Cathedral Library |h[microform] :|bcatalogue of pre-1801 printed books.
Variant title:	246	⤓	3 ⤓	Catalogue of pre-1801 printed books|h[microform]
Variant title:	246	⤓	1 ⤓	|iTitle from microfiche header: |aCanterbury Cathedral Library catalogue of pre-1801 books
Variant title:	246	⤓	3 ⤓	Rochester Cathedral Library catalogue of the pre-1901 printed books|h[microform]
Variant title:	246	⤓	1 ⤓	|iTitle from microfiche header: |aRochester Cathedral Library catalogue of pre-1901 books
Publication info:	260	⤓	⤓	Marlborough, Wiltshire :|bAdam Matthew Publications,|c[1997]
Physical descrip:	300	⤓	⤓	17 microfiche ;|c11 x 15 cm. +|e3 guides (24 p. ; 21 cm.) in folder.
General Note:	500	⤓	⤓	Pamphlet listing and guide to the microfiche collection by David Shaw and Sheila Hingley, assisted by Karen James, Margaret Brown, Lawrence Dethan and others. Pamphlet dated 1998.
General Note:	500	⤓	⤓	Rochester Cahtedral Library Catalogue of the pre-1901 printed books, by Andrew Wellard and

Figure 7-5 *Continued*

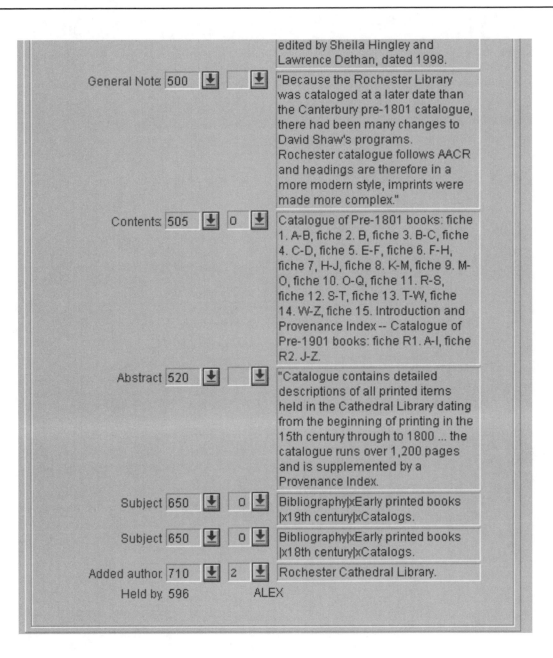

Figure 7-6 Microfilm Set

| Control | **Bib** | MARC Hldgs | All Volumes |

Fixed Fields

Rec_Type: a	Bib_Lvt m	Enc_Lvt	Desc: a	TypeCtrl
Entrd 990720	Dat_Tp: s	Date1: 1984	Date2	Ctry: nyu
Lang eng	Mod_Rec:	Source: d	Illus:	Audience:
Repr.	Cont	GovtPub:	ConfPub: 0	Festschr. 0
Indx 0	Fiction: 0	Biog:		

Bibliographic Info

Phys descrip codes:	007			hd afu---bucu
Local system #	035			(CStRLIN)NJRGa1407808
Cataloging source	040			NjR|cNjR|dNjR
Corporate author	110		20	Schomburg Center for Research in Black Culture.
Title	245		10	National Association of Colored Graduate Nurses|h[microform].
Portion of title	246		30	National Association of Colored Graduate Nurses records, 1908-1951|h[microform]
Variant title	246		1	|iTitle on container:|aThe National Association of Colored Graduate Nurses
Publication info	260			New York, N.Y. :|bNew York Public Library, Schomburg Center for Research in Black Culture,|c[1984]
Physical descrip	300			2 microfilm reels ;|c35 mm.
Contents	505		0	[Reel 1]. Minutes -- By-Laws and articles of incorporation -- Correspondence -- Memoranda -- Speeches and testimony -- Studies and reports -- [Reel 2]. Publications of the National Association of Colored Graduate Nurses -- Printed materials -- Scrapbooks and clippings.
Abstract	520			Reels contain minutes of the associations 1st annual meeting, annual meetings, and executive board meetings, correspondence of efforts to integrate black nurses into the armed forces during WWII, transcript of public hearings of the

Figure 7-6 *Continued*

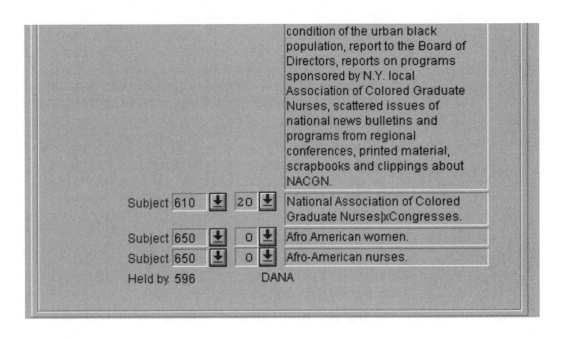

REFERENCES

Frost, Carolyn O. 1989. *Media Access and Organization: A Cataloging and Reference Sources Guide for Nonbook Materials.* Englewood, Colo.: Libraries Unlimited.

Joint Steering Committee for the Revision of AACR2. 1998. *Anglo-American Cataloguing Rules, Second Edition, 1998 Revision.* Chicago: American Library Association.

Network Development and MARC Standards Office, Library of Congress in cooperation with Standards and Support, National Library of Canada. 1999. *MARC 21 Format for Bibliographic Data Including Guidelines for Content Designation, 1999 Edition.* Washington, D.C.: Library of Congress Distribution Service.

8 INTERNET RESOURCES

OVERVIEW

The introduction of Internet resources into the collections and services of libraries has changed "traditional" librarianship: collection development, public services, and of course, cataloging. In the early 1990s, ownership and access were the biggest issues in relation to cataloging Internet resources. Since that time, the Internet has evolved from simple e-mail applications and indexing and retrieval tools such as gopher, and has grown to include the World Wide Web and a variety of services and tools. The emergence of the Web has changed how information can be made available, usually on a 24-hour basis. Libraries have increasingly turned to alternative ways to deliver information in the form of resources such as databases or serial packages available through aggregators.

"The decision to catalog Internet resources presents a number of challenges....Decisions must be made as to what types of Internet resources will receive cataloging, and what information should be included in the bibliographic record. Cataloging decisions are complicated by the fact that long-standing cataloging conventions do not readily apply to Internet resources" (Weber, 1999: 298-303).

Factors influencing cataloging decisions include: stability of a resource, whether it is freely available to the public, if the contents are full-text or full-image or partial, and restrictions on access. Since Internet resources vary greatly in presentation and content, lack of a representative type makes it difficult to apply cataloging standards. Libraries often must decide if a resource will be given monographic or serial treatment, and choose a format which most accurately represents the resource (electronic resources or serials). Standard bibliographic terms such as "author," "title," or "publication information" do not hold the same meaning for these resources as they do for other nonbook resources. Additionally, Library of Congress and other subject heading schemes may not fully represent the content of the newest technology.

Level of cataloging for Internet resources also poses problems. Libraries may use a single record to describe all formats in which a title is available, or separate records may be created for each format (journal titles available in print, microform, and electronically, for example). One advantage to the single record approach is that users are presented with all the information in one place. Some library professionals argue that creating separate records provides users with a confusing amount of information. Records including GMDs (this is true when separate records are created for print and electronic journals) will not cluster with records that do not include GMDs. This requires users to look in several places in a search results display. Additionally, not all users will possess the sophistication to realize this, and will view only the immediate search results display. Libraries may choose to use the collection level approach for databases containing a large number of titles. Level of description depends on a library's collection, available staff, and the importance of Internet resources to their collection and user community. All examples included in this chapter use full level description.

The type of classification provided for Internet resources varies with type and size of library. Libraries may provide Library of Congress Classification numbers or Dewey Decimal numbers, or some other type of classification. Many libraries provide classification numbers in their bibliographic records even if it is not their policy to classify Internet resources. This is done to facilitate searching by classification area.

The following categories of Internet resources are covered in this chapter: databases and electronic journals. Additional instruction and information are provided separately for electronic journals and aggregator databases. There is also a brief discussion of electronic books, an emerging format.

Information provided in this chapter was taken from a variety of resources, which were consulted: *AACR2R (1998)* Chapter 9, the International Standard Bibliographic Description for Electronic Resources (ISBD(ER)), CONSER's *Cataloging Manual Module 31: Remote Access Computer File Serials*, and OCLC's *Cataloging Internet Resources*. While metadata schemes are used by some libraries to describe and provide access to Internet resources, all examples in this chapter are presented in MARC format. Chapter Eight provides a discussion and examination of descriptive schemes (MARC and metadata, specifically).

ELEMENTS OF BIBLIOGRAPHIC RECORDS FOR INTERNET RESOURCES

The following information is necessary to create bibliographic records for Internet resources:

- Chief Source of Information
- Prescribed Sources of Information
- Choice of Main Entry
- Physical Description
- International Standard Serial Number (ISSN)
- Cataloging Source
- Language Code
- Geographic Information
- Library of Congress Call Number
- Title
- Title Variations
- General Material Designation (GMD)
- Statement of Responsibility
- Edition
- File Characteristics
- Place of Publication and/or Distribution, or Manufacture, etc.
- Name of Publisher(s) and/or Distributor(s)
- Date of Publication, Distribution, Copyright, Manufacture, etc.
- Series
- Notes
- Subject Access
- Added Entries (Personal and/or Corporate Names, Title Added Entries)
- Electronic Location and Access
- Classification

CHIEF SOURCE OF INFORMATION

The chief source of information for Internet resources is the title screen or main terminal display. If this yields no information, titles may be taken from "welcome" or "about" screens, or other available sources of information. In the case of electronic journals, *Module 31* stipulates that sources such as journal home pages, welcome screens, other types of opening screens, publisher information pages, table of contents screens, and browser title screens should be consulted first. The first issue of an electronic journal is the preferred source of information for description. When the first issue of an electronic journal is not available or fails to provide necessary information, the entire resource available at the time of cataloging may be used as the chief source of information. Additionally, the Joint Steering Committee for the Revision of AACR2R (JSC), in the December 1999 document regarding the harmonization of the ISBD(ER) and *AACR2*, proposes that the chief source of information for electronic resources is the resource itself; no particular part of the resource is specifically cited to take precedence over others.

PRESCRIBED SOURCES OF INFORMATION

Rule 9.0B2, *AACR2R (1998)* which covers electronic resources, may be consulted when creating bibliographic records for Internet resources. Based on this rule, use the following sources of information:

- Title/statement of responsibility- Chief source of information, accompanying documentation (if any)
- Edition- Chief source of information, accompanying documentation (if any)
- File characteristics- Any source of information may be consulted
- Publication, distribution, manufacture, etc.- Chief source of information, accompanying documentation
- Physical description- Not applicable; physical description is not provided for resources which are available remotely
- Series- Chief source of information, accompanying documentation (if any)
- Notes- Any source of information may be consulted

CHOICE OF MAIN ENTRY

Main entry may be under personal authorship or corporate authorship, or title main entry may be chosen. Some library professionals feel that the issue of main entry is not as pressing in an online environment where a variety of types of searches may be performed to locate an item. However, Rule 21.1A1, *AACR2R (1998)* defines a personal author as the individual chiefly responsible for a resource's intellectual or artistic content. Rule 21.1B1, *AACR2R (1998)* defines a corporate author as an organization or group of persons with a particular name that functions as an entity. Lastly, Rule 21.1C1, *AACR2R (1998)* states that a resource should be entered under title proper (or uniform title if appropriate) when: personal authorship is unknown or shared by a large number of individuals, and authorship can not be attributed to one particular individual or when a resource is not issued by a corporate body; or when a resource is a collection of works by different individuals or corporate bodies.

For some resources, title main entry is the most logical choice since the nonprint resource is the result of the work of many individuals and/or corporate bodies, and it is not possible to attribute authorship to a particular individual or corporate body. Lack of a statement of responsibility is another reason why title main entry is chosen for some nonprint resources. Since Internet resources are often the result of a collaborative effort, they are frequently entered under title main entry.

example

| 245 | 00 | CamdenBase‡h[electronic resource] :‡ba database of citations about Camden, New Jersey. |
| 245 | 0 | New Jersey Environmental digital library‡h[electronic resource]. |

Physical Description

The 007 field, **Physical Description Fixed Field—General Information** provides information on physical description in alphabetic coded form. This is particularly important when cataloging Internet resources, which lack a physical description.

Internet resources are coded as electronic resources. The 007 field for electronic resources has fourteen characters defined for use. The first six positions are those that are most frequently used; discussion in this text is limited to those six positions. Selected values are provided in the following text.

Position 00- Category of material; is always **c** for "electronic resource"

Position 01- SMD; **r** (remote)

Position 02- Undefined; leave blank

Position 03- Color characteristics; **b** (black and white); **c** (multicolored); **m**(mixed)

Position 04- Dimensions; **n** (not applicable)

Position 05- Sound; blank (no sound); **a** (sound); **u** (unknown)

example

```
007          cr mn
c = electronic resource
r = remote
blank
m = multicolored
n = not applicable (dimensions)
blank = no sound
```

International Standard Serial Number (ISSN)

Serials are issued an International Standard Serial Number, or ISSN. The ISSN is made up of eight digits, which are provided in two groups of four and separated by a hyphen. Provide this information in the 022 field, **International Standard Serial Number,** which is repeatable. This information can be helpful in identifying specific versions of a resource.

The following subfields are used in the 022: ‡a ISSN; ‡y incorrect ISSN; and ‡z canceled ISSN.

The initial indicator value specifies level of international interest. An initial indicator value of blank indicates that no level of interest has been specified; a value of 0 indicates that the serial is of international interest; a value of 1 indicates that the serial is not of international interest. The second indicator is undefined.
example

022		1591-9528
022	0	1046-8374

Cataloging Source

Information on the origin of a bibliographic record, plus any institutions that have modified a record, is provided in the 040 field, **Cataloging Source,** which is not repeatable.

The following subfields are available for use in the 040 field: ‡a original cataloging agency; ‡c transcribing agency (which is typically the institution in ‡a); and ‡d modifying agency. There are other subfields that may be used in the 040; this discussion is limited to those that are most predominantly used.

There are no indicators defined for the 040 field.
example

Original cataloging record created and transcribed by Rutgers University Libraries
040   NjR‡cNjR

Original cataloging record created and transcribed by Rutgers University Libraries, modified by Library X.
040   NjR‡NjR‡dXyZ
Original cataloging record created and transcribed by Rutgers University Libraries, modified at a later date by Rutgers University Libraries.
040   NjR‡NjR‡dNjR

Language Code

Provide information on language(s) present in a resource in the

041 field, **Language Code**, which is not repeatable. Information in the 041 is provided in alphabetic coded form. The 041 works in conjunction with the 546 field, **Language Note**.

Codes are provided according to their predominance in the resource (Network Development and MARC Standards Office, Library of Congress, 1999). The 041 field can provide codes for a maximum of six languages. If more than six languages are present in the resource, the language for the title is coded as "mul"(multiple) to represent all the languages.

The following subfields are used in the 041: ‡a language code for text, sound track, or separate title; ‡b language code for summary or subtitle; ‡d language code for sung or spoken text; ‡e language code for librettos; ‡g language code for accompanying materials other than librettos; ‡h language code for original and/or intermediate translations of text.

The initial indicator value indicates whether a resource is or includes a translation. An initial indicator of 0 indicates that the resource is not a translation and does not include a translation; a value of 1 indicates that the item is a translation or includes a translation.
example

```
041    0    engfre
546         Web site available to users in English or French versions.
```

Geographic Information

Provide information on the geographic area presented, described, covered, etc. by the resource in the 043 field, **Geographic Area Code**, which is not repeatable. The 043 can accommodate 1-3 codes, which are represented in alphabetic coded form. Multiple geographic codes are separated by a ‡a.

Indicator values are not defined for the 043 field.
example

Resource contains information pertaining to New Jersey, in the United States
```
043        n-us-nj
```

Resource contains information pertaining to the Great Plains region in the United States
```
043        np- - - - -
```

Resource contains information pertaining to Japan
```
043        a-ja- - -
```

Resource contains information pertaining to Spain and Mexico
043   e-sp- - -‡an-mx- - -

A full list of geographic area codes is available on the USMARC Web page at http://lcweb.loc.gov/marc/geoareas/.

Library of Congress Call Number

Provide a Library of Congress Call Number (if applicable according to the cataloging agency's policies and procedures for nonprint resources) in the 050 field, **Library of Congress Call Number**, which is repeatable. Some institutions have policies governing whether an LC Call Number is included in the bibliographic portion of a record when their records are submitted to a national online bibliographic utility such as RLIN or OCLC.

The following subfields are available for use in the 050 field: ‡a classification number; ‡b item number.

The initial indicator value indicates whether the item is in Library of Congress's collection. An initial value of blank indicates that no information is provided, and is used when libraries other than the Library of Congress provide classification numbers. The second indicator value indicates source of call number. Classification numbers provided by Library of Congress have a second indicator value of zero; classification numbers provided by other libraries have a second indicator value of 4.
example

050   0   HB1335 ‡b.M84
050   4   HD28‡b.J5987

TITLE INFORMATION

Includes title, general material designation, remainder of title, and statement of responsibility.

Title

Consult the chief source of information first. Title information should be taken from the chief source of information whenever possible. If it is lacking or provides limited or no information, consult the prescribed sources of information. In the absence of chief or prescribed sources of information, a title may be supplied by the cataloger. Supplied titles are bracketed, and the source of information is cited in a general note.

The source of title for Internet resources must always be cited regardless of whether it was taken from chief or prescribed sources of information, or supplied by the cataloger. This information is provided in the 500 field, **General Note,** and includes in parentheses the date when the resource was viewed. There is discussion within the profession that HTML headers, rather than title or introductory screens, are to be used as the chief source of information for Internet resources. At any rate, source of title and when the resources are viewed are important for verification particularly when bibliographic records are submitted to the RLIN and OCLC online union databases, and may be used by other institutions as the basis for their own catalog records.

Title information is provided in the 245 field, **Title Statement.** The following subfields are available for use in the 245 field: ‡a title; ‡b remainder of title; ‡c statement of responsibility; ‡h GMD; ‡n number of part/section; ‡p name of part/section. One method of presenting subfields is to discuss them in the order in which they are used in bibliographic records, rather than alphabetically. However, the alphabetic approach is used in this text, and has been modeled after authoritative sources of information, such as *Concise MARC Format* and the RLIN and OCLC cataloging manuals. Placement of the subfields is illustrated in examples and illustrations. There are additional subfields that may be used in the 245; this text focuses discussion and examples on those that are most predominantly used.

Rule 1.1B1, *AACR2R (1998),* instructs catalogers to transcribe the title proper exactly as to wording, order, and spelling, but not necessarily to capitalization and punctuation. Titles are provided in the 245 field, ‡a, which is not repeatable.

Indicator values in the 245 field indicates if a title added entry will be generated. Most nonprint items are cataloged using title main entry. Nonprint resources are rarely entered under an author (corporate or personal) main entry. (A discussion of choice of main entry for nonbook resources is provided in the following paragraph.) For this reason, the majority of nonprint resources will have a first indicator value of 0. A first indicator value of 1 is used when a title added entry will be generated. The second indicator specifies number of nonfiling characters, with a range of 0-9 available.

example

Title from chief source of information:

245	00	New Jersey Environmental digital library
500		Title from introductory screen.

245	00	Old English corpus
500		Title from top of Web page (viewed on Oct. 1, 1999).

```
245     00      Booksinprint.com
500             Title from HTML header (viewed April 2002).
```

Title supplied by cataloger:
```
245     00      [Documentary on Douglass College, Rutgers University]
500             Title supplied by cataloger.
```

For more information regarding source of title, consult the Web page of the Online Audiovisual Catalogers (OLAC), a group of nonbook cataloging professionals who are compiling a document for terms used in source of title note. The Web page is available at http://ulib.buffalo.edu/libraries/units/cts/olac/capc/draft1.htm.

Remainder of Title

The 245 field also provides the remainder of a title or other information, such as parallel titles. Provide this information in the ‡b, which is not repeatable.
example

```
245     00      CamdenBase‡h[electronic resource] :‡ba database of
                citations about Camden, New Jersey.
245     00      Visions of research in music‡h[electronic resource]
                :‡bVRME.
```

Title Variations

Provide title variations in the 246 field, **Varying Form of Title,** which is repeatable. The 246 provides other titles by which a resource may be known; this includes abbreviations or acronyms, parallel titles in another language, or when one title appears on external packaging and another title is given in the chief source of information. Providing access to title variations permits users to search for a resource in multiple ways.

The following subfields are available for use in the 246 field: ‡a title; ‡b remainder of title or parallel title; ‡h medium; ‡i display text; ‡n number of part/section of a work; ‡p name of a part/section of a work. There are additional subfields that may be used with the 246; this text focuses discussion and examples on those that are most predominantly used.

The initial indicator value indicates note or added entry. The second indicator value is used to provide information on type of title. A complete list of indicator values is available on the USMARC Web page at http://lcweb.loc.gov/marc/bibliographic/ecbdtils.html#mrcb246.

example

Portions of the main title

245	10	Kyushu-Okinawa Summit 2000 official guide CD-ROM‡h[electronic resource].
246	30	Kyushu-Okinawa Summit 2000 official guide‡h[electronic resource]
246	30	Kyushu-Okinawa Summit 2000‡h[electronic resource]

Other forms of title

245	00	Standard and Poor's database‡h[electronic resource].
246	3	Standard & Poor's database‡h[electronic resource]
246	3	S&P's database‡h[electronic resource]

Title on chief source and other source of information differ

245	00	Dictionary of Old English, Old English corpus‡h[electronic resource].
246	1	‡iTitle in HTML header:‡a Old English corpus

GENERAL MATERIAL DESIGNATION (GMD)

Use of a GMD is deemed optional by Rule 1.1C, *AACR2R (1998)*. There are several reasons why a library may choose to use GMDs. It indicates to users the format of a resource when a search is done in an online catalog since all resources with a specific GMD will cluster together. Additionally, the resource described in an online catalog may not readily be apparent to users even when the bibliographic record includes a physical description that includes type of resource and characteristics. Use of a GMD helps users to distinguish between different formats in which a title is available. For example, an Internet resource may be available on the Web as well as in print. Including a GMD for the Internet version will immediately indicate to users in what formats the title is available. However, there is a growing sentiment that GMDs are no longer useful, particularly in a Web-based environment in which some libraries use one bibliographic record to represent multiple manifestations of a title (a paper and an electronic version of a serial title, for example).

The GMD is included in the 245 field, ‡h and is enclosed in brackets. It immediately follows the information provided in ‡a and precedes the ‡b. It is not repeatable.

Two lists of GMDs are provided in *AACR2R (1998)*. The first list is for British cataloging agencies; Australian, Canadian, and American cataloging agencies use terms from the second list. Use the GMD "electronic resource" for Internet resources, including electronic journals.

example

245	00	Cell physiology‡h[electronic resource].
245	00	MEMDB‡h[electronic resource] :‡bMedieval and early modern data bank.

STATEMENT OF RESPONSIBILITY

The statement of responsibility for Internet resources includes the names of individuals (creators, programmers, researchers, etc.) and corporate bodies responsible for production of the resource. This information is taken from the chief or prescribed sources of information.

The statement of responsibility is included in the 245 field, ‡c, is preceded by a forward slash, and is not repeatable. Each corporate body or individual presented in the statement of responsibility is separated by semicolons. Per Rule 1.1F1, *AACR2R (1998)*, statements of responsibility are to be transcribed as they appear. Information taken from sources other than the chief source of information will be bracketed.

example

245	00	MEMDB‡h[electronic resource]:‡bMedieval and early modern data bank /‡ca Web site developed by the Scholarly Communication Center, Rutgers [University] Libraries and Rudolph M. Bell.

EDITION

Provide edition information in the 250 field, **Edition Statement**, which is not repeatable. The concept of "edition" is important for Internet resources since they often undergo many updates and changes, and typically within a short time period. Include an edition statement if appropriate and available. Edition statements are not limited to numeric terms, such as "3rd edition." The terms "release," "version," "revision" or others deemed appropriate by a cataloging agency may be used in an edition statement. Different document formats are not considered as editions. Rule 1.2B1, *AACR2R (1998)*, instructs catalogers to transcribe edition statements in the form found on the item.

The following subfields are available for use in the 250 field: ‡a edition statement; ‡b remainder of edition statement. There are additional subfields that may be used with the 250; this text focuses discussion and examples on those that are most predominantly used.

There are no indicators defined for the 250 field.
example

250	Electronic version.
250	Release 12/91.
250	News version.
250	Internet ed.

FILE CHARACTERISTICS

Provide information on file characteristics for Internet resources in the 256 field, **Electronic Resource Characteristics**, which is not repeatable. File characteristics include: designation and number of records, statements, etc. According to OCLC's *Cataloging Internet Resources: A Manual and Practical Guide*, designation is required when cataloging resources are available remotely. It should be noted that CONSER does not support use of this field for electronic journals since it is believed that bibliographic records for these resources specify type of file. *Module 31* instructs catalogers to instead use the 516 field, **Type of Electronic Resource or Data Note**, to provide information to describe electronic journals.

DESIGNATION

As instructed in Rule 9.3B1, *Amendments 2001*, the following designations are used to indicate type of file: *electronic data, electronic program(s), electronic data and program(s)*. Alternately, the International Standard Bibliographic Description for Electronic Resources (ISBD-ER), as proposed by IFLA, provides additional terms for this field. This information is available via the Internet at http://ifla.inist.fr/VII/s13/pubs/isbd.htm.
example

256	Electronic data.
256	Electronic text data.
256	Text and image data.
256	Computer online service.
516	Electronic journal.

NUMBER OF RECORDS, STATEMENTS, ETC.

Provide information on the number of files contained in an electronic resource. This portion of the 256 may also include *data* (number of records), *programs* (number of statements), or multipart files (number of records and/or bytes, or number of statements and/or bytes) (Joint Steering Committee for the Revision of *AACR2R (1998))*. OCLC's *Cataloging Internet Resources* advises against including this type of information in the 256 since the number and size of files may vary greatly from the form in which it is received to the form in which it is used and stored.
example

256   Electronic data (2 files).

PUBLICATION INFORMATION

Consult the chief and/or prescribed sources of information to obtain information on where and when a resource was published, distributed, manufactured, etc. Publication, distribution, manufacture, etc. information is provided in the 260 field, **Publication, Distribution, etc. (Imprint)**, which is not repeatable.

There are no indicators defined for the 260 field.

PLACE OF PUBLICATION, DISTRIBUTION, MANUFACTURE, ETC.

The place of publication, distribution, manufacture, etc. is provided in the 260 field, ‡a. It is repeatable if there is more than one place of publication, or if a resource is published in one location and distributed in another, for example.

Generally, the city and country or state of publication are given. If only a city name is given, and it is necessary to record the country, state, etc., for purposes of identification and clarification, record the supplied information in brackets, as per Rule 1.4C3, *AACR2R (1998)*.
example

260   Detroit, Mich.
260   Schmalkalden [Germany]

If a place of publication, distribution, manufacture, etc. is not provided, but may be ascertained, record in brackets with a ques-

tion mark. Consult Rule 1.4C6, *AACR2R (1998)*, for further discussion of this topic.
example

260   [Denver?]

If no place of publication, distribution, manufacture, etc. is provided, and may not be ascertained, the abbreviation for the term "Sine loco," [S.l.], is used per Rule 1.4C6, *AACR2R (1998)*. The abbreviation is always bracketed.
example

260   [S.l.] :‡bMedia Mix Productions

NAME OF PUBLISHER(S) AND/OR DISTRIBUTOR(S)

Consult the chief and/or prescribed sources of information first. Record the publisher's name following the place of publication as per Rule 1.4D1, *AACR2R (1998)*.

Provide this information in the 260 field, ‡c.
example

260   [S.l.] :‡bMedia Mix Productions

If there is no information provided for publisher, and it may not be ascertained, use the abbreviation for the term "sine nomine," [s.n.], as per Rule 1.4D7, *AACR2R (1998)*. The abbreviation is always bracketed.
example

260   Chicago :‡b[s.n.]

DATE OF PUBLICATION, DISTRIBUTION, COPYRIGHT, MANUFACTURE, ETC.

Provide this information in the 260 field, ‡c, which is repeatable. However, the practice of repeating the ‡c is not widely used. Multiple dates, such as for date of production and copyright, may be included in the 260 field, ‡c.

Consult the chief and/or prescribed sources of information first. Record publication date, or distribution date if publication date is not available. In the absence of either date, record copyright date, which is preceded by a lower case "c." Information on date of publication, distribution, etc. is further outlined in Rule 1.4F, *AACR2R (1998)*.

example

Publication date
260   Media, Pa. :‡bEducational Clearinghouse,‡c1990.
Copyright date
260   Oxford :‡bIRL Press Ltd.,‡cc1986.

If information on publication, distribution, etc. date is not provided in either the chief or prescribed sources of information, approximate the date of publication. Approximated dates are bracketed.
example

Approximated date
260   [S.l.] :‡bT. Meyer Publishers,‡c[ca. 1997]

Probable date
260   Cherry Hill, N.J. :‡bAriel Press,‡[1990?]

Decade certain
260   Clifton, N.J. :‡bPiermatti Educational Resources,‡c[198-]

Probable decade
260   Chicago :‡bScholars Press,‡c[199-?]

Note: More information on dates is available in *AACR2R (1998)*, Chapter 1, "General Rules for Description."
Unpublished items: All Internet resources are considered as published according to OCLC's *Cataloging Internet Resources*. If the place of publication, distribution, etc. and/or name of publisher, distributor, etc. may not be ascertained, use the abbreviations "S.l." and "s.n." as needed.
example

260   [S.l] :‡bInternet Wherehouse,‡c1999.
260   [S.l. :‡bs.n.,‡c2000?]

PHYSICAL DESCRIPTION

No physical description is provided for Internet resources, which are available remotely. Volume designators are not used for electronic serials as is the case for their print counterparts. Sound, color, or other characteristics may be provided in a note in lieu of a physical description. Any information on accompanying materials in a physical format may also be provided in a note; this note is discussed later in the chapter.

SERIES

Provide series information if appropriate and available from the chief and/or prescribed sources of information. This text provides general series information; a detailed discussion of various types of series treatments is beyond the focus of this text. Series are represented in this text by the 440 field, **Series Statement/Added Entry—Title**, which is repeatable.

The following subfields are available for use in the 440 field: ‡a title; ‡n number of part/section; ‡p name of part/section; ‡v volume or numbering designation.

Provide series title in the 440, ‡a, which is not repeatable.

The first indicator value for the 440 field is undefined. The second indicator specifies number of nonfiling characters, with a range of 0-9 available.

Detailed information on series is available on the USMARC Web page at http://lcweb.loc.gov/marc/bibliographic/ecbdhome.html#mrcb440.

example

| 440 | 0 | Inside statistics |
| 440 | 0 | BMG classics |

Provide information on numbered parts in the ‡n number of Part/Section of a Work.

example

| 440 | 0 | Langues de l'Orient.‡nI,‡pManuals |
| 440 | 0 | Baseball.‡nVolume 7,‡pFourth inning |

Provide the specific name of the part(s)/section(s) of a series in the ‡p name of Part/Section of a Work.

example

| 440 | 4 | The Great explorers.‡pThe Columbus series |
| 440 | 0 | Janua linguarum.‡pSeries minor |

Provide numbering designation, such as "volume" or "part" in the ‡v.
example

| 440 | 0 | BMG classics ;‡vvol. 32 |
| 440 | 0 | Medicine at the crossroads ;‡vMECR108 |

NOTES

Notes for Internet resources provide a variety of information, including contents, summary, file characteristics, and program language. They are also used to describe characteristics of the Internet resource or to note features unique to a library's copy of an item.

The notes in this section are provided in the order which they appear in MARC records. Notes are not arranged in numeric order by MARC tag number.

NATURE AND SCOPE

Provide a note on nature and scope of the Internet resource in the 516 field, **Type of Electronic Resource or Data Note**, only when it is not apparent from the rest of the description. This field is repeatable.
example

516	Novel.
516	Online bibliographic database.
516	Electronic newsletter.
516	Text (Electronic database).

SYSTEM REQUIREMENTS

Provide information on system requirements in the 538 field, **Systems Detail Note**, which is repeatable. Information is provided in the 538 in the following order: make and model of the computer(s) required to access the resource; required memory; operating system; software requirements, including programming language; kind and characteristics of required and recommended peripherals (Joint Steering Committee for the Revision of *AACR2R (1998)*). The description of system details may be preceded by a note specifying the type of information which follows.

Indicator values are not defined for the 538 field.

example

538	System requirements: Graphical Web browser (Netscape Navigator 3.0 or higher, or Microsoft Explorer).
538	System requirements: Internet connectivity, Java-enabled World Wide Web browser.

Mode of Access

Per Rule 9.7B1c, *AACR2R (1998)* specify mode of access for Internet resources. Provide this information in the 538 field, **System Details Note,** which is repeatable. The ISBD(ER) states that this note is mandatory for remotely accessible electronic resources, and should follow the **System Requirements** note. The ISBD(ER) also states that this will be the first note given in the absence of a System Requirements note.
example

538	Mode of access: GPO via the Internet at the GPO Web site.
538	Mode of access: Internet via World Wide Web; DJVU Plugin and Adobe Acrobat Reader required to view and print documents.

SOURCE OF TITLE PROPER

The source of title must always be provided for Internet resources, as per Rule 9.7B3, *AACR2R (1998)*. Source of title and the date when the resource was viewed are important for verification particularly when bibliographic records are submitted to the RLIN and OCLC online union databases. Provide this information in the 500 field, **General Note,** which is repeatable. At the April, 2001, JSC meeting in Washington, D.C., Rule 12.7B23, *AACR2R (1998)* was revised to clarify that the date on which a resource was viewed by a cataloger should always be provided for electronic resources that are available via remote access.
example

500	Title from HTML header (viewed Nov. 2001).
500	Description based on: Vol. 2, no. 1 (Dec. 1999); title from available issues screen (viewed Jan. 15, 2000).

CREDITS

Provide the names of individuals or corporate bodies not named in the statement of responsibility who have contributed to the production of the Internet resource. This information is provided in the 508 field, **Creation/Production Credits Note,** which is not repeatable.

example

508	Camden images courtesy of William M. Hoffman, Jr.
508	Information compiled and reported by the Scholarly Communications Center, Rutgers University Libraries.

EDITION AND HISTORY

Per Rule 9.7B7, *AACR2R (1998)* provide information on the resource, or use to provide history of the Internet resource. This note is also used to provide information on changes to the resource, to cite other works upon which it is based, or to provide date information (dates covered by resource, dates when data was collected).

This information is provided in the 500 field, **General Note**, which is repeatable, and differs from what is provided in the 250 field.

example

500	Online version includes issues from earlier titles.
500	Updated annually.
500	Inclusive dates: 1949 to the present.

FILE CHARACTERISTICS

Provide additional information on file characteristics not given in the 256 field, **Electronic Resource Characteristics**, in a 500 field, **General Note**, which is repeatable.

example

500	File size undeterminable.

PUBLICATION, DISTRIBUTION, ETC., AND DATE INFORMATION

"Make notes on publication, distribution, etc., details that are not included in the publication, distribution, etc., area and are considered to be important" (Joint Steering Committee for the Revision of *AACR2R (1998)*: 196, Rule 7.7B9).

Provide this information in the 500 field, **General Note**, which is repeatable.

example

500	Copyrighted by Bell & Howell, 2000.
500	Release notes dated January, 2001.

AUDIENCE

Provide information on the intended audience or intellectual level of an Internet resource in the 521 field, **Target Audience Note,** which is repeatable. Take this information from chief or prescribed sources of information.

The first indicator value provides an introductory phrase for the 521 field that describes audience or intellectual level of materials. A first indicator value of blank provides the display constant "Audience." The second indicator value is undefined. Additional information on indicator values for the 521 field is available on the USMARC Web page at http://lcweb.loc.gov/marc/bibliographic/ecbdnot1.html#mrcb521.
example

521	For elementary school students.
521	Intended for use by medical professionals.

OTHER FORMATS

Provide information on other formats in which an Internet resource has been issued in the 530 field, **Additional Physical Form Available Note,** which is repeatable.
example

530	Also available in a print ed.
530	Backfile also issued online via JSTOR.

SUMMARY

Provide a brief description of the scope and contents of the Internet resource in the 520 field, **Summary, Etc.,** which is repeatable. This note is particularly useful for remote users.

The first indicator value provides an introductory phrase for the 520 field. A blank first indicator value generates the display "Summary." The second indicator value is undefined. Additional information on indicator values for the 520 field is available on the USMARC Web page at http://lcweb.loc.gov/marc/bibliographic/ecbdnot1.html#mrcb520.
example

520	Summary: Provides image and full-text online access to back issues. Consult the online table of contents for specific holdings.
520	Summary: Provides access to the literature on the left, with a primary emphasis on politically and culturally engaged scholarship inside and outside the academy and a second-

ary emphasis on significant but little known sources of news and ideas.

520   Summary: "...provides access to information about New Jersey's environment in full text and graphic content. Much of the material in this collection is undocumented (aka 'grey literature')." - - Welcome screen.

CONTENTS

Information detailing the contents of an Internet resource is provided in the 505 field, **Formatted Contents Note**, which is repeatable. It provides individual titles or parts contained in the resource, and may include statements of responsibility.

Contents notes in which the various parts of the note are coded are referred to as "enhanced." Enhanced contents notes contain a ‡t (title) and ‡r (statement of responsibility).

The first indicator value for the 505 field indicates completeness of the contents. A first indicator value of 0 indicates complete contents, a value of 1 is used for incomplete contents, and a value of 2 is used for partial contents. The second indicator value provides information on content designation. A second indicator value of 0 is used for enhanced contents. A second value of blank is used for nonenhanced contents notes. The indicators for an enhanced contents note are 00 (a nonenhanced contents has a single first indicator with a value from 0-2, or 8).

While not required, a contents note is useful to providing a description since the contents of a nonprint resource may not be browsed in the manner used for print resources.
example

505   0   Introduction to Drug literature index - - Introduction to Index medicus - - Introduction to International pharmaceutical abstracts.

505   0   Currency exchanges (Metz) - - Currency exchanges (Mueller) - - Currency exchanges (Spufford) - - Prices (Metz) - - Prices (Posthumus).

Enhanced contents note

505   00   ‡tBalcony rock /‡rD. Brubeck, P. Desmond - - ‡tOut of nowhere /‡r Heyman, J.W. Green - - ‡tLe souk /‡rD. Brubeck, P. Desmond - - ‡t Take the "A" train /‡rStrayhorn - - ‡tThe song is you /‡rHammerstein II, Kern - - ‡tDon't worry 'bout me /‡rKoehler, Bloom - - ‡tI want to be happy /‡rCaesar, Youmans.

DESCRIPTIVE OR LIBRARY SPECIFIC NOTES

Provide descriptive information regarding Internet resources in a
500 field, **General Note**, which is repeatable.
example

500	Also available on the University's INFO system.
500	Available to authorized users with RU IP addresses.

RESTRICTIONS ON ACCESS NOTE

Provide information on restrictions to access in the 506 field,
Restrictions on Access Note, which is repeatable.
example

506	Restricted to use by faculty and graduate students.
506	Restricted to institutions with a site license to the JSTOR collection.
506	Access restricted by licensing agreement.

"WITH" NOTES

Provide notes for titles that are not the first in a collective title.
This information is provided in the 500 field, **General Note**, which
is repeatable. Additionally, information provided in this type of
note may also be used as the basis for a 740 field, **Added Entry—
Uncontrolled Related/Analytical Title**.
example

500	With: New Grove II, Grove Opera, and New Grove dictionary of Jazz, second edition.

Information About Documentation Note

Provide information about documentation that can be used with
electronic resources in the 556 field, **Information About Documentation Note**, which is repeatable.

The first indicator value for the 556 provides information on
the display content. A first indicator value of blank provides the
display constant "Documentation"; a value of 8 will not generate a display constant. The second indicator value is undefined.

Additional information on the 556 field is available on the
USMARC Web page at http://lcweb.loc.gov/marc/bibliographic/
ecbdnot2.html#mrcb556.
example

556		Documentation: Index guide appendixes, reference manual, user manual.
556	8	Accompanied by user guide and reference manual.

SUBJECT ACCESS

Subject access to nonprint resources helps users to identify and locate resources, particularly when resources are not available in a physical format, as is the case for Internet resources. Subject headings are used to provide access to resources through *personal names*, *corporate names*, *topical terms*, or *geographic names*. Subject headings may be further subdivided by form division (format of material), general subdivisions, chronological subdivisions, and geographic subdivisions. Meeting names and subject added entries for uniform titles are not included in this text.

PERSONAL NAME

Provide subject access to personal names in the 600 field, **Subject Added Entry—Personal Name**, which is repeatable. Personal names are included in a bibliographic record when a resource is about an individual or individuals, or contains a significant portion of information about an individual or individuals.

The following subfields are available for use in the 600 field: ‡a personal name; ‡c titles associated with a name; ‡d dates associated with a name; ‡v form subdivision; ‡x general subdivision; ‡y chronological subdivision; ‡z geographic subdivision. There are additional subfields that may be used with the 600; this text focuses discussion and examples on those that are most predominantly used.

The initial indicator value indicates type of name. An initial article value of 0 indicates entry under forename; 1 indicates entry under single surname. The second indicator value provides source of name heading. A second indicator value of 0 indicates that a name is from the Library of Congress Name Authority file. Additional information is available on the USMARC Web page at http://lcweb.loc.gov/marc/bibliographic/ecbdsubj.html #mrcb600.

example

600	00	Cher,‡d1946-
600	10	Day-Lewis, Daniel.
600	10	Weinberg, Valerie Ann.
600	10	Irving, Henry,‡cSir,‡d1838-1905.
600	10	Ellington, Duke,‡d1899-1974.
600	10	King, Martin Luther,‡cJr.,‡d 1929-1968‡xAssassination.
600	10	Krupa, Gene,‡d1909-1973‡vBiography.
600	10	Shakespeare, William,‡d1564-1616‡xStage history‡y1800-1950.

| 600 | 10 | Gogh, Vincent van,‡d1853-1890‡xMuseums‡zNetherlands‡zAmsterdam. |

CORPORATE NAME

Provide subject access to corporate names in the 610 field, **Subject Added Entry—Corporate Name**, which is repeatable. Corporate names are included in a bibliographic record when a resource is about a corporation or corporations, or contains a significant portion of information about a corporation or corporations.

The following subfields are available for use in the 610 field: ‡a corporate or jurisdiction names; ‡b subordinate units; ‡v form subdivision; ‡x general subdivision; ‡y chronological subdivision; ‡z geographic subdivision. There are additional subfields that may be used with the 610; this text focuses discussion and examples on those that are most predominantly used.

The initial indicator value indicates form of entry for names. An initial indicator value of 1 is for jurisdiction name; 2 is for a name presented in direct order. A second indicator value of 0 indicates that a name is from the Library of Congress Name Authority file. Additional information is available on the USMARC Web page at http://lcweb.loc.gov/marc/bibliographic/ecbdsubj.html#mrcb610.

example

610	20	Lyceum Theatre (London, England)
610	10	United States.‡bDept. of the Interior.
610	20	Harvard University‡xFunds and scholarships‡vHandbooks, manuals, etc.
610	20	Microsoft Corporation‡xHistory.
610	20	Grand Central Terminal (New York, N.Y.)‡xHistory‡y20th century.
610	20	Salvation Army‡zEngland.

TOPICAL TERMS

Provide subject access to topical terms in the 650 field, **Subject Added Entry–Topical Term**, which is repeatable. Terms used in the 650 may describe form of the resource (Motion pictures, Spanish) or content (Jazz, Bicycle touring).

The following subfields are available for use in the 650 field: ‡a topical term or geographic name as entry element; ‡v form division; ‡x general subdivision; ‡y chronological subdivision; ‡z geographic subdivision. There are additional subfields that may be used with the 650; this text focuses discussion and examples on those that are most predominantly used.

The initial article value indicates level of subject; blank indicates that no information has been provided. In most cases, subject headings supplied by catalogers or provided in records available through union databases will have an initial indicator value of blank. A second indicator value of 0 indicates that a name is from the Library of Congress Name Authority file. Additional information is available on the USMARC Web page at http://lcweb.loc.gov/marc/bibliographic/ecbdsubj.html#mrcb650.
example

650	0	Violence in art.
650	0	Grandparents as parents‡xServices for‡zNew Jersey ‡vDirectories.
650	0	Crime prevention‡xCitizen participation.
650	0	American prose literature‡y19th century.
650	0	Catalogs, Publishers'‡zUnited States.

GEOGRAPHIC TERMS

Provide subject access to geographic terms in the 651 field, **Subject Added Entry—Geographic Name**, which is repeatable.

The following subfields are available for use in the 651 field: ‡a geographic name; ‡v form division; ‡x general subdivision; ‡y chronological subdivision; ‡z geographic subdivision. There are additional subfields that may be used with the 651; this text focuses discussion and examples on those that are most predominantly used.

The initial indicators are undefined for this field. A second indicator value of 0 indicates that a name is from the Library of Congress Name Authority file. Additional information is available on the USMARC Web page at http://lcweb.loc.gov/marc/bibliographic/ecbdsubj.html#mrcb651.
example

651	0	Brooklyn (New York, N.Y.)
651	0	United States‡vBibliography.
651	0	United States‡xImprints.
651	0	United States‡xHistory‡yCivil War, 1861 1865.
651	0	United States‡xHistory‡xStudy and teaching (Higher) ‡zNew Jersey

ADDED ENTRIES

Added entries provide access to personal and corporate names that are not main entries yet serve as important additional access points. Title added entries provide additional access for titles related to the main work. This information is provided in the 7XX fields, which are discussed in detail in the following paragraphs as they relate to Internet resources.

PERSONAL NAME

Provide access to personal names in the 700 field, **Added Entry— Personal,** which is repeatable. It is used to include additional access points in the form of names taken from the 245, **Title Statement,** or other fields deemed appropriate by the cataloging agency. Personal name added entries differ from personal names in the 600 in that they provide different types of information, and would be found in an online catalog using different types of searches (subject versus personal name).

The following subfields are available for use in the 700 field: ‡a personal name; ‡c titles or other words associated with a particular name; ‡d dates; ‡4 relator code. A list of relator codes is available on the USMARC Web page at http://lcweb.loc.gov/marc/ relators/. It is not typical to include relator codes in name added entries for Internet resources. There are additional subfields that may be used with the 700; this text focuses discussion and examples on those that are most predominantly used.

The initial indicator value indicates type of name. An initial article value of 0 indicates entry under forename; 1 indicates entry under single surname. A blank second indicator value indicates that no information is provided; a second indicator value of 2 indicates an analytical entry, and means the item in the bibliographic record contains the work represented by the added entry. Additional information is available on the USMARC Web page at http://lcweb.loc.gov/marc/bibliographic/ ecbdadde. html#mrcb700.
example

700	0	Liberace,‡d1919-
700	1	Glenn, Tyree.
700	1	Irving, Henry,‡cSir,‡d1838-1905.
700	1	Severinsen, Doc,‡d1927-
700	1	Fellini, Federico.‡4drt
700	1	Binoche, Juliette,‡d1964- ‡4prf

CORPORATE NAME

Provide access to corporate names in the 710 field, **Added Entry—Corporate Name**, which is repeatable. It is used to include additional access points in the form of names taken from the 245, **Title Statement**, 260, **Publication, Distribution, etc. (Imprint)**, or other fields deemed appropriate by the cataloging agency. Corporate name added entries differ from corporate names in the 610 in that they provide different types of information, and would be found in an online catalog using different types of searches (subject versus corporate name).

The following subfields are available for use in the 710 field: ‡a corporate name or jurisdiction name; ‡b subordinate unit; and ‡4 relator code. There are additional subfields that may be used with the 710; this text focuses discussion and examples on those that are most predominantly used.

The initial indicator value indicates type of corporate name. An initial article value 1 indicates entry in jurisdiction order; a value of 2 indicates entry in direct order. A blank second indicator value indicates that no information is provided; a second indicator value of 2 indicates an analytical entry, and means the item in the bibliographic record contains the work represented by the added entry. Additional information is available on the USMARC Web page at http://lcweb.loc.gov/marc/bibliographic/ecbdadde.html#mrcb710.
example

710	1	United States.‡bArmy.
710	2	Warner Home Video.
710	2	United States.‡bBureau of the Census.
710	2	Beatles.‡4prf

UNIFORM TITLE

Provide access to uniform titles in the 730 field, **Added Entry—Uniform Title**, which is repeatable. Uniform titles provide a title related to the resource being cataloged. Examples include earlier manifestations of a work.

The following subfields are available for use in the 730 field: ‡a uniform title; ‡f date of a work; ‡h medium; ‡k form subheading; ‡l language. There are additional subfields that may be used with the 730; this text focuses discussion and examples on those that are most predominantly used.

The initial indicator value indicates number of nonfiling characters (0-9). A blank second indicator value indicates that no information is provided; a second indicator value of 2 indicates an analytical entry, and means the item in the bibliographic record contains the work represented by the added entry. Additional information is available on the USMARC Web page at http:// lcweb.loc.gov/marc/bibliographic/ecbdadde.html#mrcb730. example

245	00	Journal of management inquiry‡h[electronic resource].
730	0	ABI/INFORM (Global ed. : Online)
245	04	The collected works of Thomas Hobbes.
730	0	Thucydides.‡tHistory of the Peloponnesian War. ‡lEnglish.‡f1992.
245	00	Blade runner.
730	0	Blade runner.‡hMotion picture.
245	00	James Joyce's "Anna Livia Plurabelle"
730	0	Finnegan's wake.‡kSelections.
245	00	65 songs, for voice and piano.
730	0	Songs.‡lEnglish & German.‡kSelections.

RELATED TITLES

Provide access to titles related to the work described in the 245 field, **Title Statement**, using the 740 field, **Added Entry—Uncontrolled Related/Analytical Title**, which is repeatable.

The following subfields are available for use in the 740 field: ‡a uncontrolled related/analytical title; ‡h medium; ‡n number of part/section of a work; ‡p name of part/section of a work. There are additional subfields that may be used with the 740; this text focuses discussion and examples on those that are most predominantly used.

The initial indicator value indicates number of nonfiling characters (0-9). A blank second indicator value indicates that no information is provided; a second indicator value of 2 indicates an analytical entry, and means the item in the bibliographic record contains the work represented by the added entry. Additional information is available on the USMARC Web page at http:// lcweb.loc.gov/marc/bibliographic/ecbdadde.html#mrcb740. example

245	00	Cape Fear.
500		Based on the novel "The Executioners" by John D. MacDonald.
740	0	Executioners.
740	0	Isis current bibliography of the history of science‡h [electronic resource].
740	0	Against all odds : inside statistics ;‡nprogram 15–16.
740	0	America by design.‡pThe workplace.

ELECTRONIC LOCATION AND ACCESS

Provide information on electronic location and access (Uniform Resource Locator or URL, etc.) in the 856 field, **Electronic Location and Access,** which is repeatable. This field may also describe type of resource, mode of access, or restrictions on access.

The following subfields are available for use in the 856 field: ‡a domain name of host; ‡b host's access number, which can be an IP address or telephone number; ‡d path, or directory or subdirectory names; ‡f a file's electronic name listed in a directory or subdirectory; ‡h processor of request, which includes user names; ‡i instruction required for a remote host to process requests; ‡k password if needed to access a resource or to issue a command; ‡l logon needed to connect to a remote resource or FTP site; ‡m contact name for assistance; ‡n name and geographic location of host; ‡q electronic format type; ‡s file size; ‡u uniform resource identifier, or URI; ‡z public note. There are additional subfields that may be used with the 856; this text focuses discussion and examples on those that are predominantly used.

Both indicators are defined for the 856 field. The first indicator value specifies type of access. In most cases, it will be 4 for "HTTP." Other first indicator values include 0 (email), 1 (FTP), 2 (Telnet), and 3 (dial-up). The second indicator value specifies relationship between the resource provided in the URI and the item described in the record as a whole. A second indicator value of 0 is used when an item is the original version or the only manifestation of a resource. A second indicator value of 1 specifies that the resource is a version of a resource (an electronic version of a print resource, or portions of a print resource made available online). A second indicator value of 2 specifies that there is a related resource available. Additional information on the 856 field is available on the USMARC Web page at http://lcweb.loc.gov/marc/bibliographic/ecbdhold.html#mrcb856.
example

856	41	‡uhttp://scc01.rutgers.edu/memdb/
856	42	‡zRelated resource available at:‡uhttp://lcweb.loc
856	41	‡uhttp://www.hti.umich.edu/english/oec/‡zAccess restricted to Rutgers University faculty, staff, and students.

The 856 field is repeatable when multiple modes of access (table of contents, index pages, etc.) are available for a resource, when the resource is available from a mirror site, or when a related version of a resource is available. Libraries must decide which location(s) to include to best serve users. In the case of mirror sites, libraries must decide if it is beneficial to provide access to mirror sites. Mirror sites are helpful when access to one location is slow or unavailable. However, including a large number of mirror sites can also mean more catalog maintenance or lack of access when URLs change quickly. Some utilities, such as OCLC, place limits on the number of fields in a record (Beck, 2001).

Module 31 specifies that the 856 field is also repeatable when: (1) an electronic journal is available by more than one mode of access, or (2) when multiple file formats exist with different file names or groups of files. This criteria is applicable to other types of electronic resources.

example

245	00	Prices (Metz)‡h[electronic resource] /‡cRainer Metz ; editors, Rudolph M. Bell and Martha C. Howell.
856	41	‡uhttp://scc01.rutgers.edu/memdb/uhttp://scc01.rutgers.edu/memdb/databasesSpecificFiles/SearchForm/SearchForm_Metzpr.asp?provenance=databaseList/
856	42	‡uhttp://scc01.rutgers.edu/memdb/
245	00	International journal of the sociology of law.
856	41	‡uhttp://www.idealibrary.com/cgi-bin/links/toc/sl ‡zAccess from campus or login via Rutgers account.
856	41	‡uhttp://www.europe.idealibrary.com/cgibin/links/toc/sl ‡zAccess from campus or login via Rutgers email account.
856	00	‡zemail subscription‡umail subscription requests to: LISTSERV@VTVM1 or NELSON.L@PLU‡iSUB AIR-L your name and institution command (e.g. DOE@UMICHUM)

For more examples of 856 fields with various access modes (ftp, gopher, etc.), consult the USMARC Web page at http://lcweb.loc.gov/marc/bibliographic/ecbdhold.html#mrcb856 and CONSER's *Module 31* at ww.loc.gov/acq/conser/module31.htm.

CLASSIFICATION

Libraries may choose to classify their Internet resources using a scheme such as LCC or DDC. Classifying electronic resources provides access to their subject content. Libraries may provide classification for Internet resources much as they would for electronic resources available on disks/discs and serial publications. However, the number of Internet resources now made available in libraries, combined with factors such as vendor instability, numerous updates and changes, etc. may also lead to assign accession numbers or other local schemes to these resources.

INFORMATION SPECIFIC TO ELECTRONIC JOURNALS AND AGGREGATORS

CONSER refers to electronic journals as "remote access computer file serials," and provides the following definition in *Module 31* (2001): "A remote access computer file serial is a work issued in designated parts for an indefinite period of time, in electronic resource format, and accessed 'via input/output devices connected electronically to a computer.'" Current CONSER policy advocates creating one record (or modifying an existing record for a print journal) to represent all formats in which a journal is available. The basic principle is to use the single-record approach if the bibliographic record for the original provides sufficient access for the electronic version. The single record approach may be used when: (1) the electronic version contains enough full text to be a satisfactory substitute for the print, and contains no additional content; or (2) when the electronic version lacks full text or provides selected full text from the original print version, and is not considered as a substitute for the original. Creation of separate records is advised when the electronic journal provides significant additional content not provided by the original print version.

It should be noted that *Module 31* will be updated in conjunction with Chapter 12, *AACR2R (1998)*, in 2002. CONSER is currently in the process of updating and revising the entire CONSER manual. Additionally, since *Module 31* specifically deals with serials that are issued remotely, it is expected that the terminology "remote access computer file serial" (including that used in the title *CONSER Cataloging Manual Module 31: Remote Access Computer File Serials)* will not change in light of the changes to Chapter 9 as reflected in the *Amendments 2001*.[1] It is likely that future CONSER modules will cover topics such as Web sites and databases, which have not always fallen neatly under the rules for monographic electronic resources or serially issued electronic resources.

SEPARATE RECORD APPROACH

This approach requires catalogers to create separate records for each version of a title (print, electronic, microform, etc.). See figure 8-1 for information on which fields must be added to the existing bibliographic record for the print original as well as the record created for the electronic version.

SINGLE RECORD APPROACH

This approach requires the cataloger to modify an existing record (or records) to accommodate information for all formats in which a title is available. See figure 8-1 for information on which fields must be added to the existing bibliographic record for the print original.

AGGREGATORS

Electronic journal titles may be offered by vendors in a variety of packages or databases. These vendors are referred to as "aggregators," which may be defined as "An intermediary service which offers subscribers electronic titles from different publishers through one interface" (Fecko, 1997: 134).

A library may have access to a particular title through more than one aggregator or as part of a database package. In such cases, a library may use the single-record approach, or may provide separate records for each aggregator or database. Current CONSER policy prohibits creation of a separate record to describe all aggregator or database versions of an electronic journal.

See figure 8-1 for guidelines to apply (per current CONSER policy) when separate records are created for titles available through aggregator packages or databases.

An explanation of the fields to be used for the separate and single records approach and for aggregator titles is provided below.

Code the 008/22 fixed field (form of original) and 008/23 (form of item) for the original. The code will be "as" for printed language material (a) and serial (s). The 008 field provides information about bibliographic records as a whole plus any special bibliographic characteristics of the item being cataloged (Network Development and MARC Standards Office, Library of Congress).

Optionally, provide a 007 field, **Physical Description Fixed Field—General Information** for the electronic version. Consult the beginning of this chapter for a detailed description of the 007 field.

Figure 8-1 Comparison of Possible Approaches for Cataloging Electronic Journals		
SEPARATE RECORD APPROACH	SINGLE RECORD APPROACH	AGGREGATORS
Add the following fields to an existing record for the print original:	Code 008/22 (form of original) and 008/23 (form of item) for original	130 Uniform Title, Main Entry
530 Additional Physical Form	Provide an 007 Physical Description Fixed Field for electronic version (optional)	260 Publication, Distribution, Etc. Information
730 Uniform Title	530 Additional Physical Form	362 Dates of Publication and/ or Sequential Designation
776 Additional Physical Form	740 Related/Analytical Title	776 Additional Physical Form
856 Electronic Location and Access	856 Electronic Location and Access	856 Electronic Location and Access
Add the following fields to the record for the electronic version:		
730 Uniform Title		
776 Additional Physical Form		
856 Electronic Location and Access		

example

```
007          cr mn
c = electronic resource
r = remote
blank
m = multicolored
n = dimensions not applicable
blank = no sound (silent)
```

Uniform Title, Main Entry

Provide a 130 field **Main Entry Uniform Title** when the title is the same as that of the print version. Qualify the uniform title with the phrase "Online." When records are created for multiple aggregator/database versions of an electronic journal, distinguish the versions further with qualifiers. The 130 field is not repeatable.

The first indicator value for the 130 field specifies number of nonfiling characters, with a range of 0-9 available. The second indicator is undefined.

Additional information on the 130 field is available on the USMARC Web page at http://lcweb.loc.gov/marc/bibliographic/ecbdmain.html#mrcb130.

example

130	0	INSPEC (Online)
130	0	American quarterly (Online : Project Muse)
130	0	ERIC (Online : OVID)
130	0	Portal (Baltimore, Md. : Online)

Publication, Distribution, Etc.

Record publication information for the print version as well as for aggregators.

example

| 260 | | Philadelphia :‡bUniversity of Pennsylvania ;‡aBaltimore, MD :‡bJohns Hopkins University, |

Dates of Publication and/or Sequential Designation

Provide an unformatted 362 field, **Dates of Publication and/or Sequential Designation,** if electronic coverage does not begin with the first issue. Provide a 500 note specifying the source of description in cases when the first issue is not available. The 362 field is repeatable.

There are a number of subfields that may be used in the 362 field. Additional information on the 362 field is available on the USMARC Web page at http://lcweb.loc.gov/marc/bibliographic/ecbdphys.html#mrcb362.

The first indicator value for the 362 provides format of date used in the note. A first indicator value of 0 indicates that the note is in a formatted style; a value of 1 indicates that the note is in an unformatted style. The second indicator value is undefined.

example

362	0	Vol. 1, no. 1 (Jan. 2001)-
362	0	Vol. 1- Oct. 1925-
362	1	Vol. 1 (1972)-v. 18, no. 5 (Nov. 1989).

Additional Physical Form

Provide a 530 field, **Additional Physical Form Available Note,** which is repeatable, for the electronic version of the title. Con-

sult the beginning of this chapter for a detailed description of the 530 field.
example

530	Also available online on Internet via WWW; access restricted to institutions with a subscription to ProQuest Direct, ABI/ INFORM, Project Muse database.
530	Also available online on Internet via WWW; access restricted to institutions with a site license to the JSTOR collection.

Uniform Title

Provide a 730 field when the electronic title differs from that of the original.
example

245	00	Journal of management inquiry‡h[electronic resource].
730	0	Management inquiry (Online)

Related/Analytical Title

Provide a 740 field when the title of the electronic version differs from that of the original.
example

245	00	Ancient philosophical literature review.
740	0	Philosophical review.

Additional Physical Form

Provide 776 fields to link from electronic versions to print, and vice-versa. Do not provide links to the various electronic versions of a title. Consult the preceding section for a detailed description and examples of the 776 field. This field is repeatable.

The first indicator value for the 776 field indicates whether a note will be displayed from data contained in the field. A first indicator value of 0 is used when a note is displayed; a note will not be displayed with a first indicator value of 1. The second indicator value controls the display constant. A second indicator value of blank specifies when the item is available in another format; no display constant is generated with a second indicator value of 8.

A number of subfields are available for use in the 776 field. This discussion will concentrate on those predominantly used. The following subfields may be used in the 776 field: ‡a main entry; ‡b edition; ‡t title; ‡w record control number; ‡x International Standard Serial Number (ISSN); and ‡z ISBN. Additional information on the 776 field is available on the USMARC Web page at http://lcweb.loc.gov/marc/bibliographic/ecbdlink. html#mrcb776.

example

| 776 | 1 | ‡tAnnual review of anthropology (Online) |
| 776 | 1 | ‡tJournal of American history (Bloomington, Ind. : Online)‡w(DLC)sn 97023007‡w(OCoLC)35782298 |

Electronic Location and Access

Provide 856 fields as needed for the electronic version of a title. Consult the preceding section for a detailed description and examples of the 856 field. This field is repeatable.

Additionally, libraries, regardless of choice of single or separate record approach, may also provide a separate bibliographic record, created using the electronic resources format, for aggregator packages or databases.

ELECTRONIC BOOKS

Libraries have begun to acquire electronic books, also known as "e-books." E-books are created using an encrypted format, require a download, and must be "unlocked" to a specific device, or are authenticated to a specific reader's computer (DeCandido, 2001). They are readable on a computer screen, may be downloaded to a PC or a digital assistant, such as a PalmPilot, or may be placed on a reader specifically designated for that purpose. Some vendors that provide e-books are netLibrary, ebrary, Ibooks, and Books24x7.

Cataloging e-books provides a number of challenges for libraries. The large number of titles available, and often on a limited time basis, make libraries reluctant to spend staff resources and funds to catalog e-book titles from large packages. In some cases, vendors (netLibrary, for example) provide MARC records to libraries. However, MARC records provided by vendors may not contain full-level cataloging or standardized subject headings. Some libraries are following the single or separate record approach used for electronic journals available from aggregators. Libraries may also opt to create a record for the e-book package, and include the e-book titles in a 505 field, **Formatted Contents Note**, and provide 700 fields, **Added Entry, Personal Name**, and 740 fields, **Added Entry, Uncontrolled Related/Analytical Title**, for each title. Since e-book cataloging standards are evolving, and no definite guidelines have been proposed within the profession, this discussion will not provide further information, instruction, or examples.

EXAMPLES OF BIBLIOGRAPHIC RECORDS

Examples follow on the next page.

Figure 8-2 Database Available Via the World Wide Web

| Control | **Bib** | MARC Hldgs | Vol/Copy |

Fixed Fields

Rec_Type: a	Bib_Lvt m	Enc_Lvt	Desc a
TypeCtrl	Entrd 010126	Dat_Tp c	Date1 2000
Date2 9999	Ctry nju	Lang eng	Mod_Rec
Source d	Illus	Audience	Repr
Cont j	GovtPub	ConfPub 0	Festschr 0
Indx 0	Fiction 0	Biog	

Bibliographic Info

001			a1507898
007			cr cn
040			NjR|cNjR
130	0		Books in print (Online)
245	10		Booksinprint.com|h[electronic resource].
246	3		booksinprint.com|h[electronic resource]
246	1		|iTitle in HTML header:|aBowker's BooksinPrint.com
246	30		Bowker's Books in print|h[electronic resource]
246	30		Books in print with reviews|h[electronic resource]
246	30		R.R. Bowker's Books in print|h[electronic resource]
256			Computer data
260			New Providence, N.J. :|bR.R. Bowker,|cc2000-
500			Title from welcome page (viewed Jan. 26, 2001).
505	0		In the media -- Publisher homepages -- Publisher spotlight -- Our resource guides -- What's new -- Bowker's Bookwire -- Bowkerlink -- Ulrichsweb.com -- Literary market place -- Quick search -- Forthcoming book room -- Children's room -- Bowker's fiction room.
520			Automated version of Books in print offering information on books, sound recordings, and videorecordings. Searchable by keyword, author, title, ISBN, or UPC. May also be browsed by general subject, or using the following indexes: author, title, publisher, performer, or video subjects.
530			Also available in print.
538			Mode of access: World Wide Web.
596			RU-ONLINE

Figure 8-2 *Continued*

Figure 8-3 Electronic Journal

| Control | **Bib** | MARC Hldgs | Vol/Copy |

Fixed Fields

Rec_Type: a	Bib_Lvl: s	Enc_Lvl:	Desc: a
TypeCtrl:	Entrd: 910510	Dat_Tp: c	Date1: 1992
Date2: 9999	Ctry: cau	Lang: eng	Mod_Rec:
Source: d	Frequn: q	Regulr: r	ISDS: 1
Ser_Type: p	Phys_Med:	Repr:	Pub_Type:
Cont:	GovtPub:	ConfPub: 0	Alphabt: a
S/L_Ent: 0			

Bibliographic Info

Tag	Ind	Data
001		a1393818
007		cr mnu
030		JMNIE6
037		|bSage Publications, 2455 Teller Rd., Thousand Oaks, CA 91320
040		NjR|cNjR
050	4	HD28|b.J5987
130	0	Journal of management inquiry (Online)
245	00	Journal of management inquiry|h[electronic resource].
246	13	JMI|h[electronic resource]
260		Newbury Park, CA :|bSage Periodicals Press,
310		Quarterly
362	1	Began publication with: Vol. 1, no. 1 (Mar. 1992).
500		Published: Thousand Oaks, CA, 1996-
500		Description based on online display of: Vol. 8, no. 1 (Mar. 1999); title from title screen.
506		Access restricted to institutions with a subscription to ProQuest Direct, ABI/INFORM.
516		Electronic journal.
530		Also issued in a print version.
538		Mode of access: Internet through ProQuest Direct.
550		Sponsored by the Western Academy of Management.
596		RU-ONLINE
650	0	Management|vPeriodicals.
650	0	Organizational behavior|vPeriodicals.
710	2	Western Academy of Management.
710	2	ProQuest Direct.
730	0	ABI/INFORM (Global ed. : Online)
776	1	|tJournal of management inquiry|x1056-4926
856	40	|zAccess from campus or login via Rutgers account.|uhttp://www.umi.com/pqdauto

Figure 8-4 Electronic Journal

Control	**Bib**	MARC Hldgs	Vol/Copy

Fixed Fields

Rec_Type: a	Bib_Lvl: s	Enc_Lvl:	Desc: a
TypeCtrl:	Entrd: 010717	Dat_Tp: c	Date1: 1999
Date2: 9999	Ctry: nju	Lang: eng	Mod_Rec:
Source: d	Frequn: u	Regulr: u	ISDS:
Ser_Type:	Phys_Med:	Repr:	Pub_Type:
Cont:	GovtPub: s	ConfPub: 0	Alphabt:
S/L_Ent: 0			

Bibliographic Info

001			a1611579
007			cr mnu
040			NjR|cNjR|dNjR
043			n-us-nj
050		4	MT18|b.V58
130		0	Visions of research in music education (Online)
245		00	Visions of research in music|h[electronic resource] : |bVRME.
246		30	VRME|h[electronic resource]
260			New Brunswick, N.J. :|bNew Jersey Music Educators Association,|cc1999-
362			Vol. 1 (1999)-
516			Electronic journal.
538			Mode of access: World Wide Web via the Internet.
550			"Made possible through the facilities of the Mason Gross School of the Arts of Rutgers, The State University of New Jersey."
596			RU-ONLINE
650		0	Music|xInstruction and study|vPeriodicals.
650		0	School music|xInstruction and study|zNew Jersey |vPeriodicals.
650		0	Music in universities and colleges|vPeriodicals.
710		2	New Jersey Music Educators Association.
710		2	Mason Gross School of the Arts (Rutgers University)
710		2	Rutgers University.
856		40	|uhttp://musicweb.rutgers.edu/vrme/|zAccess restricted tp Rutgers University faculty, staff, and students.
978			ls|d20010717

Figure 8-5 Electronic Journal

| Control | **Bib** | MARC Hldgs | Vol/Copy |

Fixed Fields

Rec_Type: a	Bib_Lvl: s	Enc_Lvl: 4	Desc: a
TypeCtrl:	Entrd: 010717	Dat_Tp: c	Date1: 2001
Date2: 9999	Ctry: gw	Lang: eng	Mod_Rec:
Source: d	Frequn: u	Regulr: u	ISDS:
Ser_Type: p	Phys_Med:	Repr:	Pub_Type:
Cont:	GovtPub:	ConfPub: 0	Alphabt:
S/L_Ent: 0			

Bibliographic Info

001			a1611369
007			cr mnu
022			1591-9528
040			NjR|cNjR
050		4	RB40|b.C5811
130		0	Clinical and experimental medicine (Online)
245		00	Clinical and experimental medicine|h[electronic resource].
246		13	Clin exp med|h[electronic resource]
260			Milano, Italy :|bSpringer-Verlag Italia,
362		0	Vol. 1, no. 1 (2001)-
500			Title from journal's general information screen (viewed July 17, 2001).
506			Subscription and registration required for access.
516			Electronic journal.
530			Also available in print ed.
538			Mode of access: World Wide Web via Internet.
550			Digitized and made available by Springer LINK Online Service.
596			RU-ONLINE
650		0	Medicine, Experimental|vPeriodicals.
650		0	Medicine|vPeriodicals.
650		0	Clinical chemistry|vPeriodicals.
710		2	LINK (Online service)
776		1	|tClinical and experimental medicine|x1591-8890
856		40	|uhttp://link.springer-ny.com/link/service/journals/10238/index.htm|zAccess restricted to Rutgers University faculty, staff, and students.
978			cb|d20020110|nrecat.

Figure 8-6 Electronic Journal

Control	**Bib**	MARC Hldgs	Vol/Copy

Fixed Fields

Rec_Type: a	Bib_Lvt: s	Enc_Lvl:	Desc: a
TypeCtrl	Entrd: 960430	Dat_Tp: c	Date1: 199u
Date2: 9999	Ctry: ja	Lang: eng	Mod_Rec:
Source: d	Frequn: q	Regulr: r	ISDS:
Ser_Type: p	Phys_Med:	Repr:	Pub_Type:
Cont:	GovtPub:	ConfPub: 0	Alphabt:
S/L_Ent: 0			

Bibliographic Info

001			a1610257
003			CStRLIN
005			20010227084830.0
007			cr mnu
022			1616-3915
040			NjR|cNjR
043			a-ja---
050		4	QL614|b.I29
130		0	Ichthyological research (Online)
245		00	Ichthyological research|h[electronic resource].
260			Tokyo, Japan :|bIchthyological Society of Japan,
310			Quarterly
506			Access restricted by licensing agreement.
515			Carries the vol. numbering of: Gyoruigaku zasshi.
516			Electronic journal.
530			Also issued in a print version which started with vol. 43, no. 1 (Feb. 20, 1996).
538			Mode of access: World Wide Web via the Internet.
550			Digitized and made available by Springer LINK Online Service.
596			RU-ONLINE

Figure 8-6 *Continued*

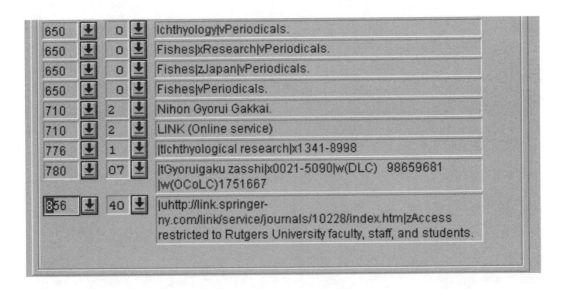

Figure 8-7 Single Record Approach for Journal Available in Print and Electronically

| Control | **Bib** | MARC Hldgs | All Volumes |

Fixed Fields

Rec_Type: a	Bib_Lvt: s	Enc_Lvt:	Desc: a
TypeCtrl:	Entrd: 970716	Dat_Tp: c	Date1: 19uu
Date2: 9999	Ctry: nju	Lang: eng	Mod_Rec:
Source: d	Frequn: a	Regulr: r	ISDS:
Ser_Type:	Phys_Med:	Repr:	Pub_Type:
Cont:	GovtPub:	ConfPub: 0	Alphabt:
S/L_Ent: 0			

Bibliographic Info

001			a1250459
005			19970717134403.0
007			cr mnu
035			(CStRLIN)NJRG97-S846
040			NjR|cNjR
050		4	QA75.5|b.D56
090			QA75.5|b.D56|i07/17/97 T
110		2	DIMACS (Group)
245		10	DIMACS annual report.
246		14	Annual report for National Science Foundation
260			[S.l.] :|bDIMACS, Center for Discrete Mathematics and Theoretical Computer Science,
300			v. ;|c28 cm.
440		0	DIMACS technical report
500			"DIMACS is a cooperative project of Rutgers University, Princeton University, AT&T Bell Laboratories and Bellcore".
500			"DIMACS is an NSF Science and Technology Center".
530			Also available online on Internet via WWW.
536			Supported in part by the NSF.|bSTC-91-19999
536			Supported in part by the New Jersey Commission on Science and Technology
590			Also available on the University's INFO system.
596			LSM RU-ONLINE

Figure 8-7 *Continued*

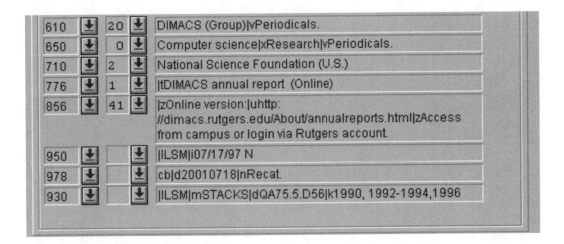

Figure 8-8 Single Record Approach for Journal Available in Print and Electronically

| Control | **Bib** | MARC Hldgs | All Volumes |

Fixed Fields

Rec_Type: a	Bib_Lvl: s	Enc_Lvl:	Desc: a
TypeCtrl:	Entrd: 830914	Dat_Tp: c	Date1: 1967
Date2: 9999	Ctry: nju	Lang: eng	Mod_Rec:
Source: d	Frequn: q	Regulr: r	ISDS:
Ser_Type: p	Phys_Med:	Repr: a	Pub_Type:
Cont:	GovtPub:	ConfPub: 0	Alphabt: a
S/L_Ent: 0			

Bibliographic Info

001			a36682
005			19910828121514.0
007			hdrafb---buca
011			769450
022	0		0022-4529
035			(CStRLIN)NJRG83-S1955
040			NjR|cNjR
090			HN1|b.J6|i08/28/91 CT|h09/16/83 CT
245	00		Journal of social history|h[microform].
260	00		New Brunswick, N.J. :|bRutgers University ;|bdistributed by Transaction Periodicals Consortium,
300			v. :|bill. ;|c24 cm.
362	1		Began with: Vol. 1, no. 1 (fall 1967).
500			Imprint varies.
500			Description based on: Vol. 7, no. 1 (fall 1973).
530			Also available online on Internet via WWW.
533			Microfilm.|bAnn Arbor, Mich. :|cUniversity Microfilms International.|e microfilm reels : negative ; 16 mm. |f(Current periodicals series ; publication no. 2504-5)
596			DGLSS KLMR
650	0		Social history|vPeriodicals.
650	0		Political sociology|vPeriodicals.
760	1		|tCurrent periodicals series
8	41		|uhttp://www.umi.com/pqdauto|zAccess restricted to Rutgers University faculty, staff, and students.

Figure 8-8 *Continued*

Figure 8-9 Database Available Via the World Wide Web

| Control | **Bib** | MARC Hldgs | Vol/Copy |

Fixed Fields

Rec_Type: m	Bib_Lvt: s	Enc_Lvt:	Desc: a
TypeCtrl:	Entrd: 000807	Dat_Tp: c	Date1: 2000
Date2: 9999	Ctry: nju	Lang: eng	Mod_Rec:
Source: d	Frequn:	Regulr:	Audience:
FileType: e	GovtPub: s		

Bibliographic Info

001			a1480912
007			cr nn
040			NjR|cNjR|dNjR
043			n-us-nj
245		1	CamdenBase|h[electronic resource] :|ba database of citations about Camden, New Jersey /|ca joint project of Rutgers University Libraries' Scholarly Communication Center and Paul Robeson Library.
246		3	Camden Base|h[electronic resource]
246		1	|iTitle in HTML header:|aCAMDEN database
246		30	Database of citations about Camden, New Jersey |h[electronic resource]
260			New Brunswick, N.J. :|bRutgers University Libraries, Scholarly Communicaton Center ;|aCamden, N.J. : |bRutgers University Libraries, Paul Robeson Library, |c[2000?-
500			Title from introductory screen (viewed Aug. 7, 2000).
500			Camden images courtesy of William M. Hoffman, Jr.
500			Database.
505		0	Search -- Help -- Examples -- Paul Robeson Library -- SCC -- About -- Feedback.
520			A database of selected citations of journal, book and newspaper articles about the city of Camden, New Jersey. The documents cover economic, political, and social events in the city from 1945 to the present. Provides bibliographic access to over 4,000 articles; searchable by keyword, or may be browsed using specific themes.
538			Mode of access: World Wide Web browser.
596			RU-ONLINE

Figure 8-9 *Continued*

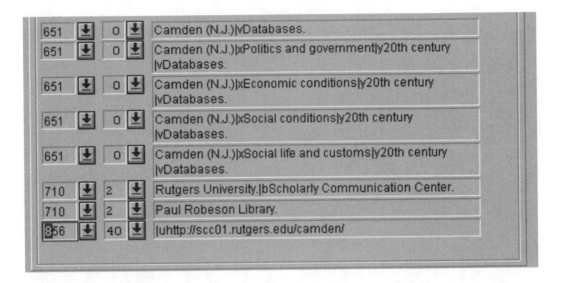

Figure 8-10 Database Available Via the World Wide Web

| Control | **Bib** | MARC Hldgs | Vol/Copy |

Fixed Fields

Rec_Type: m	Bib_Lvt: s	Enc_Lvt:	Desc: a
TypeCtrl:	Entrd: 000523	Dat_Tp: c	Date1: 2000
Date2: 9999	Ctry: nju	Lang: eng	Mod_Rec:
Source: d	Frequn:	Regulr:	Audience:
FileType: e	GovtPub: s		

Bibliographic Info

001			a1468277
007			cr nn
040			NjR|cNjR|dNjR|dNjR
043			n-us-nj
245		00	New Jersey environmental digital library|h[electronic resource] /|csponsored by the New Jersey Department of Environmental Protection and the Scholarly Communication Center, Rutgers University Libraries.
246		30	NJ environmental digital library|h[electronic resource]
246		30	Environmental digital library|h[electronic resource]
246		30	NJEDL|h[electronic resource]
260			New Brunswick, N.J. :|bScholarly Communication Center, Rutgers University Libraries,|c[2000-
500			Title from welcome screen (viewed July 24, 2000).
500			Samples from the collection include the NEPPS reference collection from NJ DEP, documents from NGOs and municipal governments, maps, and multimedia materials.
505		0	Home -- Search library -- Find organizations -- Enter records -- Contact us -- About -- Help -- Partners -- Feedback.
520			"...provides access to information about New Jersey's environment in full text and graphic content. Much of the material in this collection is undocumented (aka 'grey literature')."--Welcome screen
538			Mode of access: World Wide Web browser.
596			RU-ONLINE

Figure 8-10 *Continued*

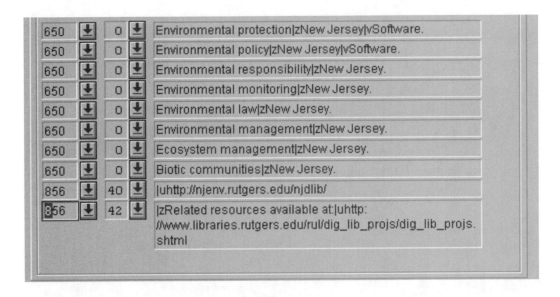

Figure 8-11 Database Available Via the World Wide Web

| Control | **Bib** | MARC Hldgs | Vol/Copy |

Fixed Fields

Rec_Type: m	Bib_Lvt: s	Enc_Lvt:	Desc: a
TypeCtrl:	Entrd: 000126	Dat_Tp: c	Date1: 1999
Date2: 9999	Ctry: nju	Lang: eng	Mod_Rec:
Source: d	Frequn: u	Regulr: n	Audience:
FileType: m	GovtPub: s		

Bibliographic Info

001	⬇		⬇	a1441623
007	⬇		⬇	cr cn
040	⬇		⬇	NjR|cNjR|dNjR|dNjR
245	⬇	00	⬇	Alcohol Studies database|h[electronic resource] / |cdeveloped by the Scholarly Communication Center and the Center of Alcohol Studies.
246	⬇	3	⬇	Center of Alcohol Studies library database web site |h[electronic resource]
260	⬇		⬇	New Brunswick, N.J. :|bRutgers University Libraries, |c1999-
500	⬇		⬇	Title from introductory screen (viewed January 26, 2000).
516	⬇		⬇	Database
520	⬇		⬇	This site provides access to the Alcohol Studies Database. The database contains over 50,000 citations for journal articles, books, book chapters, dissertations, conference papers, and audio-visual materials.
538	⬇		⬇	Mode of acess: Internet via the World Wide Web.
596				RU-ONLINE
650	⬇	0	⬇	Alcohol.
650	⬇	0	⬇	Alcoholics.
650	⬇	0	⬇	Alcoholism|xStudy and teaching.
650	⬇	0	⬇	Alcoholism|xTreatment.
710	⬇	2	⬇	Rutgers Center of Alcohol Studies.
710	⬇	2	⬇	Rutgers University.|bScholarly Communication Center.
856	⬇	40	⬇	|uhttp://scc01.rutgers.edu/alcohol_studies/

REFERENCES

Beck, Melissa, Bill Anderson, Les Hawkins, and Regina Reynolds. "CONSER Cataloging Manual Module 31: Remote Access Computer File Serials" Washington, D.C.: Library of Congress. (June 2001) Available at: *www.loc.gov/acq/conser/module31.htm.*

DeCandido, Grace. "PLA Tech Note: E-Books" Chicago: Public Library Association. (August 2001) Available at: *www.pla.org/technotes/ebooks.htm*

Fecko, Mary Beth. 1997. *Electronic Resources: Access and Issues.* London: Bowker-Saur.

Joint Steering Committee for the Revision of AACR2. 1998. *Anglo-American Cataloguing Rules, Second Edition, 1998 Revision.* Chicago: American Library Association.

Network Development and MARC Standards Office, Library of Congress in cooperation with Standards and Support, National Library of Canada. 1999. *MARC 21 Format for Bibliographic Data Including Guidelines for Content Designation, 1999 Edition.* Washington, D.C.: Library of Congress Distribution Service.

Weber, Mary Beth. 1999. "Factors to be Considered in the Selection and Cataloging of Internet Resources." *Library Hi Tech* 17, no. 3, 298-303.

ENDNOTE

1. E-mail correspondence in November, 2001, with Jean Hirons, Coordinator, CONSER Office, Library of Congress.

9 METADATA AND MARC FORMATS

OVERVIEW

This chapter provides a brief overview of metadata in relation to MARC format as used in libraries. It provides a point of information in the overall discussion of cataloging nonbook resources and is not meant to be all encompassing.

MARC format has been the predominant scheme used by libraries to represent and exchange information in machine-readable form for a number of years. MARC is an acronym for "Machine-Readable Cataloging," and was developed as an automated alternative to printed catalog cards. The format and presentation of information in MARC bibliographic records closely resembles that of the printed catalog card. MARC is a "...system by which data elements within bibliographic records are uniquely labelled for computer handling" (British Library, 2001).

There are five implementations of MARC format: authority data, bibliographic data, classification data, community information, and holdings data. This discussion is limited to MARC 21 Format for Bibliographic Data which is used in the United States and Canada, and will soon be used in the United Kingdom as the result of international efforts to realign the various versions of MARC. Since many of the variable fields used in the MARC bibliographic format have been discussed in earlier chapters, this chapter will not outline the numerous available variable fields in the detail which this chapter provides for metadata.

METADATA

Metadata is described as information that qualifies other information. Typical examples include bibliographic description, information about intellectual property rights, terms of use, reviews, abstracts and summaries, and provenance information (Lynch, 2001). Metadata is available in many different forms. Descriptive cataloging is one form of metadata. Carl Lagoze describes MARC records in this manner, "MARC records are generally the domain of professional catalogers because of the complex rules and arcane structure of the MARC record. In addition there are a number of simpler descriptive rules, such as that suggested by the Dublin Core. These are usable by the majority of authors, but do not offer the degree of precision and organization that characterizes library cataloging" (2001).

Dublin Core was originally created for author-generated description of Web resources. It is now used by libraries and museums, and other institutions that provide formal resource description. Dublin Core is an "unqualified" metadata standard, meaning that it is not specific to any discipline or resource description set. It was designed to serve as the lowest form of resource description. Dublin Core was designed so that the data elements could be defined by document authors or site managers, and does not require a trained cataloger or indexer.

There are two types of library applications of Dublin Core: (1) the first permits libraries to participate in network search services, and (2) the second permits libraries to provide patrons with seamless access to both libraries and non-library resources. The second application allows description of new resources that can not be described adequately or cost-effectively by traditional MARC cataloging (Lynch, 2001).

METADATA ELEMENTS

Metadata elements fall into 3 categories: (1) elements related to *content*, (2) elements related to *intellectual property aspects*, and (3) elements related to *instantiation*, or representation, of the resource. Elements related to content are: title, subject, description, source, language, relation, and coverage. Elements related to intellectual property aspects are: creator, publisher, contributor, and rights. Elements related to instantiation are: date, type, format, and identifier. Metadata elements are designed to permit users to find, identify, select, obtain, and use resources. An explanation of the elements of the Dublin Core follows.

Title- Refers to the resource name provided by the creator or publisher.
example

John Muir exhibit.
Woodcut portrait by Michael McCurdy.

Subject- Refers to the resource topic, and is defined by keywords or phrases that describe the resource's subject or content.
example

Sierra Club.
Muir, John, 1838-1914.

Creator- Refers to the person or organization with primary responsibility for the resource's intellectual content.
example

Sierra Club.
Wood, Harold.

Publisher- The party, organization, or corporate body responsible for making the resource available in its present form.
example

Sierra Club.

Contributor- Person or organization that has made significant (but not primary) intellectual contributions to the resource.
example

Chinn, Harvey.
McCurdy, Michael.

Date- Refers to the date when the resource was created or made available.
example

1994-06-00

Type- Refers to a resource category. Examples cited by OCLC include home page, novel, technical report, essay, and dictionary.
example

Compound/mixed.
Image.

Format- Refers to the nature of the resource, rather than type. This element describes a resource's data format, and identifies software and/or hardware requirements.
example

World Wide Web resource.
JPEG image (file size = 2 kilobytes)

Identifier- Refers to the unique identifier given to the resource. Typical examples are a URI or an ISBN.

example

www.sierraclub.org/john_muir_exhibit/
www.sierraclub.org/john_muir_exhibit/pictures/graphics/
woodcut_portrait_of_john_muir_by_michael_mccurdy

Relation- This element identifies a second resource, and describes its relation to the resource being described.
example

Web page is for Portraits in art and sculpture of John Muir.

Source- Provides information about a second resource from which the present is derived.
example

Sierra Club Web Server.
John Muir Exhibit: Images and Pictures.

Language- This element provides information on the language of the resource.
example

English.

Coverage- Describes the extent or scope of a resource's content, and describes spatial or temporal characteristics or jurisdiction.
example

2000-2001

Rights- Provides a statement or link to information about a rights statement for the resource.
example

Copyright held by Scholarly Communication Center, 2001.

For additional information on the Dublin Core, see the home page of the Dublin Core Metadata Initiative at http://dublincore.org/.

METADATA CREATION

CORC (Cooperative Online Resource Catalog) is a service provided by OCLC that enables libraries to create metadata for bibliographic records. The service was first made available in July, 2000. CORC provides multi-record creation that automatically generates records for all the links on Web pages. This product is intended for noncatalogers as well as resource description specialists. OCLC states that CORC is international, and provides an alternative to more costly description models such as full-level cataloging using MARC format.

OCLC is working to introduce a single interface for cataloging and metadata services. The interface will provide the benefits of a Web browser and the functionality of Windows-based software. It will also provide multiple user-defined views of records, automatic record creation for electronic resources, and URL checking and notification. The service will be phased in, and is expected to be fully operational by 2003.

MAPPING BETWEEN METADATA AND MARC

There are cases when a library will need to convert metadata information into MARC format in order to provide cataloging treatment. Cataloging Web resources or other nonstandard resources are two such examples. Several "crosswalks" are available that provide mapping between MARC format and various metadata schemes. Consult the Appendix for more information. In addition to crosswalks, there are products that will assist with the conversion. Two are described in the following paragraphs.

d2m converts Dublin Core metadata to MARC. The converter was developed by the Nordic Metadata Project, and is available at www.bibsys.no/meta/d2m.

MARCit is a tool that permits libraries to catalog Internet resources. It converts metadata, and creates a MARC record that includes an 007, **Physical Description Fixed Field**, an 040, **Cataloging Source**, a 245, ‡a, ‡h, **Title Statement** and **General Material Designation**, a 256, ‡a, **Computer File Characteristics**, a 516, ‡a, **Type of Computer File or Data Note**, a 538, ‡a, **Systems Detail Note**, and an 856, ‡u, **Electronic Location and Access** and **Uniform Resource Identifier**. More information on MARCit is available at www.marcit.com/.

COMPARISON OF MARC AND METADATA

Libraries are exploring alternative ways to provide access to materials in their collections, including materials available through external databases and sources. Traditional MARC format may not adequately describe these resources, or may prove too costly and labor intensive. In such cases, metadata may provide a viable alternative. Some online catalogs as well as databases can map various metadata schemes into MARC, and vice-versa. Mapping works by finding common elements between the schemes. Metadata provides more flexibility in description than MARC, and can be adapted to the specific needs of a particular user community. However, the lack of structure in metadata schemes can result in data inconsistency.

A comparison of metadata and MARC, illustrated using formatted records, follows.

Figure 9-1, Comparison of Metadata and MARC Format	
METADATA	MARC FORMAT
15 elements (unqualified Dublin Core)	Numerous elements
Intended for use by non-catalogers as well as those experienced with using formal description models	Requires specialized training and expertise
Commonly understood set of descriptors, increases possibility of interoperability across disciplines	Internationally known and recognized data
Built on international consensus	Realignment of MARC taking place internationally
Well-suited for description of Web-based resources	Best suited to print resources; well suited to resources in a tangible, physical form
Flexible	Greater flexibility provided through format integration
No limits to field length	Changes and develops slowly; outpaced by technology; often provides inadequate means for access and description of Web-based resources
All fields optional and repeatable as needed	Some fields optional, others required; only some fields are repeatable

EXAMPLES OF MARC AND METADATA RECORDS

Figure 9-2 MARC and Metadata Records

MARC Record for John Muir Exhibit

245 00	John Muir exhibit ‡h[electronic resource] : ‡bpictures and images.
246 3	Pictures and images of John Muir ‡h[electronic resource]
260	[San Francisco] : ‡bSierra Club, ‡c[199-?]
500	World Wide Web resource.
500	Title taken from Web document (viewed August 3, 2001).
600 10	Muir, John, ‡d1838-1914.
610 20	Sierra Club.
650 0	Naturalists ‡zUnited States.
710 2	Sierra Club.
856 40	‡uhttp://www.sierraclub.org/john_muir_exhibit/pictures/

Dublin Core Metadata Record for John Muir Exhibit

Title	John Muir Exhibit : Pictures and Images.
Subject	Muir, John, 1838-1914.
Subject	Sierra Club.
Subject	Naturalists.
Subject	Conservationists.
Description	Internet collection of materials on the life and legacy of John Muir, conservationist and founder of the Sierra Club.
Description	Harold Wood has served as the Content Editor of the Exhibit since its inception in 1994 and has been its Webmaster since 1997. Send suggestions, comments, and corrections about the Web server or pointers to Muir-related resources on the Internet to Harold Wood at harold.wood@sierraclub.org. Harvey Chinn originated the concept of a John Muir exhibit in 1994, and created all the original HTML formatting of the website, and maintained the Exhibit until 1997.
Creator	Sierra Club.
Publisher	Sierra Club.
Contributor	Chinn, Harvey.
Contributor	Wood, Harold.
Date	1994-06-00.
Type	compound/mixed.
Format	World Wide Web resource.
Identifier	http://www.sierraclub.org/john_muir_exhibit/
Source	Sierra Club Web Server.

Figure 9-3 MARC and Metadata Records

MARC Record for Woodcut Portrait of John Muir

100	1	McCurdy, Michael.
245	10	[Woodcut portrait of John Muir] ‡h[electronic resource] / ‡cMichael McCurdy.
245	30	Woodcut of John Muir ‡h[electronic resource]
260		[S.l. : ‡b.n., ‡c19- - ?]
500		World Wide Web resource (viewed on August 3, 2001).
500		Title supplied by cataloger.
520		Woodcut portrait of Sierra Club founder John Muir featured in the online exhibit "John Muir : Images and Pictures."
600	10	Muir, John, ‡d1838-1914.
610	20	Sierra Club.
650	0	Naturalists ‡zUnited States.
856	41	‡chttp://www.sierraclub.org/john_muir_exhibit/pictures/graphics/woodcut_portrait_of_john_muir_by_michael_mccurdy.jpg

Dublin Core Record for Woodcut Portrait of John Muir

Title	Woodcut portrait by Michael McCurdy.
Subject	Woodcut portrait of John Muir by Michael McCurdy.
Subject	Muir, John, 1838-1914.
Description	Woodcut portrait by artist Michael McCurdy of Sierra Club founder John Muir. Provided to the John Muir Exhibit by the artist.
Creator	Wood, Harold.
Publisher	Sierra Club.
Contributor	McCurdy, Michael.
Type	Image.
Format	JPEG image (file size = 22 kilobytes).
Identifier	www.sierraclub.org/john_muir_exhibit/pictures/graphics/woodcut_portrait_of_john_muir_by_michael_mccurdy.jpg
Source	John Muir Exhibit : Images and Pictures.
Language	English.

REFERENCES

British Library. "MARC Home Page." London: British Library. (July 2001) Available at: *http://minos.bl.uk/information/marc.html*.

Lagoze, Carl. "The Warwick Framework: A Container Architecture for Diverse Sets of Metadata." Reston, Va.: Corporation for National Research Initiatives. (July 2001) Available at: *www.dlib.org/dlib/july96/lagoze/07lagoze.html*.

Lynch Clifford. "The Dublin Core Descriptive Metadata Program: Strategic Implications for Libraries and Networked Information Access." *D-Lib Magazine* Issue 196 (February 2001) Available at: *www.arl.org/newsltr/196/dublin.html*.

A FINAL WORD

The purpose of this text is to assist catalogers of nonbook resources with bibliographic description. This text is intended to be used in conjunction with standard cataloging sources such as *AACR2R (1998)*, Library of Congress's *Subject Cataloging Manual*, and *MARC21 Bibliographic Format*. Cataloging policies, including level of description, choice of access points, and classification type are driven by local needs, user communities, and available staff and financial resources. This text is aimed at providing catalogers with information that will help them to make those decisions and to create high-quality bibliographic records.

This is a time of great change in the area of cataloging. Professionals are devising solutions to help keep pace with emerging technologies, which in turn place an enormous burden on cataloging departments. Technologies such as electronic journal titles available through aggregator databases make it nearly impossible for even the best-staffed and well-equipped cataloging department to keep pace with the workflow in a timely manner. One solution to this type of problem is for vendors to provide bibliographic records or record maintenance. This is a radical departure from the past, when catalogers sought help from copy in the bibliographic utilities or from committee discussions at professional conferences. Cataloging will remain an integral part of the infrastructure of libraries. How it is perceived, who handles it or directs the workflow, and how it is made available to users is slowly changing. Internet resources and 24/7 availability of library catalogs on a global basis has changed how cataloging is perceived. What was once made available to users on a very local (and on site) basis is now available to anyone who gains access to a given collection or resource. When the first edition of this book was published, the "hot topics" at that time were developing procedures and practices for nonbook resources (computer files, particularly CD-ROMs, were the newest and problematic material type), the question of ownership versus access, considering the option of vendor supplied cataloging, and accepting the idea of cataloging items that did not exist in a physical format. These issues seem so dated and small in comparison to the issues libraries are now facing.

It is hoped that this text provides catalogers with useful information and the tools needed to catalog nonbook resources. Lastly, cataloging should be fun, and it is also hoped that this text will help individuals to reach that conclusion.

APPENDIX

SUGGESTED READINGS

All Media Guide. "All Movie Guide." Ann Arbor, Mich.: All Media Guide. (May 2001) Available at: *www.allmovie.com*.

All Media Guide. "All Music Guide." Ann Arbor, Mich.: All Media Guide. (July 2001) Available at: *http://almusic.com/*.

Andrew, Paige G., and Mary Lynette Larsgaard, editors. 1999. *Maps and Related Cartographic Materials: Cataloging, Classification, and Bibliographic Control.* New York: Haworth Press.

Anglo-American Cataloging Committee for Cartographic Materials. 1982. *Cartographic Materials: A Manual of Interpretation for AACR2.* Chicago: American Library Association.

Archival Moving Image Materials: A Cataloging Manual, 2nd edition. 2000. Washington, D.C. . Library of Congress, Cataloging Distribution Service.

Association for Library Collections and Technical Services, American Library Association. "ALCTS Publications & Resources, Cataloging Resources." Chicago: American Library Association. (February 2001) Available at: *www.ala.org/alcts/publications/index.html*.

Association for Library Collections and Technical Services, American Library Association, Committee on Cataloging: Description and Access. "Task Force on Metadata Summary Report, June 1999." Chicago: American Library Association. (July 2001) Available at: *www.ala.org/alcts/organization/ccs/ ccda/tf-meta3.html*.

Association for Library Collections and Technical Services, American Library Association, Committee on Cataloging: Description and Access. "Task Force on Specific Characteristics of Electronic Resources, Interim Report: February version." Chicago: American Library Association. (July 2001) Available at: *www.ala.org/alcts/organization/ccs/ccda/tf-scer1.html*.

Association for Library Collections and Technical Services, American Library Association, Committee on Cataloging: Description and Access. "Task Force on the VRA Categories." Chicago: American Library Association. (July 2001) Available at: *www.ala.org/alcts/organization/ccs/ccda/tf-vra1.htm*.

Association for Library Collections and Technical Services, American Library Association, Committee on Cataloging: Description and Access. "Task Force on Uniform Resource Identifiers and AACR2." Chicago: American Library Association. (July 2001) Available at: *www.ala.org/alcts/organization/ccs/ ccda/tf-uri1.htm*.

Association of American Publishers. "AAP Releases Recommendations for Ebook Standards" New York: Association of American Publishers, Inc. (July 2001) Available at: *www.publishers.org/home/press/ebookpr.htm*.

Association of Moving Image Archivists Web. "Compendium of Cataloging Practice." Beverly Hills, Calif.: Association of Moving Image Archivists. (March 2001) Available at: *www.amianet.org/*.

Association of Research Libraries. "Directory of Scholarly Electronic Journals and Academic Discussion Lists." Washington, D.C.: Association of Research Libraries. (July 2001) Available at: *www.arl.org/scomm/edir/index.html*.

Beacom, Matthew. "Crossing a Digital Divide: AACR2 and Unaddressed Problems of Networked Resources." Washington, D.C.: Library of Congress. (July 2001) Available at: *http://lcweb.loc.gov/catdir/bibcontrol/beacom_paper.htm.*

Beck, Melissa, Bill Anderson, Les Hawkins, and Regina Reynolds. "CONSER Cataloging Manual Module 31: Remote Access Computer File Serials." Washington, D.C.: Library of Congress. (June 2001) Available at: *www.loc.gov/acq/conser/module31.htm.*

British Library. "MARC Home Page." London: British Library. (July 2001) Available at: *http://minos.bl.uk/information/marc.html.*

Calhoun, Karen. "Redesign of Library Workflows: Experimental Models for Electronic Resource Description." Washington, D.C.: Library of Congress. (July 2001) Available at: *http://lcweb.loc.gov/catdir/bibcontrol/calhoun_paper.htm.*

Carey, Karen, Elaine Day, and Jackie Shieh. "Guidelines for Cataloging VIVA Electronic Collections." Richmond: Library of Virginia. (July 2001) Available at: *www.lib.virginia.edu/~ejs7y/vivacat/guidelines.html.*

"Cataloging Electronic Resources: OCLC-MARC Coding Guidelines." Buffalo, N.Y.: University of Buffalo Libraries. (July 2001) Available at: *http://ublib.buffalo.edu/libraries/units/cts/olac/new/oclcmarc.html.*

Cataloging Policy and Support Office, Library of Congress. 2000. *Library of Congress Rule Interpretations, Cataloger's Desktop Edition* (CD-ROM). Washington, D.C.: Library of Congress.

Cataloging Policy Committee, Online Audiovisual Catalogers. "Definitions for Terms Used in the Source of Title Note for Internet Resources." Buffalo, N.Y.: University of Buffalo Libraries. (July 2001) Available at: *http://ublib.buffalo.edu/libraries/units/cts/olac/capc/def.html.*

Cataloging Service Bulletin. 1978–. Washington, D.C.: Library of Congress Processing Service.

Chan, Lois Mai. "Exploiting LCSH, LLC, and DDC to Retrieve Networked Resources: Issues and Challenges." Washington, D.C.: Library of Congress. (July 2001) Available at: *http://lcweb.loc.gov/catdir/bibcontrol/chan_paper.htm.*

Chan, Lois Mai. 1999. A *Guide to the Library of Congress Classification.* Englewood, Colo.: Libraries Unlimited.

Cole, Jim E. 1999. "Augmented Title: Adapting Rules for Cataloging Microforms." *Cataloging & Classification Quarterly* 28, no. 3: 45–54.

Colgate University Libraries. "Documents Classification System." Hamilton, N.Y.: Colgate University Libraries. (August 2001) Available at: *http://exlibris.colgate.edu/services/departments/govdocs/govdocs2.html.*

Committee on Cataloging: Description and Access, Task Force on the Harmonization of ISBD(ER) and AACR2. "Final Report (Penultimate Draft)." Chicago: Association for Library Collections and Technical Services, American Library Association. (June 2001) Available at: *www.library.yale.edu/cataloging/aacrer/tf-harm2l.htm.*

Delsey, Tom for the Joint Steering Committee for the Revision of AACR with the assistance of Beth Dulabahn, Michael Heaney, and Jean Hirons. "The Logical Structure of the Anglo-American Cataloguing Rules—Part I." Ottawa, Canada: National Library of Canada. (May, 2001) Available at: *www.nlc-bnc.ca/jsc/aacr.pdf.*

Delsey, Tom for the Joint Steering Committee for the Revision of AACR with the assistance of Beth Dulabalm, Michael Heaney, and Jean Hirons. "The Logical Structure of the Anglo-American Cataloguing Rules—Part II." Ottawa, Canada: National Library of Canada. (May, 2001) Available at: *www.nlc-bnc.ca/jsc/aacr2.pdf.*

Diekema, Anne. "Dewey Decimal Classification Websites." Syracuse, N.Y.: School of Information Studies, Syracuse University. (July 2001) Available at: *http://istweb.syr.edu/~isdp561/Dewey/websites.html.*

Dillon, Martin. "Metadata for Web Resources: How Metadata Works on the Web." Washington, D.C.: Library of Congress. (July 2001) Available at: *http://lcweb.loc.gov/catdir/bibcontrol/dillon_paper.htm.*

"Discussion Paper 2001-DP01: Recording Narrators in Fields 508 and 511." Washington, D.C.: Library of Congress. (June 2001) Available at: *http://lcweb.loc.gov/marc/marbi/2001/2001-dp01.html.*

Dublin Core Metadata Initiative. "DCMI Frequently Asked Questions (FAQ)." Chilton, Didcot, Oxon, United Kingdom: JISCmail, Information Technology Department, Rutherford Appleton Laboratory. (July 2001) Available at: *http://dublincore.org/resources/faq.*

Dublin Core Metadata Initiative. "DCMI Moving Pictures Special Interest Group." Chilton, Didcot, Oxon, U.K.: JISCmail, Information Technology Department, Rutherford Appleton Laboratory. (July 2001) Available at: *http://dublincore.org/groups/moving-picture.*

Dublin Core Metadata Initiative. "Dublin Core Metadata Element Set, Version 1.1: Reference Description." Chilton, Didcot, Oxon, U.K.: JISCmail, Information Technology Department, Rutherford Appleton Laboratory. (July 2001) Available at: *http://dublincore.org/documents/dces.*

Federal Depository Library Program. "GPO Classification Manual (Revised January 1993)." Washington, D.C.: Government Printing Office. (August 2001) Available at: *www.access.gpo.gov/su-docs/fdlp/pubs/classman/class93.thm.*

Geography and Map Division, Library of Congress. 1991. *Map Cataloging Manual.* Washington, D.C.: Cataloging Distribution Service, Library of Congress.

Hillmann, Diane. "Using Dublin Core." Chilton, Didcot, Oxon, U.K.: JISCmail, Information Technology Department, Rutherford Appleton Laboratory. (July 2001) Available at: *http://dublincore.org/documents/2001/04/12/usageguide/.*

Hirons, Jean and Members of the CONSER AACR Review Task Force. "Revising AACR2 to Accommodate Seriality: Rule Revision Proposals." Ottawa, Canada: National Library of Canada. (June 2001) Available at: *www.nlc-bnc.ca/jsc/ch12.pdf.*

Hollywood Entertainment Corporation. "Reel.com." Wilsonville, Oreg.: Hollywood Entertainment Corporation. (May 2001) Available at: *www.reel.com/.*

International Federation of Library Associations and Institutions. "Digital Libraries: Metadata Resources." Valley Forge, Pa.: Blue Angel Technologies. (July 2001) Available at: *www.ifla.org/II/metadata.htm.*

International Federation of Library Associations and Institutions. "Universal Bibliographic Control and International MARC Core Programme." Valley Forge, Pa.: Blue Angel Technologies. (July 2001) Available at: *www.ifla.org/ VI/3/p1996-1/unimarc.htm*.

Internet Movie Database Limited. "Internet Movie Database." Seattle, Wash.: Amazon.com. (May 2001) Available at: *www.imdb.com/*.

Intner, Sheila S., and William E. Studwell, with the assistance of Simone E. Blake and David P. Miller. 1992. *Subject Access to Films and Videos*. Lake Crystal, Minn.: Soldier Creek Press.

J. Paul Getty Trust, Getty Standards Program. "Metadata Standards Cross-walks." Los Angeles: Getty Center. (July 2001) Available at: *www.getty.edu/ research/institute/standards/intrometadata*.

James Hardiman Library. "Dewey Decimal System." Galway, Ireland: James Hardiman Library, National University of Ireland. (July 2001) Available at: *http://sulacco.library.ucg.ie/misc/dewey.html*.

Joint Steering Committee for the Revision of AACR. 1998. *Anglo-American Cataloguing Rules, Second Edition, 1998 Revision*. Chicago: American Library Association.

Joint Steering Committee for the Revision of AACR. 1999. *Anglo-American Cataloguing Rules, Second Edition, 1998 Revision, Amendments, 1999*. Chicago: American Library Association.

Joint Steering Committee for Revision of Anglo-American Cataloguing Rules. "Home page." Ottawa, Canada: National Library of Canada. (June 2001) Available at: *www.nlc-bnc.ca/jsc/index.htm*.

Kuyper-Rushing, Lois. "Reference Works Used for Music Cataloging as Listed in the Music Cataloging Bulletins, current through Vol. 30, no. 3." Bloomington, Ind.: Indiana University School of Music. (March 2001) Available at: *www.music.indiana.edu/tech_s/mla/reflist99.htm*.

Kwasnik, Barbara. "IST561 Online Lecture Series: Dewey Decimal Classification." Syracuse, N.Y.: School of Information Studies, Syracuse University. (July 2001) Available at: *http://istweb.syr.edu/~isdp561/Dewey/dui.html*.

Kwasnik, Barbara. "IST561 Online Lecture Series: Library of Congress Classification." Syracuse, N.Y.: School of Information Studies, Syracuse University. (July 2001) Available at: *http://istweb.syr.edu/~isdp561/LCC/ lcc.html*.

Lagoze, Carl. "The Warwick Framework: A Container Architecture for Diverse Sets of Metadata." Reston, Va.: Corporation for National Research Initiatives. (July 2001) Available at: *www.dlib.org/dlib/july96/lagoze/ 07lagoze.html*.

Larsgaard, Mary, and Katherine Rankin. "Helpful Hints for Small Map Collections." Stony Brook, N.Y.: State University of New York at Stony Brook. (November 2001) Available at: *www.sunysb.edu/libmap/larsg.htm*.

Lavole, Brian, and Henrik Frystyk Nielsen, eds. "Web Characterization Terminology & Definitions Sheet." Cambridge, Mass.: Massachusetts Institute of Technology, Laboratory for Computer Science. (June 2001) Available at: *www.w3.org/1999/05/WCA-terms/01*.

Library of Congress, Cataloging Directorate. "Bibliographic Control of Web Resources: A Library of Congress Action Plan, Revised July 25, 2001." Washington, D.C.: Library of Congress. (November 2001) Available at: *www. loc.gov/catdir/bibcontrol/draftplan.htm*.

Library of Congress, Cataloging Directorate, Program for Cooperative Cataloging. "Program for Cooperative Cataloging Home Page." Washington, D.C.: Library of Congress. (August 2001) Available at: *http://lcweb.loc.gov/ catdir/pcc.*

Library of Congress, Cataloging Directorate, Program for Cooperative Cataloging. "Most Frequently Asked Questions About Joining BIBCO (BIBCO FAQ)." Washington, D.C.: Library of Congress. (August 2001) Available at: *www.loc.gov/catdir/pcc/bibcofaq.htm.*

Library of Congress, Cataloging Directorate, Program for Cooperative Cataloging. "Program for Cooperative Cataloging BIBCO Home Page." Washington, D.C.: Library of Congress. (August 2001) Available at: *www.loc.gov/ catdir/pcc/bibco.htm.*

Library of Congress, Network Development, and MARC Standards Office. "MARC 21 Concise Format for Bibliographic Data." Washington, D.C.: Library of Congress. (March 2001) Available at: *http://lcweb.loc.gov/marc/ bibliographic/ecbdhome.html.*

Library of Congress, Network Development, and MARC Standards Office in cooperation with Standards and Support, National Library of Canada. 1999. *MARC 21 Format for Bibliographic Data including Guidelines for Content Designation, 1999 Edition.* Washington, D.C.: Library of Congress Distribution Service.

Lynch, Clifford. "The Dublin Core Descriptive Metadata Program: Strategic Implications for Libraries and Networked Information Access." Washington, D.C.: Association of Research Libraries. (July 2001) Available at: *www.arl.org/newsltr/196/dublin.html.*

"MAGERT (ALA Map and Geography Round Table) [Home page]." Stony Brook, N.Y.: State University of New York at Stony Brook. (November 2001) Available at: *www.sunysb.edu/libmap/magert1.htm.*

"Map Cataloging Manual." Inwood, W. Va.: The Library Corporation. (November 2001) Available at: *www.tlcdelivers.com/tlc/crs/map0001.htm.*

MARCit, Inc. "MARCit Welcome Page." Minneapolis, Minn.: Sagebrush Technologies. (July 2001) Available at: *www.marcit.com/index.html.*

Maxwell, Robert L., and Margaret F. Maxwell. 1997. *Maxwell's Handbook for AACR2R: Explaining and Illustrating the Anglo-American Cataloging Rules and the 1993 Amendments.* Chicago: American Library Association.

McMullen, Jennifer, and David J. Miller, eds. "The Superintendent of Documents Classification System." Wooster, Ohio: College of Wooster Libraries. (August 2001) Available at: *www.wooster.edu/library/gov/guides/ sdexplain.html.*

Music Library Association Bibliographic Control Committee, Working Group on Popular Music Sources. "Sources for Authority Work in Cataloging Popular." Bloomington, Ind.: Indiana University School of Music. (March 2001) Available at: *www.music.indiana.edu/tech_s/mla/wgpms/wgpms.htm.*

Myers, Florence S. 1998. "Microforms Cataloging: A Brief Overview." *Mississippi Libraries* 62, no. 3: 61–63.

Network Development and MARC Standards Office, Library of Congress. "MARC to Dublin Core Crosswalk, February, 2001." Washington, D.C.: Library of Congress. (February 2001) Available at: *www.loc.gov/marc/ marc2dc.html.*

Nordic Metadata Project. "d2m: Dublin Core to MARC Converter." Helsinki: Helsinki University Library. (July 2001) Available at: *www.bibsys.no/meta/d2m/*.

OCLC. "CORC Home Page." Dublin, Ohio: OCLC. (July 2001) Available at: *www.oclc.org/corc//3_crosswalks/index.html*.

OCLC. "Dewey Decimal Classification Home Page." Dublin, Ohio: OCLC. (July 2001) Available at: *www.oclc.org/dewey/*.

OCLC. "OCLC CORC." Dublin, Ohio: OCLC. (July 2001) Available at: *www.oclc.org/corc/*.

Olson, Nancy B., ed. "Cataloging Internet Resources: A Manual and Practical Guide, Second Edition." Dublin, Ohio: OCLC. (July 2001) Available at: *www.oclc.org/oclc/man9256cat/toc.htm*.

Online Audiovisual Catalogers, Cataloging Policy Committee. "AV Authority Tools." Buffalo, N.Y.: University of Buffalo Libraries. (February 2001) Available at: *http://ublib.buffalo.edu/libraries/units/cts/olac/capc/authtools.html*.

Online Audiovisual Catalogers, Cataloging Policy Committee. "General Material Designations in the Twenty-First Century: Results of a Survey by Jean Weihs." Buffalo, N.Y.: University of Buffalo Libraries. (November 2001) Available at: *http://ublib.buffalo.edu/libraries/units/cts/olac/capc/gmd.html*.

Online Audiovisual Catalogers, Cataloging Policy Committee. "Useful Websites for AV Catalogers." Buffalo, N.Y.: University of Buffalo Libraries. (November 2000) Available at: *http://ublib.buffalo.edu/libraries/units/cts/olac/websites.html*.

Program for Cooperative Cataloging. "PCC Task Force on Multiple Manifestations of Electronic Resources." Washington, D.C.: Library of Congress (July 2001) Available at: *http://lcweb.loc.gov/catdir/pcc/tgmuler.html*.

Program for Cooperative Cataloging Standing Committee on Automation, Task Group on Journals in Aggregator Databases. "Final Report, January 2000." Washington, D.C.: Library of Congress. (July 2001) Available at: *www.loc.gov/catdir/pcc/aggfinal.htm*.

Sak, Lida, and Kenneth Karol. "Cataloging Electronic Resources." New Brunswick, N.J.: Rutgers University Libraries. (July 2001) Available at: *www.libraries.rutgers.edu/rul/staff/staff.html*.

Sak, Lida, and Kenneth Karol. "Multiformat Serials Treatment at Rutgers University Libraries." (July 2001) Available at: *www.libraries.rutgers.edu/rul/staff/staff.html*.

Shook, John R. "A Guide to Philosophy in the Library of Congress Classification: How to Find Philosophical Works in the Library." Columbus, Ohio: OhioLINK. (July 2001) Available at: *http://karn.ohiolink.edu/philosophy/shook.htm*.

Smiraglia, Richard P. 1997. *Describing Music Materials: A Manual for Descriptive Cataloging of Printed and Recorded Music, Music Videos, and Archival Music Collections: For Use with AACR2 and APPM*. Lake Crystal, Minn.: Soldier Creek Press.

Subcommittee on Authority Tools, Cataloging Access and Policy Committee, Online Audiovisual Catalogers. "Authority Tools for Audio-Visual Catalogers: An Annotated List of Useful Resources." Buffalo, N.Y.: University of Buffalo Libraries. (July 2001) Available at: *http://ublib.buffalo.edu/libraries/units/cts/olac/capc/authtools.html*.

Taylor, Arlene G. 2000. *Wynar's Introduction to Cataloging and Classification.* Englewood, Colo.: Libraries Unlimited.

Weber, Mary Beth. 1999. "Factors to be Considered in the Selection and Cataloging of Internet Resources." *Library Hi Tech* 17, no. 3: 298–303.

Working Group on Types of Compositions, Online Audiovisual Catalogers, Cataloging Policy Committee. "Types of Compositions for Use in Music Uniform Titles: A Manual for Use with AACR2 Chapter 25, 2nd, Updated Edition, June 1997, Revised 2000." New Haven, Conn.: Yale University Library. (April 2001) Available at: *www.library.yale.edu/cataloging/music/types.htm.*

INDEX

ABOUT THE AUTHOR

Mary Beth Weber has worked as the Special Formats Catalog Librarian in Technical and Automated Services at Rutgers University Libraries since 1989. She has also worked as the Head of Copy Cataloging, and served as the Acting Head of the Cataloging Department at Rutgers University Libraries. As Special Formats Catalog Librarian, she has shaped cataloging policies and procedures for nonprint resources.

Ms. Weber published an earlier edition of this book in 1993, as well as *Electronic Resources: Access and Issues*, in 1997. She has written numerous reviews of nonprint resources, and has served on the editorial boards of the electronic journals *McJournal: Journal of Academic Media Librarian* and *LIBRES: Library and Information Science Research Electronic Journal* since the early 1990s. Ms. Weber has been an active participant in the American Library Association, both as a speaker as well as serving as chair of the Audiovisual Cataloging Committee (now the Media Resources Committee), co-chair of the Computer Files Discussion Group, and Audiovisual Committee Representative to the Committee on Cataloging: Description and Access. In addition, she has served on the Online Audiovisual Catalogers Cataloging Description and Policy Committee, and has given numerous presentations on cataloging nonprint resources to various groups.